Through the Thicket

Through the Thicket

A Tangle with End Times

Ivan W. Bowden

RESOURCE *Publications* · Eugene, Oregon

THROUGH THE THICKET
A Tangle with End Times

Copyright © 2017 Ivan W. Bowden. All rights reserved. Except for brief quotations in critical publications or reviews, no part of this book may be reproduced in any manner without prior written permission from the publisher. Write: Permissions, Wipf and Stock Publishers, 199 W. 8th Ave., Suite 3, Eugene, OR 97401.

Resource Publications
An Imprint of Wipf and Stock Publishers
199 W. 8th Ave., Suite 3
Eugene, OR 97401

www.wipfandstock.com

PAPERBACK ISBN: 978-1-5326-3439-0
HARDCOVER ISBN: 978-1-5326-3441-3
EBOOK ISBN: 978-1-5326-3440-6

Manufactured in the U.S.A.   NOVEMBER 27, 2017

Unless otherwise stated, biblical quotations are taken from the HOLY BIBLE, NEW INTERNATIONAL VERSION, copyright © 1973, 1978, 1984, International Bible Society, and used by permission of Zondervan Bible Publishers.

> From the cowardice that shrinks from new truth,
> From the laziness that is content with half-truths,
> From the arrogance that thinks it knows all truth,
> O God of truth, deliver us.
>
> —An Ancient Hebrew Prayer

Contents

Abbreviations | ix

1. An Unexpected Dismissal | 1
2. A Shocking Possibility | 4
3. Relocation | 8
4. A Conservative Church | 12
5. Tangled in the *Little Apocalypse* | 17
6. Questioning the Signs | 21
7. Historical Support for the Signs | 25
8. No to a New Pastor | 28
9. Yes to a New Pastor | 32
10. The Last Days | 35
11. Universal Language | 40
12. An Unsettling Address | 45
13. At the Surf Club | 52
14. Coffee Club and the Antichrist | 56
15. Apocalyptic Language | 60
16. Conflict at a Barbecue | 63
17. In Big Trouble | 68
18. A Statement of Faith Proposed | 72
19. Reconciliation | 75
20. The Rationale for Our Beliefs | 79
21. Still Tangled in the *Little Apocalypse* | 82
22. A Statement of Faith Adopted | 88
23. A Debate with an Atheist | 94
24. Question Time at the Debate | 98
25. Changes in the Church | 102

26 The Integrity of Jesus | 107
27 This Generation | 111
28 The Kingdom of God | 115
29 The Doctor and the Atheist | 121
30 The Growth of the Kingdom | 128
31 A Three-fold Package | 135
32 At the Traffic Lights | 142
33 A Very Little While | 147
34 The Pastor's Concerns | 152
35 Escape or Endure? | 157
36 Home Group | 163
37 Is Abraham in Heaven? | 171
38 Just Around the Corner | 177
39 Conference Preparations | 183
40 A Panoramic View of Revelation | 190
41 Questioning the Panoramic View | 195
42 The Rapture and the Tribulation | 200
43 Jesus' Teaching Raises Doubts | 207
44 The Harlot and the Bride | 214
45 Babylon is Not Rome | 222
46 A Better Hope | 227
47 The Millennium and the New Jerusalem | 233
48 Highlight of the Conference | 242
49 Dodgy Means to the End | 248
50 Eschatological Dangers | 255
51 Inauguration or Consummation? | 264
52 Fantastic News | 271
53 One Coming, Two Outcomes | 278
54 A Startling Revelation | 284
55 The Jigsaw Comes Together | 291

Epilogue | *299*

Study Guide | *301*

Bibliography | *321*

Abbreviations

AIMS	Australian Institute of Ministry Studies
CV	curriculum vitae
ESRD	End Stage Renal Disease
FRACP	Fellow of the Royal Australasian College of Physicians
GP	General Practitioner
KJV	King James Version
MBA	Master of Business Administration
MDiv	Master of Divinity
NIV	New International Version
PTSD	Post-Traumatic Stress Disorder
SCIF	Sunshine Coast Independent Fellowship
USC	University of the Sunshine Coast

1

An Unexpected Dismissal

Early retirement was not on my mind. The college had no mandatory retirement policy, I was very fit for my sixty-four years, and I enjoyed my work as lecturer in New Testament at the Australian Institute of Ministry Studies, known to the college community as AIMS. I might retire in five or six years but not before. As the longest-serving faculty member, I was part of the place. How would they survive without Dr. Edward J. Sutherland, popular lecturer in student opinion polls, successful recruiter of new students, and national conference speaker? The letter from the chairman of the college board was unexpected, inexplicable, and curt:

> Dear Dr. Sutherland,
>
> As you know, your present three-year contract with the college expires at the end of the current academic year. I regret to advise that the board has decided not to renew your contract.
>
> The board expresses its gratitude for your contribution to the life of the college and wishes you a happy retirement.
>
> Yours truly,
> Alex Symons.
> (Chairman)

Alex Symons had been chairman of the board for ten of my seventeen years at the college. A successful businessman and company director, he was invited onto the board during a period of declining student numbers and accompanying loss of income, with the hope that his marketing skills and financial aptitude would reverse the trend. The fortunes of the college improved so markedly, he was soon appointed chairman. I knew him through my rostered attendance at board meetings as a faculty representative but we were not close.

Most board members were in awe, if not fear, of his manipulative management style. Only the resolute remained composed when bald-headed Alex glared disapprovingly over the top of his half-frame spectacles. In spite of his short stature and slight build, his intimidating personality meant he usually got his way. In the early days, I spoke up when I disagreed with him but the tension generated on the board disturbed my phlegmatic temperament and made me a silent observer.

Although Alex's letter had shocked me, I would have been content to slink quietly into retirement at the end of the semester with barely a chip on my shoulder. Not so Charlotte, my wife of thirty-eight years, who has a commendable sense of justice and a strong compulsion to expose injustice. When she read the letter she was incensed.

"This is outrageous, Ed! He's given no reason for your dismissal and you have a right to know. I for one am not going without a fight."

"The decision may have originated with another member of the board," I said meekly. "*You* weren't at the meeting to know if it was Alex's idea."

"You always refuse to face the obvious," Charlotte said acerbically. "You can't let him get away with it." I *could* but she was not about to let me. She continued: "I'm going to phone him now and demand an explanation." She lifted the telephone receiver as she looked for the Symons's number. I began to feel apprehensive and quickly said I would email him and ask to meet with the board at its next meeting even though I was not rostered to attend. Charlotte hesitated as if considering whether my offer to cooperate in the fight against injustice was adequate to assuage her annoyance. My blood pressure went down with the telephone receiver.

In a more conciliatory tone, she said, "Ed, you know he's had it in for you ever since he attended one of your courses."

I had to admit she was right. Months earlier I had given an evening public lecture series on the topic, *Jesus' Discipling Method in the Gospel of Matthew*. Alex enrolled and took advantage of my participatory lecturing style to ask more questions than anyone else and, not infrequently, to challenge my views when they clashed with his. In an attempt to elicit responses from other members of the class, I would say, "Does anyone *else* have a comment?" and when nothing was said within five seconds, Alex would jump in as if he had not heard the word "else," in spite of my having stressed it. I sensed other members of the class were inwardly moaning, "Oh no, here he goes again," every time he opened his mouth.

Alex's ultra conservative theology was coupled with an arrogant dogmatism that seemed to say two things: one: that any position other than his own smacked of heresy; and, two: that he was under divine orders to expose the heresy and denounce the heretic. Little did I know that I would be one of his victims.

2

A Shocking Possibility

The clash with Alex occurred during week 7 of the series. I was working through Matthew 10, a chapter containing instructions Jesus gave his disciples prior to sending them out in pairs on a preaching and healing mission. When we reached verse 23, I thought it might stimulate some class discussion:

> When you are persecuted in one place, flee to another. I tell you the truth, you will not finish going through the cities of Israel before the Son of Man comes.

"Do you find anything surprising in these words?" I asked the class. For once Alex was not the first to speak. I could only assume that he did not see anything surprising in the text. Luke, a bearded young man whom I knew to be a lawyer by day and a part-time student by night, *did*.

"The verse suggests that Jesus returned while some at least of the disciples were still living." Alex came to life.

"I hope you're not suggesting that the second coming of Christ has already occurred!" he yelled, glaring over his half-frames.

"I'm only suggesting that the *text* is suggesting that," said Luke.

"Nonsense!" said Alex, voice still raised.

Hoping to keep the discussion amicable and to prevent Alex from continuing, I asked Luke, his composure slightly ruffled by Alex's blast, "What do you see in the text in support of your statement?"

"Well," he said, "the repeated use of the word 'you' makes it clear that the words are addressed to Jesus' disciples in the first century, not to us in the twenty-first century. Even if his disciples hurry from town to town, they will not finish their task before Christ returns. They're urged not to waste time where they're not wanted because time is short. Furthermore, when Jesus said, 'I tell you the truth,' it was as if he were saying, 'I'm about to tell you something surprising. You're going to find it hard to believe but it's true.'"

Luke's response challenged conventional eschatology but I was impressed with his thoughtful observations. Alex was not. He proceeded to correct the implied heresy: "All Jesus meant was that Jewish evangelism would continue right till the end. It is still continuing, the end has not come, and neither has Jesus." He spoke with an air of finality that assumed the matter would be put to rest. Luke, who had been thoughtfully stroking his beard, was preparing to speak so, wanting to get on with the exposition and not wanting to prolong acrimonious debate, my phlegmatic temperament kicked in and I said, "Each of the comments we have heard is interesting but we run the risk of being side-tracked. If we don't move on we'll not finish the chapter tonight." Alex lowered his head and glared at me over his glasses as if to say, "You haven't heard the last of this." I didn't have to wait long.

As I shut down my laptop and disconnected the data projector at the end of the lecture, the firm footsteps of an unsmiling Alex approached and, leaving me no time for pleasantries, he got stuck into me: "How could you let that bearded idiot get away with such garbage? You're a disgrace to the college." I'd had a long day, had not eaten since lunch, and was anxious to get home so I simply said, "Alex, you and I have this in common that we both respect the Scriptures as the authority for what we believe. We are obliged to listen to what they say. I have to confess that I felt the so-called bearded idiot—his name's Luke Rodman by the way—was listening to the text more than you were. You rattled off a pat interpretation designed to make the text fit your predetermined eschatology as if what you believe has greater authority than the word of God."

For once Alex was speechless—with anger. He didn't need to say anything; his scowl said everything. Had I spoken too strongly? I tried to excuse myself on the grounds of hunger, tiredness, and the need to put him in his place but as he stomped away, I was left unsettled.

The following morning, Charlotte greeted me at breakfast with a blunt, "What's up with you?" She's pretty good at interpreting my face, not that on this occasion special hermeneutical skills were required. I tried to pass her off with "a bit more sleep would help" but she continued to probe until I told her of my run-in with Alex Symons. Not being a fan of Alex, she was quite pleased at my assertiveness and gave me a veiled compliment: "It's not like you to take such a strong stand."

The incident with Alex was not the only thing that disturbed me. I could not stop thinking about the implications of Luke's comments on Matthew 10:23. I would email Alex and apologize for my lack of respect and the off-handed way I had treated him but what was I to do with the shocking possibility that Christ had already returned? The least I could do was explore relevant texts and practice what I had preached to Alex the previous night: listen to the text of Scripture without trying to make it fit my theological preconceptions. Sadly, my good intentions evaporated in the heat of end-of-semester pressures.

Alex did not return to the lecture series. I had no further contact with him until I received the letter of dismissal. I had promised Charlotte I would visit the board to ask for an explanation. The board met on the first Tuesday of each month which meant the October meeting was only days away. In my email to Alex I requested attendance on the grounds that my next rostered board meeting would fall after the end of the semester and that I would like to speak with the board prior to my departure.

Although I arrived five minutes early, the board members were seated in silence, four on each side of a large oblong table. Alex Symons sat at the head of the table with a severity matching the board room itself. Its walls were lined on the lower half with reddish-brown Tasmanian oak. Above the wainscoting, on all four walls, life-size head-and-shoulders photographs of board chairmen looked sternly down on proceedings so that one felt surrounded by a "great cloud of witnesses." Ironically, Alex sat beneath his own photograph. From the atmosphere that prevailed, I wondered if the board had met earlier and whether I had been the topic of discussion.

David Barnes, the faculty member due to attend that month, had not yet arrived. I presumed his seat was the one with the agenda in front of it so I took the adjacent seat at the end of the table opposite Alex. A couple of board members looked in my direction. I responded with a nod and a forced smile. Alex was about to open the meeting when his mobile phone rang. Excusing himself, he withdrew to an adjoining room. I would like to have cracked a joke to lighten the atmosphere but Alex's photographic proxy restrained me. Instead, I took the opportunity to glance at the agenda items beside me. My name headed the list. The remaining items were routine except one: "Appointment of Dr. Robert Donaldson." The door behind me opened and David Barnes entered, a little out of breath. After he settled, I pointed to the agenda item and, looking at him, raised my eyebrows as if to ask, "Who's Robert Donaldson?" Before he could reply, Alex returned through the door at the other end of the room.

After the minutes of the preceding meeting were approved, Alex said, "Dr. Sutherland has asked to attend tonight's meeting so I'll invite him to speak for a few minutes before we proceed with the agenda."

"Thank you, Mr. Chairman," I began. "I leave my position within a matter of weeks with a great deal of sadness." The hush that pervaded the room became palpable. I continued: "It has been a privilege to serve the institute these last seventeen years doing what I love doing. As you can imagine, the termination of my contract came as a shock. I asked to come here this evening hoping to receive an explanation for the dismissal that would ease my mind for I am not conscious of having failed in my academic responsibilities." I paused to allow opportunity for people to respond. No one did and the pause, though brief, seemed long. I expected some affirmation from those board members who had supported me over the years. Though none was given, I thanked them for their support and told of our plans to move to the Sunshine Coast where we had bought a retirement home.

Alex stood to speak. I feared he might ground my dismissal in a defection from theological orthodoxy or a failure to contend for the faith as he understood it. He merely said, "The board felt that after seventeen years it was time for a change and that a younger man should be appointed." He thanked me for coming and said I was free to leave.

Glad to get out of the stuffy atmosphere, I couldn't help feeling that most of the board members disapproved of my dismissal but had been pressured by Alex to toe his line. But what *was* his line? Surely if he wanted to move me on because of the altercation in the lecture on Matthew's gospel, he'd have done it before now. I was puzzled.

Charlotte was not impressed with my report on the meeting with the board. "You let him get away with it," she said. "'Time for a younger man!'" she scoffed. "That's not the real reason." I remembered the agenda item about the appointment of Robert Donaldson and mentioned it to Charlotte. "Robert Donaldson," she reflected. With furrowed brow she repeated the name. "Robert Donaldson. That name rings a bell." She began to rummage through a pile of papers on the office desk and soon produced a copy of *Aiming Higher,* the monthly college magazine. "Listen to this," she said, pointing to a picture of a wedding. 'The chairman of the college board, Mr. Alex Symons, and his wife, Natalie, celebrated the marriage of their daughter, Roslyn, to Dr. Robert Donaldson who recently completed his PhD in New Testament in the United States.' That's why we're leaving, Ed." She was right again. Alex Symons may well have wished me gone earlier but he decided to wait till his future son-in-law finished his studies and then created a vacancy for him at my expense. My dismissal was not just about eschatology but nepotism.

3

Relocation

Loading my extensive personal library into cartons as I cleaned out my office was a dismal task that brought a tear or two to my generally unemotional eyes. I had contemplated, as an act of exceptional grace, donating the books to the college library, partly to save having to clog up our retirement home with academic books I might never touch again, and partly to heap coals of fire on Alex Symons's head. Suddenly I imagined Charlotte's voice on learning of my generosity: "You gave your books to the AIMS library! No way!" I saw myself humbly asking the librarian if I could please have my books back. It was all too much. Grace lost the day but I didn't feel too bad about it: I just might need those books down the track.

Charlotte was less disappointed than I about leaving AIMS. She had come into an inheritance following the death of her father two years earlier and had invested the money in a house at Maroochydore on the Sunshine Coast, about an hour-and-a-half's drive north of Brisbane. At last she was living in it rather than letting it. An old Queenslander built in 1937, the weatherboard house stood tall on its ten-foot stumps overlooking the Maroochy River. From the front veranda we could relax on low-slung canvas deckchairs and watch pelicans aquaplane across the surface of the river, paddle towards the bank, and score a free feed from fishermen gutting their catch. I began to believe Alex Symons was my benefactor.

Charlotte was an architect and the old Queenslander offered scope for her skills. She was excited at the opportunity of designing new features for her own house rather than someone else's. Surrounded by empty space, the supporting stumps under the house stood silently waiting for her creative talents. They did not have to wait long. Within six months of our moving in, the posts were supporting walls encasing a spacious rumpus room, an extra bedroom and bathroom for visitors, a studio for Charlotte the architect and

Charlotte the talented oil painter, and an office for me with a wall-to-wall desk, a generous set of bookshelves, and a picture window overlooking the river. A workshop fitted with a bench and shelving for tools and gardening accessories was provided with two doors, one offering access from under the house and the other access from the backyard.

Upstairs, Charlotte modernized the kitchen with a granite-topped island, teak-paneled cupboards, recessed down-lights and European appliances. Halfway along the wide hall that ran through the middle of the house from the front veranda to the back veranda, she installed an internal staircase to the rooms below. The wide verandas on all four sides of the house were left open. She rightly deplored the common, ugly, and stupid practice of enclosing heat-reducing verandas in a sub-tropical climate.

With the renovations complete, Charlotte and I revived a garden left to run down by disinterested tenants. My contribution to the project was more as a laborer, my knowledge of growing things barely extending to the difference between cobblers' pegs and chrysanthemums. I dug, carted, weeded, watered, and pruned. Later, when accompanying Charlotte as she tour-guided visitors around the garden, I would say to myself, too modest to say it out loud, "I dug the hole for that frangipani tree; I built the trellis for that passionfruit vine; I re-potted those poinsettias." While not particularly practical, I did enjoy working with tools and having something to show for my efforts at the end of the day.

One morning, Charlotte said, "We need a bird table. Yesterday I saw galahs foraging in the grass over the road in the picnic grounds and this morning I saw a couple of rainbow lorikeets in the banksias." I sensed an opportunity to make use of my new workshop. After two or three hours' work, the poinciana trunk sported a waist-high wooden collar complete with birdbath and containers for avian food and water. Pride in my work led me to expect immediate patronage so I was disappointed that it took a week for the lorikeets to appreciate that the cuisine on offer in our backyard was superior to the competition in the banksia bushes by the Maroochy River.

Once they began to dine at our bird table, their numbers increased in spite of territorial opposition from our dog Chuffey, named after a character in Dickens's *Martin Chuzzlewit*. We'd wanted a dog for years but college rules forbade the keeping of pets on campus. My sacking and our own enclosed backyard made way for Chuffey, a tan-colored Cavoodle, a cross between a cavalier King Charles spaniel and a poodle. Chuffey's objection to the intrusion of parakeets reflected his prowess as a watchdog, an asset in excluding less-welcome visitors. Another asset was his need for daily walks which ensured Charlotte and I exercised regularly, usually along the river bank.

Our neighbors, Jack and Carol Wilson, more than compensated for my horticultural ignorance. For generations the Wilson family had farmed on the Buderim plateau only twenty-minutes' drive from Maroochydore in the Sunshine Coast hinterland. The red volcanic soil, regular rainfall, and subtropical climate helped give Buderim an international reputation for ginger. Charlotte and Carol soon became friends and spent a lot of time swapping plants and advice. Jack and I spent a lot of time fishing, a common interest supported by his three-meter aluminum dinghy, a fifteen-horsepower Yamaha outboard motor, and the nearby Maroochy River.

Nothing was more relaxing on a brisk morning than to drift downstream toward the river's mouth, throw in a line and watch the sun rise warmly over the Pacific Ocean. At such times Jack and I chatted as we waited for a bite. I had assumed that having come from Buderim he'd been a ginger farmer. On our first trip, I wondered why he had retired so early as he appeared to be only in his mid-fifties. "Jack," I asked, "Buderim's such a beautiful place and the ginger industry's been so profitable, I'm surprised you could let it go."

"Ed, ginger hasn't been grown commercially on Buderim for decades. My father and his father grew it but when I was only a toddler, Dad sold our thirty-acre property to developers except for five acres around our home."

"What did he do after that?" I asked.

"He foresaw that Buderim would become a haven for tourists and retirees so he set up a coffee shop and outlet for ginger products."

"I thought you said ginger was no longer grown at Buderim."

"True, but it was grown in the region—still is—and since ginger and Buderim were historically linked, tourists and locals were pleased to buy items from Dad's shop in the main street."

"Ginger is ginger," I said. "He can't have had much variety in his product line."

"Don't you believe it," said Jack with some emphasis. "He sold not only crystallized ginger but ginger marmalade, ginger sauces, ginger beer, ginger chutney, ginger health products, chocolate-coated ginger, and ginger recipe books. I followed him in the business but three years ago I sold the shop after succumbing to an irresistible offer on our five acres (now a retirement village) and we moved here. It's just as well because neither of our kids was interested in the shop. Josh is an accountant in Nambour and Lauren is in the United States."

"What's she doing there?" I asked.

"She's taking a gap year at a Bible college in Tennessee."

"Lauren's obviously a Christian girl?"

"She sure is," he said. "We all are actually. Carol and I attend the Sunshine Coast Independent Fellowship, known to the members as SCIF. My father and his father went there and I serve as an elder. Why don't you come along some Sunday?"

"We just might do that," I said. "Charlotte and I have been shopping around for a church since we came to the coast but so far haven't settled in one."

When I told Charlotte my conversation with Jack, she thought it would be a good idea to try the Wilsons' church. I felt it would be too conservative for me but I knew Charlotte liked small rather than large churches so I agreed to go. The Wilsons were delighted and offered to drive us in their Land Rover, a 1970's relic from their Buderim property.

Sunday morning was warm so I dressed in an open-necked shirt and light sports trousers only to discover Jack was wearing a suit complete with coat and tie. I got the feeling I was going to stand out in the congregation as a newcomer. When Charlotte noticed Carol was wearing a hat, her body language said she too felt under-dressed. What had I let myself in for?

4

A Conservative Church

The Sunshine Coast Independent Fellowship met in an all-timber construction, apart from its steep-pitched corrugated iron roof. The building seemed to have been built inside out, its exterior planks being attached to the inside of the studs. At the top of a short set of wooden stairs, we entered a foyer with barely space for the four of us. A weathered man in a double-breasted suit with wide lapels, warmly welcomed the Wilsons as Brother Jack and Sister Carol, then looked at us, not unkindly, but as if the presence of strangers was an uncommon occurrence. After Jack introduced us to Brother Arthur, who gave us a red Sankey's *Sacred Songs and Solos*, the Wilsons led us to a hard, high-backed wooden pew with a comfort level arguing a strong case for a short sermon. I had a good idea of what to expect in the service.

I was not wrong. The average age of the twenty or so adults present was sixty or more. One younger couple had two small children but any lowering of the average age of the congregation by their presence was partially offset by an octogenarian at a pedal organ of similar vintage.

The order of service was of the "hymn-sandwich" variety: hymn, prayer, hymn, reading, hymn, announcements, hymn, sermon, hymn, benediction. As each hymn was announced, there was a delay as the organist found the page in the thick Sankey's music book with its 1,200 tunes, and then attached two large wooden clothes pegs to hold the pages in place. I was rather surprised at the volume she extracted from the organ given the amount of pedal power needed to activate the bellows. I was even more surprised at the volume of the congregational singing. The hymns were clearly well-known and loved, even by the children. I glanced at Charlotte whose enthusiasm made her look like one of the regulars. I feared our church hopping was at an end.

Though the service was old-fashioned and the sermon prosaic and predictable, the genuineness of the worshippers and the passion of the lay preacher lent a sense of the presence of God. After the service we retired to a hall behind the pulpit where Charlotte and I were royally treated to tea brewed in a blue, willow-pattern teapot and served in matching cups and saucers. Side plates were loaded with homemade pumpkin scones topped with ginger jam and whipped cream. I was in no doubt we were the only visitors in a long while. The door steward, Arthur Bradford, and his wife, Robyn, invited us and the Wilsons to their home for lunch.

Though I had over-indulged on the pumpkin scones, I still managed to do justice to Robyn's shepherd's pie and home-grown salad followed by freshly picked strawberries and ice-cream.

In addition to their similar age and church affiliation, the Wilsons and Bradfords had much in common. Both families were descended from Buderim pioneers and had grown up on adjacent ginger-farming properties. Ginger was in their blood. Jack and Arthur talked at length about it, having kept a keen interest in the industry over the years. Charlotte and I could contribute little to the conversation apart from questions that betrayed our ignorance. My feelings of social isolation were relieved when Robyn Bradford steered the conversation in a totally new direction.

"Guess what?" she said. "We've got a computer." I judged by the tone of her comment that a computer in the home was an innovation. She continued: "I've been attending U3A, the University of the Third Age. It's an organization of volunteers offering classes for the mature-aged. I've taken courses in quilting, landscape painting, and nutrition. Two months ago I enrolled in a course run at the local high school called 'First steps in computing.' I had never sat in front of a computer before but I didn't feel out of place because we were all in the same boat and the instructor was very patient with us. By the end of the fourth week he had us searching the internet. It's amazing! My excitement at how easily I picked up the basics so overcame Arthur's nonchalance that he took me to Office Works and bought me a computer. I've never looked back. When Arthur's pottering in the garden, I'm on the computer. We've been doing a Bible study on the second coming of Christ at our mid-week prayer meeting so the other day I did a search on the word 'rapture.' One of the sites had a rapture index. It analyzes world events in terms of biblical signs heralding the return of Christ and summarizes the results mathematically. Last year the index reached a high of 163 and anything over 160 is regarded as a prepare-for-lift-off score."

"What sort of factors are analyzed?" I asked.

"The incidence of earthquakes, local and international conflicts, events in the Middle East, particularly in Israel, developments in the European

Union, and so on. It's five minutes to midnight for this old world. The last days are upon us; no doubt about that."

Jack and Arthur nodded in agreement but said nothing. Ginger seemed to make them garrulous and theology taciturn. Carol Wilson spoke up: "Jack and I subscribe to a magazine called *Last Days Bulletin* that confirms what Robyn is saying. Every month there are reports from around the world that the signs heralding the second coming of Christ are being fulfilled." I was tempted to keep the conversation going by cautioning against matching headlines in the newspaper with prophetic texts, on the grounds that in the past authors had generated anticipation of an imminent rapture in the light of current events but the predictions failed. I was about to speak but resisted the temptation, partly because I felt it inappropriate as a guest to oppose my hostess and mainly because a diversionary kick under the table from Charlotte suggested it would be unwise to continue. Robyn looked disappointed. Perhaps she thought a retired lecturer in New Testament would have more to say on the matter.

It was mid-afternoon before we got home. I was about to doze off when Charlotte asked, "What did you think?" In spite of the brevity of her question, I knew she wanted a report on the SCIF experience.

"I felt I was back in the church of my childhood and that time had stopped." I hoped she would sense my reluctance to make SCIF our spiritual home.

"Weren't the people lovely?" she beamed.

"They were nice enough," I mumbled, an intentional understatement. I had actually been impressed with the people whose obvious love for one another outweighed their outmoded worship style. I began to ponder community versus contemporaneity but was interrupted.

"I also enjoyed singing songs I knew and that had substance in them," said Charlotte. "I find I can't sing the songs in the larger churches we've visited recently."

Charlotte and I had often engaged in vigorous debates on music matters and I was too tired for another one so responded with a cliché: "Whatever floats your boat." She let me sleep.

The following Sunday we were back at SCIF and over ensuing weeks we experienced a growing acceptance by the community. For Charlotte's sake I wore a mask of enthusiasm but the ultra-conservatism and lack of intellectual stimulation taxed my church commitment on a weekly basis.

I began to worry that my mind was beginning to atrophy. I no longer had lectures to prepare or assignments to mark. Gardening and fishing were fine but they did not occupy all of my days. Charlotte made good use of her studio, designing part-time for a local architect and transforming colored photos of the Sunshine Coast into saleable oil paintings. The big question for me was what to do with *my* days. Jack and I usually fished in the early morning or late afternoon so I had plenty of time to fill. Aware of statistics about retirees going to an early grave for lack of challenging pursuits, I feared the onset of Alzheimer's and a short retirement if I didn't commence a project soon. An email from David Barnes prevented my becoming a statistic.

David was the theologian at AIMS and we had been close colleagues, often engaging in theological disagreements yet never disagreeably. His email began with pleasantries about how we were missed at AIMS, inquiries about our health, and how the fish were biting. He then asked, "Do you remember Luke Rodman, the lawyer who attended some of your public lectures? He's now enrolled part-time at AIMS in an MDiv. He keeps me on my toes with well-considered questions that stimulate vigorous class discussions as well as my own thinking. Last Wednesday the theology lecture was about eschatology. I presented the commonly accepted paradigms about the second coming of Christ and related matters. You know, pre-millennial, post-millennial, a-millennial, along with variations of each, when Luke recounted an incident in one of your public lectures last year in relation to Matthew 10:23. He then asked where I thought it fitted into the scheme of things. I gave a couple of 'safe' interpretations consistent with a still-future return of Christ but I could tell by the way he stroked his beard that he wasn't convinced. He said nothing more in class but the following morning he came to my office and asked if he could share some concerns arising from his studies. I was happy to oblige and listened as he related, to the best of my recollection, what follows:

> In addition to your theology subject, I'm studying hermeneutics. It's certainly sharpening my interpreting skills but it has also unsettled me theologically. A couple of weeks ago, I was browsing in the college library for help with an assignment on apocalyptic and came across a book called *Biblical Hermeneutics*, a reprint by Zondervan of a nineteenth-century work by Milton Terry. I have always found Zondervan's books to be conservative so imagine my shock as I read a chapter entitled, "The Gospel Apocalypse," to be confronted with a disturbing eschatological position. I'm confused. Terry's views are at variance with the systematic theologies in the college library, with what I have been taught over the years in my own church, and with what you are teaching me in class. What particularly disturbs me is that his arguments are very convincing and seem to be grounded in solid biblical exegesis of Matthew 24. I need your help because I'm beginning to feel like a theological loner.

"Ed, my reason for writing like this is to ask a favor. I promised Luke I would address his problem but I'm snowed under with work at AIMS. You're the New Testament expert. Would you mind if I passed your email address on to Luke so he can interact with you about Matthew 24? Luke has a sharp mind and he won't be put off easily so you'll need to be convincing in your rebuttal of any aberrant views he comes up with. And rebut we must. Luke is a good guy and we can't let him get caught up in an off-beat eschatology bordering on heresy."

I remembered my good but unfulfilled intentions of the previous year to follow up Luke's provocative eschatological comments so replied positively to David's email. The following day I heard from Luke. After thanking me for my willingness to chat with him online and repeating the concerns David had already shared, he said, "My reading of Matthew 24 and the parallel passages in Mark 13 and Luke 21 leads me to believe there is a connection between the destruction of the temple in AD 70 and the second coming of Christ. What do you think?"

5

Tangled in the *Little Apocalypse*

With Luke's challenge as my project and my new office under the house in which to pursue it, I considered how best to begin my rebuttal. A copy of Milton Terry's *Biblical Hermeneutics* was available on the internet and I was tempted to read the chapter that had unsettled Luke and simply pick holes in it. I thought better of it as I remembered how I had reprimanded Alex Symons for mouthing pat answers, not listening to the text, and making it fit preconceived ideas. I needed to study Matthew 24 with an open mind before consulting the opinions of others.

I read the chapter, sometimes called the *Little Apocalypse*, over and over to get the big picture and then began to look at the parts. The first three verses set the scene:

> Jesus left the temple and was walking away when his disciples came up to him to call his attention to its buildings. [2]"Do you see all these things?" he asked. "I tell you the truth, not one stone here will be left on another; every one will be thrown down." [3]As Jesus was sitting on the Mount of Olives, the disciples came to him privately. "Tell us," they said, "when will this happen, and what will be the sign of your coming and of the end of the age?"

The parallel chapters in Mark 13 and Luke 21 began similarly with the disciples' admiration of the temple, Jesus' bombshell prediction of its destruction, and questions by the disciples. While there were minor verbal differences in each account, I noticed a more substantial difference: the questions in Mark and Luke were limited to the destruction of the temple but the questions in Matthew appeared to go beyond that event to the second coming and the end of the age.

How was I to account for the differences? I noted that in all three gospels Jesus' response to the disciples' questions included references to his second coming. That suggested Matthew had given a fuller account of the questions but all three had covered the answers. However, one thing puzzled me: Why did the disciples respond to a prediction about the destruction of the temple with a question about the second coming and the end of the age unless there was a connection between all three events? The destruction of the temple occurred in AD 70. Almost 2,000 years later we were still waiting for the other two events. It seemed that the conversation with Jesus went along the following lines:

> Disciples: "Teacher, isn't this an amazing building?"
>
> Jesus: "Surprise, surprise! It's all going to come tumbling down."
>
> Disciples: "When is this going to happen and, by the way, while you're answering that question, can we throw in a totally unrelated question?"

The shock announcement of the destruction of the temple would have kept the disciples focused on that event. Of course, they may have mistakenly believed that the second coming and the end of the age would occur at the same time as the destruction of the temple and hence have regarded their second question as relevant. But what if the disciples were correct in associating the second coming and the end of the age with the destruction of Jerusalem and I was mistaken in thinking the questions related to events widely separated? I had to admit that when reading Matthew 24 in the past I had always found it difficult to decide which parts of the chapter answered which question.

A turning point in my thinking came through recalling that the King James Version had translated "the end of the age" as "the end of the world." I knew the Greek word for "age" was in the original, not the Greek word for "world," but I had been brought up on the older version and it was possible it had subconsciously influenced my thinking that the "end of the age" and the "end of the world" were coterminous. The world had not come to an end but could an age have come to an end in AD 70? If so, what age?

To answer that question, I put myself in the shoes of the disciples and considered AD 70 from a Jewish point of view. The destruction of Jerusalem and its temple in AD 70 under the Roman general Titus was, for the Jews, far more than the mere sacking of a city and burning of a building: their center of worship, their priestly ritual, their sacrificial system, were at an end. It was indeed the end of an age. There *were* grounds for the disciples to include a question linking the destruction of the temple with the end of the age, the end of the age *they* were living in, and not the end of the age *I* was living in. I could accept that in AD 70 an age came to an end but surely Christ did not return at that time. The mere suggestion smelt of heresy. My mobile rang.

"Ed, the whiting are running and the tide's just right." It was Jack Wilson. Correctly interpreting his report as an invitation to go fishing, I gladly accepted. A dose of salt air would be an effective prophylactic against unhealthy eschatological ideas. By the time we had pulled in a dozen winter whiting of legal size I was settling comfortably back into orthodoxy.

Jack had a policy of not over-fishing so we headed for the bank and began gutting and filleting our catch. As he lobbed the tail of a whiting into the cavernous mouth of a pelican, Jack announced, "Carol and I are taking a trip to the United States to visit Lauren next month. Would you be willing to preach at the church on the Sundays in July?" I was a little surprised at the offer since we had only been attending since March. Besides, Charlotte and I were divided over whether to remain with the church beyond the end of the month. I felt I had demonstrated outstanding loyalty to my wife and the church in having endured slow songs and soporific sermons for so long. Jack's invitation to preach tipped the scales in Charlotte's favor. I accepted. The quality of preaching at SCIF was about to improve.

I regarded the church to be as relevant to the community as a golf ball to a soccer match. The congregation was greying not growing. Most of the members were cocooned from the rest of the world with little hope of metamorphosis so I embraced the challenge over the four Sundays at my disposal to help the church move into the twenty-first century. On reflection, I wondered if *twentieth* century might not be a more realistic goal.

On the first Sunday, I announced that the theme for the month would be "Openness" and preached from Acts 15 about being "Open to the Holy Spirit" as the Council of Jerusalem had been in the face of pressures for change with the influx of Gentiles into the church. That week I received several emails—I was wrong in thinking Robyn Bradford was the only computer owner in the church—none of them positive. One accused me of being a "change agent," apparently a dirty word; another suspected me of being a "closet charismatic" (an even dirtier word) because of my emphasis on the Holy Spirit.

On the second Sunday I spoke from Acts 18 about being "Open to learning from others" like Apollos who, though a learned man, was willing to be taught by Priscilla and her husband Aquila. The emails continued in similar vein. One felt I was approving of female pastors; another criticized me for suggesting we could learn from Bill Hybels and Rick Warren, each apparently persona non grata. I had publicly committed myself to the series and determined to see it through, optimistically believing that it could not get worse.

Using Jesus' metaphor of putting new wine in new wineskins, on the third Sunday I urged the congregation to consider being "Open to new worship styles" including the use of more contemporary music as a means of reaching today's youth. I was wrong: it *could* get worse. I received a package in the mail containing a book about the satanic origins of rock music (although the word "rock" had not been in my sermon) and another containing a DVD upholding the King James Version as the only reliable English version of the Bible. I had not targeted the KJV specifically so could only presume it was my use of the New International Version that had motivated the donor. My phlegmatic temperament was severely tested but with only one Sunday to go, I decided to persevere.

I was pleasantly surprised to see Jack and Carol in the congregation on the fourth Sunday. At first I didn't recognize them: I did not expect them home till the following week and their attire, noticeably American, made them look like visitors. In my message from Acts 6, I mentioned how, at a time of internal crisis, an innovative leadership appointment led to significant church growth. I suggested that *our* (a brave word-choice) church should be open to leadership change as a catalyst for growth.

At morning tea after the service, I was pleased that the focus was on the Wilsons and not on my sermon. Surrounded by a welcoming group of church members, Jack was regaling them, in between bites on a pumpkin scone, with news of Lauren and their experiences in America. The keen interest in the Wilsons' travels made me think the locals viewed them like Christopher Columbus returning to Spain from the New World. When I finally had an opportunity to speak with Jack alone, he began by praising my sermon, the first compliment I had received in a month. He could, of course, have been merely making conversation but when he said, "I'd like to catch up with you this week to explore your topic further," I was doubly encouraged.

At home there was an email from David Barnes: "Ed, Luke Rodman is complaining that he hasn't had an answer to his question about Matthew 24. Where are you at with it?" In working on the August sermons, I had put Matthew 24 on hold. I wrote a note of apology with a promise to contact Luke by the end of the week.

6

Questioning the Signs

Early Monday morning I helped Charlotte plant a couple of frangipani trees, sprayed the lawn against bindii prickles so we could walk barefoot on the grass in summer, and then went to my office. The traffic outside our house had died since the weekend day-trippers had vacated the river parklands and, apart from some lorikeets squawking over the honey-flavored bread Charlotte had placed on the bird table, all was quiet. I began with an email to Luke Rodman in response to his question about a connection between the destruction of Jerusalem and the second coming of Christ. I told him that any suggestion that the second coming occurred in AD 70 went counter to the teaching of the New Testament, the creeds of the church, and to the truth that sound Christians have agreed on over the centuries. I acknowledged the possibility that an age came to an end in AD 70, hoping that conceding such a link would settle Luke and get him off my back. Such optimism was short-lived. Luke must have been sitting at his computer and have responded immediately to the "You've-got-mail" popup because within minutes I received the following message:

> The disciples asked about the sign of Christ's coming and of the end of the age. If they believed the age would finish with the destruction of Jerusalem but that the second coming would occur later, would you not expect them to reverse the order of the events, end of the age, second coming? Furthermore, the singular use of the word "sign" before both events and the structure of the Greek phrase, suggest an expectation that the two events would occur together. Speaking of signs, my reading of Matthew 24 and of the history of the time indicates that the signs popularly associated with a future coming of Christ were to be

fulfilled in the first century not the twenty-first century. What do you think?

Fearing a prolonged and unproductive correspondence with Luke, I was tempted simply to trash his email—end of story—or at least write and tell him that I wished to end the conversation to protect him from becoming theologically entangled. On reflection, I acknowledged that our limited interaction had forced me to accept that the disciples may have been correct in linking the end of the age with the destruction of Jerusalem. I also admitted that I was really trying to protect myself not Luke. He was asking good questions and I was afraid of the answers. For the sake of my own integrity I had to continue. Resisting the temptation to read Milton Terry on the subject, I read Matthew 24 listening to what it said rather than imposing my preconceptions on it.

When teaching my New Testament exegesis students at AIMS, I had often urged them to ask questions of the text. "If you want good answers *from* the Bible," I'd say, "you must ask good questions *of* the Bible." I put my advice into practice as I read the chapter. The pronoun "you" kept recurring in Matthew 24 so I asked, "Whom does 'you' represent?" I created a new document on my computer and downloaded part of the text dealing with signs and italicized some of the occurrences of "you."

> [3]As Jesus was sitting on the Mount of Olives, the disciples came to him privately. "Tell us," they said, "when will this happen, and what will be the sign of your coming and of the end of the age?" [4]Jesus answered: "Watch out that no one deceives *you*. [5]For many will come in my name, claiming, "I am the Christ," and will deceive many. [6]*You* will hear of wars and rumors of wars, but see to it that *you* are not alarmed. Such things must happen, but the end is still to come. [7]Nation will rise against nation, and kingdom against kingdom. There will be famines and earthquakes in various places. [8]All these are the beginning of birth pains. [9]Then *you* will be handed over to be persecuted and put to death, and *you* will be hated by all nations because of me. [10]At that time many will turn away from the faith and will betray and hate each other, [11]and many false prophets will appear and deceive many people."

Most contemporary preachers included their congregations in the "you." I'd been guilty of doing so myself but there seemed to be several reasons for thinking I was wrong: The persons represented by the pronoun "you" would normally be found earlier in the sentence or in a preceding sentence. The only candidate for "you" in verse 4 was "disciples" in verse 3.

Furthermore, the disciples said, "Tell *us* . . . " It made sense for the "us" and the "you" to refer to the same people. According to verse 3, the conversation with Jesus was private so Jesus' use of "you" would appropriately refer to those present.

Jesus was telling the disciples the signs *they* would experience in advance of the events they had asked about, signs such as messianic claims, wars, famines, earthquakes, persecution, martyrdom, apostasy, betrayal, false prophets. These signs were popularly cited in *our* day as heralding the second coming of Christ. I recalled our lunch with the Bradfords when Robyn had spoken about the incidence of earthquakes and wars as signs of the end. I remembered her saying, "It's five minutes to midnight for this old world. The last days are upon us." Robyn Bradford seemed to think the "you" included her. I wasn't so sure anymore.

The questions were piling up in my mind: *Did* the disciples experience the things that the "you" implied they would experience? If so, did they, like Robyn Bradford, think they were in the last days? My thoughts were interrupted by Jack Wilson's face appearing at the window. He asked if I could spare a minute. I signaled him in and quickly jotted down "earthquakes/wars/first century/last days" to remind me to seek answers to my questions. I wasn't expecting Jack so early in the week since he'd only been back from the States for three days. He explained:

"Carol wants me out of the house; thinks she can put things away more quickly without me. I'm keen to talk about something you said last Sunday."

"Can't it wait?" I said. "*I'm* keen to hear about your trip."

"We'll have you and Charlotte over later in the week when we've sorted out our photos. What I want to talk about is not unrelated to our trip."

"Fire away, Jack."

"Last Sunday you spoke about how the early church made an innovative decision to appoint leaders to solve a problem and how the church grew after that. Our church has a problem. We're not growing and I've been thinking it's because we haven't got good leadership. While we were visiting Lauren, we went to several different churches that were flourishing. In each case they had a gifted pastor. We've been limping along for years with untrained lay leaders maintaining the status quo. Someone told me status quo is 'Latin for the mess we're in.'"

I interrupted: "I'm sure the church would benefit from a visionary pastor who could give time to pastoral and evangelistic work. You don't have to be Sherlock Holmes to see a connection here in Australia between growing churches and good leadership." I wanted to go on but Jack was as excited as if he had just hooked a three-pound flathead.

"I've had a great idea. Lauren has been attending a Bible Chapel in Chattanooga, Tennessee, where she has become friends with a girl called Anna Zimmerman. Her father, Andy Zimmerman, is the assistant pastor of the church. Carol and I got to know the family quite well and they asked lots of questions about Australia and also about our church."

"But what's your great idea?" I asked.

"Andy said he's always wanted to come to Australia to which I jokingly responded, 'Our church could do with a pastor.' He must have taken me seriously because when I got home there was an email waiting for me from Andy. Here's a copy of it."

"But what's your great idea?" I asked again.

"Read the email," he said.

I skipped over the small talk at the beginning of the email and read the section Jack had highlighted: "Jack, you commented when you were here that your church needed a pastor. I've been assistant pastor here for seven years and feel it's time for a change. When I shared my feelings with our senior pastor and mentioned your need for a pastor, he was encouraging to the point of offering to recommend to our mission board that the church support such a move should you be interested in our coming."

I hardly needed Jack to spell out his great idea but he did anyway: "I believe Andy Zimmerman would be a wonderful asset to our church. He's a trained pastor, preaches well, is personable, has a lovely family, and is on the same theological page as we are. My idea is to recommend to the elders that we invite him to become the pastor of SCIF. They will see it as a radical suggestion but I believe I can make a strong case on the grounds of declining numbers and an aging congregation. I've got some photos of his family and a CD of some of his sermons. I think they'll be impressed."

"I suggest you get some information about Andy," I said. "*You* know him, but the elders don't. Ask Andy for a copy of his CV and for some references."

"What's a CV?"

"A curriculum vitae is a document that outlines a person's qualifications, experience, and character qualities that can be used when applying for a job. It would give the elders a snapshot of him and make it easier for them to make a decision."

"Good idea. I'll get right onto it so I have something for the elders' meeting tomorrow week. I'll also ask for a reference from his senior pastor and one or two others who know him well." After lending me Andy's CD and family photos, Jack left and I went back to Matthew 24.

7

Historical Support for the Signs

I found the piece of paper that reminded me of the questions I had asked myself. If the "you" in Matthew 24 referred to the disciples of the first century, it was reasonable to ask if they experienced the phenomena recorded in the chapter as Jesus said they would. I was not going to find all the answers to this question in the Bible but with the help of an old commentary by Adam Clarke, the works of Josephus (the first century Jewish historian), and the internet, I did find some answers.

I began with the incidence of false Christs and false prophets. Josephus wrote of men "who deceived and deluded the people under pretense of divine inspiration . . . and these prevailed with the multitude to act like madmen, and went before them into the wilderness, as pretending that God would there show them the signals of liberty." He also wrote of "an Egyptian false prophet that did the Jews more mischief than the former; for he was a cheat, and pretended to be a prophet also, and got together thirty-thousand men that were deluded by him." According to Adam Clarke, "About twelve years after the death of our Lord, when Cuspius Fadus was procurator of Judea, arose an impostor of the name of Theudas, who said he was a prophet, and persuaded a great multitude to follow him with their best effects to the river Jordan, which he promised to divide for their passage; and saying these things, says Josephus, he deceived many: almost the very words of our Lord." Clarke went on to write, "A few years afterwards, under the reign of Nero, while Felix was procurator of Judea, impostors of this stamp were so frequent that some were taken and killed almost every day."

"Wars and rumors of wars" was a phrase often quoted in anticipation of the second coming of Christ whenever newspaper headlines recorded or threatened even a minor skirmish somewhere in the world. My question concerned the relevance of the phrase for the disciples in the first century.

How peaceful *was* the Pax Romana? I discovered there were plenty of wars at that time, as reflected in the title of Josephus's book, *The Wars of the Jews*. But what about rumors of wars? Even that prediction was fulfilled in the days of the disciples. Josephus wrote: "Now as to the Jews, some of them could not believe the stories that spake [sic] of a war; but those that did believe them were in the utmost distress how to defend themselves, and the terror diffused itself presently through them all: for the army [Roman] was already come to Ptolemais."

As for famines, in addition to Christ's prediction, Acts 11:28 records, "One of them, named Agabus, stood up and through the Spirit predicted that a severe famine would spread over the entire Roman world. (This happened during the reign of Claudius)." But *did* it happen? According to Adam Clarke, independent sources, Suetonius, Tacitus, and Eusebius confirmed the fulfilment of Agabus's prophecy.

I was beginning to doubt the modern application of the signs in Matthew 24 to my generation and my doubts only increased as I read the evidence supporting "earthquakes in various places": Crete, Smyrna, Miletus, Chios, Samos, Rome, Laodicea, Campania, and Judea. It was becoming clear that the signs predicted in Matthew 24 occurred during the lifetime of the apostles. What right did we have to give them an application beyond that specified by Christ? If the shock of dismissal from AIMS had unsettled me, the apprehension about where my eschatological reflections might lead smacked of a rumble before a seismic upheaval greater than earthquakes at Smyrna or Samos.

To alleviate my apprehension I picked up the photos Jack had left: a family shot and separate photos of each member with name and age on the back. I was impressed. The smiles on each face seemed not to be the result of saying "cheese" but to come from within. Andy, forty years old, was a head taller than his wife Linda, thirty-seven. Their strikingly handsome features required no imagination to believe that mutual attraction had helped bring them together. Daughter Anna was seventeen and shared the good looks of her parents. A mini-version of his father, eleven-year-old Sam's smile differed from the others' in betraying a mischievous streak.

However, the church needed more than the addition of some pretty faces. What did Andy Zimmerman have to offer as a pastor? I reached for the CD player on top of my bookshelf, plugged it in and inserted the disc. Again I was impressed. Andy's first sermon began with an attention-grabbing introduction and continued with a well-structured exposition of John 15:1–8. He tellingly illustrated the message, not with cut-and-paste stories from the internet but from his own observations and experience. Particularly impressive was his warm personality that radiated pastoral concern as he showed the relevance of his message to contemporary needs. The whole was interspersed with a judicious use of humor. I was encouraged. If the Zimmerman family *did* come to SCIF, the church might gain more than a drop in the average age of the congregation.

A few days later, as I continued to wrestle with Matthew 24, I was pleased to be interrupted by a phone call from Jack asking if I would look over Andy Zimmerman's CV and a couple of references that had arrived by email. Andy was certainly keen to come to Australia and as I read about his academic qualifications and fifteen years of pastoral experience, I became almost as excited as Jack. The prospect of a trained pastor whose sermons were mentally and spiritually stimulating might induce me to hang in at SCIF with Charlotte after all. Both the referees were very affirming of Andy as a suitable pastoral candidate: visionary leader, powerful preacher, empathetic listener, loving husband and father.

"Jack, SCIF could be on a winner here," I said. "Go ahead and put your case at the elders' meeting next week."

"I've already asked Stan Mullins to put it on the agenda. He said he would but I could tell he wasn't too excited about a pastor at SCIF. As chairman of the board of elders, he is responsible for drawing up the preaching roster. He fancies himself as the best preacher on the roster so I suspect he's afraid he'll rarely be in the pulpit if Andy comes. Stan's rating of his own sermons is not shared by most in the congregation who find his sermons too long and boring and too short on substance and relevance. By the way, could I have Andy's CD and photos back to support my case?"

I was more pessimistic than Jack about a positive decision by the board but did not want to discourage him. I said, quite sincerely, "It will be a great leap forward for the church if you *can* persuade the elders."

8

No to a New Pastor

Having come to the conclusion that there was a good case for a first-century fulfilment of the signs Jesus had predicted in Matthew 24, I felt I owed it to Luke to acknowledge that he could be onto something. I had mixed feelings as I wrote to him. On the one hand, there was a sense of satisfaction that in reading the text in the light of the contemporary history, it was making more sense than it ever had; on the other hand, I felt a strong allegiance to the eschatological paradigm I had personally embraced and taught for more than thirty years.

Jack was disappointed when I declined an invitation to go fishing—he hadn't thrown in a line since he went to America—but I needed time to resolve my frustrations. I thought of him out in the tinnie reeling in the winter whiting. I was an idiot to be shut up in my office wrestling with someone else's problem on a day that justified Sunshine Coast as the name of our region. I was under no obligation to get involved with Luke: I was retired; the issue was theological; David Barnes was the theologian; Luke Rodman was *his* student, not mine; and, unlike me, David Barnes had not been sacked. It was a problem for AIMS, not me. Thus I reasoned with myself—but not successfully. Had I not urged my students to be true to the text of Scripture even if it put them offside with others? I knew I could not rest personally with the problem unresolved so I began to see Luke's request for answers as a means of motivating me to find answers for myself. One part of me wanted to find answers while another part of me feared the answers might be theologically unsettling and distance me from my heritage and my contemporaries. A measure of courage was needed. I was reminded of the words of the ancient Rabbi Hillel: "A timid student does not learn."

I returned to Matthew 24, questioning if its statements were really as plain as I had imagined and looking for material that allowed me to retain my traditional views and associated orthodoxy. I was encouraged: I found a number of predictions in the chapter that so far had not been fulfilled. They clearly proved that the unsettling train of thought that conflicted with the generally accepted eschatology could not be true. I was no longer on the back foot; I had enough ammunition to permanently silence Luke Rodman; and I could continue my retirement with eschatological respectability and the freedom to accept all of Jack's fishing invitations. Relieved, I sent off an email to Luke with a blind copy to David Barnes:

> Hi Luke,
>
> I've been looking seriously into Matthew 24 and agree with you that parts of it were fulfilled during the lifetime of the disciples. However, parts of it have not yet been fulfilled so we must avoid relegating the whole chapter to the first century.
>
> As an example of a yet-to-be-fulfilled prophecy, look at verse 14: "And this gospel of the kingdom will be preached in the whole world as a testimony to all nations, and then the end will come." The whole world hasn't heard the gospel so the end hasn't come. We only need to listen to the concerns of contemporary missionaries who tell us of unreached tribes with no part of the Bible in their language to know that this prophecy has not been fulfilled.
>
> Clearly, some of Matthew 24 is still future so let's not unsettle ourselves or others by casting doubts on our hope of a future return of Christ.
>
> Kind regards,
> Ed Sutherland.

A prompt reply from David Barnes applauded my effort to straighten Luke out, affirmed the unfulfilled prediction I had mentioned and, like me, anticipated Luke would let the matter rest.

I put Matthew 24 behind me and turned to local matters, not least SCIF's leadership meeting at which Jack was to present a case for the pastoral appointment of Andy Zimmerman. In the days before the meeting, we talked at length about it. Jack's enthusiasm was somewhat dampened by my ambivalence. While I supported the idea of a pastoral appointment and was impressed with Andy's preaching ability, I had misgivings about importing an American into an Australian context. Contrary to my earlier resolve not to discourage Jack, I raised a number of questions: Would Andy be accepted by the average Aussie? Would they take to his Southern drawl? Would his family miss their social network and shorten his tenure?

On the Tuesday night when Jack dropped in on the way to the elders' meeting, I was pleased to sense his resilience had restored his optimism about the outcome of the meeting, in spite of my reservations.

"This is an historic meeting, Ed, a significant turning point for our church. Andy Zimmerman and his family will be like a miracle cure for a chronic fatigue victim, generating fresh vigor and motivating us to fulfil a vision for numerical and spiritual growth. Before long we'll need to extend the church building to accommodate the new members." I hoped he was right and wished him well as he left for the meeting, not before arranging a dawn trip the following day to the Cod Hole, a popular spot in the river for flathead and whiting.

An hysterical kookaburra laughed me into wakefulness at ten to five, ten minutes before my alarm clock was due to go off, so I was in good time for my 5:30 a.m. appointment with Jack at the jetty. He was late and looked disheveled and bleary-eyed. I was unsure whether his lugubrious demeanor was due to the lateness of the meeting or its outcome. It *was* a late meeting but his somber mood mainly reflected the Zimmerman decision as I soon learned from Jack's report:

"The appointment of Andy Zimmerman was near the end of a long agenda. Most of the elders were tired and I was only given five minutes to speak to the topic. I tried to paint a glowing picture of Andy and his family, of his preaching and pastoral gifts, and of his suitability to meet the needs of our church. When I spoke of our aging congregation and dwindling numbers, Stan Mullins sat back with his hands clasped over his ample abdomen and a complacent look on his face that suggested we didn't have any needs. Although I had sent Stan a copy of Andy's CV, the CD of his sermons, and photos of his family, not only had he not shared them with the other elders but the air of unfamiliarity with which he took them out of the envelope said he had not done much with them himself. Mark Mullins, Stan's son, and the youngest member of the leadership team, revived my spirits with an impassioned speech that made such an impression on me I think I can retell it with a fair degree of accuracy. He said:

> The other day I told my children the old story of the Pied Piper of Hamelin, the story about the traveling musician who cleared the town of its rat infestation but was not paid by the civic authorities as agreed. In retaliation, he piped all of Hamelin's children from the town and they were never seen again. They lost a generation because they were not prepared to pay the price. Our

church has lost a generation with little hope of regaining it short of radical change.

Change comes at a price: the relinquishing of power; the intrusion of the unfamiliar; the struggle by old dogs to learn new tricks; a bigger budget; the construction of a larger church building; a renewed mindset that stops harking back to the "good old days" and begins to look optimistically to better days ahead. Andy Zimmerman may well be the man for such a time as this. I move that we invite him to be pastor of the Sunshine Coast Independent Fellowship to commence from the start of next year.

"I gave a loud 'Amen' and was encouraged when others followed suit. No 'Amen' came from Stan who was visibly miffed by what he'd heard. Without asking if someone wished to second the motion, he said:

All this talk about declining numbers, a lost generation, growth, and a larger church building betrays ignorance of the times. We are in the last days, brothers, when decline is expected. Jesus said, "When the Son of Man comes, will he find faith on the earth?" This is the Laodicean age, the age of lukewarmness, the age immediately before the return of Christ. We need to be suspicious of large numbers. The mega-churches are apostate with their shallow sermons and their emphasis on entertainment rather than edification, on worldly music rather than godly worship. We are privileged to be part of the remnant. We must maintain what we have and heed Paul's warnings to Timothy about conditions in the last days when people will "depart from the faith" and will have only an outward "form of godliness." Paul goes on to say, "From such turn away." Gentlemen, it's late; let's close the meeting and go home.

"Ed, I went home angry with Stan Mullins for railroading the meeting and not following due process. I'm still angry! We have lost a wonderful opportunity to reverse the decline in our church—all because of one man. Needless to say, I didn't sleep well last night."

No pious it-must-be-the-Lord's-will comment was going to calm Jack. He was convinced that Stan Mullins was wrong and that the Zimmermans were meant to come to Buderim. We set off on the planned fishing trip, albeit in silence. The Cod Hole lived up to its reputation by delivering five flathead and seventeen whiting into our Esky but they were not enough to brighten Jack.

9

Yes to a New Pastor

It was Friday before I saw Jack again, a very different Jack. He rushed excitedly into our kitchen while Charlotte and I were eating a salad that an hour before was growing in our vegie plot. In one hand he held a letter and in the other a CD. Without a conventional greeting, he said, "Listen to this," and proceeded to read the letter in his hand:

> Dear Elders,
>
> I am writing to apologize for my mishandling of the meeting on Tuesday night. I confess that I went to the meeting with a negative attitude towards a pastoral appointment and without having studied the materials Jack Wilson gave me.
>
> On Wednesday morning I thought I should at least listen to one of Zimmerman's sermons. I considered the embarrassment, if asked what I thought of them, of having to say I hadn't listened to them. Unexpectedly, I enjoyed the first sermon so much that I listened to a second. What a message! He's on the same page as I am. He would, I am sure, endorse the comments I made about the apostasy of the last days.
>
> I have made you all a copy of the sermon CD. Please listen, particularly to the second sermon, in preparation for an extraordinary meeting of the board next Tuesday when we will revisit the matter of the pastoral appointment of Andy Zimmerman.
>
> Yours sincerely,
> Stan Mullins.

"What a turn-around!" said Jack. I was pleased for him and said so. He wanted me to go next door and listen to the CD immediately. Charlotte told me to finish my lunch first. Dutiful husband that I am, I obeyed and joined Jack twenty minutes later to find him standing near the CD player ready to push the start button. The sermon Stan wanted the elders to hear was based on 2 Timothy 3:1–5:

> But mark this: There will be terrible times in the last days. People will be lovers of themselves, lovers of money, boastful, proud, abusive, disobedient to parents, ungrateful, unholy, without love, unforgiving, slanderous, without self-control, brutal, not lovers of the good, treacherous, rash, conceited, lovers of pleasure rather than lovers of God—having a form of godliness but denying its power. Have nothing to do with them.

With powerful and passionate rhetoric, Andy Zimmerman argued that phrase after phrase in the text referring to the last days aptly described today's society. We were therefore in the last days and the second coming of Christ was at hand. His descriptions of narcissism, corporate greed, rebellious youth, broken relationships, drug abuse, domestic and international violence, hedonism, and lifeless religion were reinforced by headlines from the *New York Times*, quotations from *Newsweek*, references to Islamic State, and escalating divorce statistics and crime rates.

I could imagine Stan nodding in approval and even, uncharacteristically, uttering a loud "Amen," especially when Andy spoke of large churches that pandered to the congregation's love of pleasure by replacing good old hymns with rock music and dance troupes.

The parallels between Paul's account of the last days and life in today's world as reported in the media and known to most of us by experience, certainly came across strongly in support of our being in the last days, but one thing worried me. The last sentence in the text suggested otherwise: "Have nothing to do with them." Paul clearly expected Timothy to experience the conditions listed in the text. *Timothy*, not Stan Mullins or Andy Zimmerman, was to face the problems of the last days. Paul's intention was not to describe society in the twenty-first century but in the first century. He was warning of conditions Timothy would face in his day.

To Andy's credit, his manner, though forceful, was not aggressive; his criticism, though pointed, was not vitriolic. I didn't agree with everything he said but, at the same time, I didn't find him offensive. Mixed with his pessimism was a desire to grow the church and a challenge to reach out to neighbors and friends with the truth because the time was short. Though I hadn't met Andy, he came across as a nice guy.

After Jack pressed the stop button, he said, "What did you think of that, Ed?"

"He's a very engaging speaker," I replied.

"But what did you think of the points he made?"

Not wanting to get involved with Jack in an argument about the last days or to dampen his enthusiasm about the prospect of a new pastor for SCIF, I replied objectively: "He vividly described conditions in our world and even though his message was critical of our society, his manner was gracious—an admirable skill in preachers. He's a gifted communicator, Jack."

"Can I quote you on that at the leadership meeting on Tuesday night?" asked Jack.

"If you think it will help your case, go ahead," I replied. Jack jotted down a few notes as, with some misgivings, I hoped he would minimize the use of my name at the meeting. I did not want any impression given that a newcomer to SCIF was pulling strings behind the scene. I was also concerned that Jack might get into trouble for leaking leadership information.

The special elders' meeting the following Tuesday was dedicated to the question of Andy's appointment as pastor. It was much shorter than the previous meeting so I did not have to wait till Wednesday morning for Jack's report. He noticed my office light on so dropped in before going home. I read the decision of the meeting in his face before he opened his mouth. "SCIF is about to get a pastor," he said. "All the elders had listened to Andy preach; all were impressed and felt he would fit into our church. Stan, who clearly came to the meeting with his mind made up, followed due process for a change by seconding Mark's motion for Andy's appointment and by inviting discussion. It was all positive and the motion passed unanimously. Since I am the only elder who knows Andy, I am to write him a letter of invitation to serve as pastor of SCIF from next January."

I curbed any mention of my ambivalence over the appointment of an American fundamentalist, rejoiced with Jack over the elders' decision, and hoped with him for a new day at the Sunshine Coast Independent Fellowship.

10

The Last Days

The following Sunday Stan announced the invitation to appoint a pastor. The church members turned to one another as if surprised, but they were no more surprised than children opening Christmas presents they had secretly observed their parents wrapping the night before. The confidentiality of elders' decisions was a stated policy rarely observed. A leak to only one elder's wife guaranteed total dissemination within twenty-four hours, or even less with the help of Robyn Bradford's new computer.

Mark Mullins was rostered to preach that morning. He did well. He included his Pied Piper of Hamelin story and hoped God would use Andy Zimmerman to pipe a youthful generation back to SCIF. As he preached, I looked around at the faces of his listeners, most of them wrinkled and serious. They appeared to be concentrating on Mark but I sensed many were distracted with questions about the future.

After the service, the animated conversation over tea and pumpkin scones was about one topic. I overheard questions I had imagined in members' minds during the service. Mrs. Beecroft, the aged organist, asked if she would be out of a job should the minister's wife be musical. Her ninety-year-old husband, Matthew, stammered his concerns about the church's capacity to pay the pastor's salary. Carol Wilson asked where the family would live and my Charlotte suggested they buy an old Queenslander and do it up. Jack was encouraged at the generally positive response to the announcement but reminded everyone that the Zimmermans had yet to reply.

Day after day, Jack inspected his letterbox in anticipation of a reply from Andy only to be disappointed. In the mornings Charlotte and I extended our vegie garden and built a chook pen. In the afternoons, I took a nap, spent time on my computer making notes on my eschatological journey, and went fishing with Jack. One afternoon, while tidying my office, I found the scrap of paper on which I had written "earthquakes/wars/first century/last days." I had yet to explore the question, "Did New Testament Christians believe they were in the last days?" According to Robyn Bradford, Stan Mullins, and Andy Zimmerman, *we* were in the last days. I had already begun to doubt that while listening to the CD of Andy's sermon on 2 Timothy 3. Paul's warning to Timothy to have nothing to do with the decadence of the last days indicated that Timothy would be confronted with such conditions and therefore lived in the last days. I checked out other references to the last days.

The apostle Peter made reference to them in his sermon on the day of Pentecost. He began the sermon with a response to the criticism that he and the other disciples were drunk because they spoke in tongues under the power of the outpoured Holy Spirit (Acts 2:15–17):

> These men are not drunk, as you suppose. It's only nine in the morning! No, this is what was spoken by the prophet Joel: "In the last days, God says, I will pour out my Spirit on all people."

Peter was convinced he was in the last days. He saw the phenomena on the day of Pentecost as the fulfilment of Joel's prophecy about the last days. If Robyn Bradford was in the last days then the last days had been running for almost 2,000 years. "Last days" seemed an inappropriate description of such a long period.

The book of Hebrews begins with a reference to the last days that unmistakably places them in the first century:

> In the past God spoke to our forefathers through the prophets at many times and in various ways, but in these last days he has spoken to us by his Son.

In calling them "*these* last days," he implied that they had already begun. At the time of writing, the author was conscious of living in the last days. He also makes clear that when Jesus was on earth, he too was living in the last days. Whenever I heard people talk about *our* living in the last days, I knew they believed the end was near. Surely if that's how the words should be understood, then that's how the early Christians would have understood them. But they both can't be right. The question remained, "How *should* they be understood?"

I was aware that commentators regularly applied the last days to the whole period beginning with the first coming of Christ and extending to the second coming of Christ. I wondered if they were conveniently stretching days into centuries to conform to their eschatological paradigm. Again I questioned how "last days" could embrace such a long period of time. A verse in John's first letter only confirmed my doubt:

> Dear children, this is the last hour; and as you have heard that the antichrist is coming, even now many antichrists have come. This is how we know it is the last hour (1 John 2:18).

If "last days" was a strange way to describe 2,000 years, how much more "last hour!" Had *I* lived in John's day and read his "we know it is the last hour," I would have felt I was living on the edge of something momentous. And if, 2,000 years later, it had not arrived, I would have felt not only that he had abused the use of the word "hour" but that he had deceived me. Robyn Bradford had used the phrase "five minutes to midnight" in the context of "last days." When John wrote "last hour," his readers could have been excused for thinking it was close to midnight then.

As I reflected on the words "last days," I realized that while they were used in a technical sense by commentators and exponents of end-time scenarios, they were also used in everyday speech: the last days of the conference, the last days of summer, the last days of Pompeii. I could not insist that the technical meaning must be the same as the everyday meaning but, given the various contexts in which the words "last days" were used, I was entitled to ask, "The last days of what?" Depending on the context, the answer could be conference, summer, Pompeii, or even "this old world," to quote Robyn Bradford. "Last days" implied something was coming to an end.

I recalled that the disciples in Matthew 24, when told of the coming destruction of the temple, had asked about the sign of the end of the age. They linked the fall of the temple with the end of an age. An age did come to an end at that time, an age associated with Jewish worship in the temple, involving Jewish priests and Jewish rituals; in short, the age of the old covenant. With the demolition of the temple, these things were no more. As part of Jesus' answer to the disciples' question, he said, "You will hear of wars and rumors of war, but see to it that you are not alarmed. Such things must happen, but the end is still to come." Was it still to come 2,000 years down the track or in just a few years? The latter seems more likely. A Jewish revolt in AD 66 provoked war with Rome. In just a few years of wars and rumors of war, in AD 70, the end came.

I shut down my computer feeling more satisfied with my understanding of the last days than I was with some of the prophetic views of end-time scaremongers. AD 70 marked an end, not the end of the world, not the end of human history, but the end of an age, the age that ended with the fall of Jerusalem. "Last days" and even "last hour" were suitable terms in the context of that impending disaster.

The following morning as I continued working on the chook pen, I heard the postman's motorbike stop at our letterbox, downed tools and went to collect the mail. Most of it was for Charlotte, apart from a bankcard bill for me. As I opened it to check our debt level, I heard a loud "Yippee!" from next door. Jack was standing by *his* letterbox waving an envelope in one hand and a letter in the other. "The Zimmermans are coming!" he yelled. "The Zimmermans are coming!" Charlotte heard the yell from the backyard and came running. The three of us moved to the Wilsons' kitchen to share the news with Carol over coffee. Jack began by reading Andy's letter.

Dear Jack and Carol,

What a pleasant surprise to receive your letter! You must be wondering why I have not replied before this, given my earlier email and the CV and references I sent. I confess my own interests failed to respect the impact on our family of relocating to another country: the children's education, separation from friends and relatives, and adjustment to a different culture.

Now that I have reined in my enthusiasm and engaged in vigorous discussions with Linda and the children, as well as consultation with friends and colleagues, I am able to give you a more considered response: we are all happily agreed that it is right for us to come.

We would appreciate any information you can supply about educational opportunities for the children. Anna recently graduated from senior high and is interested in studying to be a science teacher; Sam is in the first year of middle school, grade six. Linda and I are keen to know about accommodation options for the family.

Our thought is to arrive mid-January to allow time to settle in before we commence pastoral duties and the children embark on their study courses. Be assured that we come with the support of our church and a sense of God's call to serve in your community to the best of our ability.

Kind regards to you both,
    Andy Zimmerman.

PS: We enjoyed Lauren's company at lunch on Sunday. She is excited at our decision, particularly because she and Anna will be able to continue their close friendship. Now that Lauren's year at college is over, I expect you'll be seeing her soon.

Our coffees went cold as we interacted over the letter. We discussed what needed to happen *before* they came and what might happen *after* they came. For an older congregation, it was overwhelming. The letter augured change and "change" had not been part of SCIF"s vocabulary in decades. The Pied Piper of Hamelin came to mind and the four of us committed to paying the price to regain a lost generation.

Jack phoned Stan with the news. Within hours, every SCIF member knew the Zimmermans were coming. To prepare for their coming, a church business meeting met a fortnight later when members willingly offered to help where they could. Mr. and Mrs. Beecroft, who planned to enter a retirement village within weeks, offered their home for the Zimmermans at a rate very kind to the church budget. Arthur Bradford said he would recruit a team of men to renovate the sixty-year-old home if Jack would act as project manager and Charlotte as architect. She agreed and also offered to organize a team to work on the garden. Stan Mullins would provide all materials at cost from his hardware store. Robyn Bradford would organize a team to create a homely atmosphere after the renovations were complete. Mark Mullins's wife Cathy, a primary school teacher, offered to check out schooling for Sam Zimmerman and I agreed to research Anna's eligibility to study science at the University of the Sunshine Coast, better known as USC.

Over the next three months, members cheerfully fulfilled their commitments and by mid-December all was ready for the Zimmermans' arrival at Brisbane airport on January 15.

11

Universal Language

The Wilson's daughter Lauren returned home late October after her year's study in Tennessee during which she acquired traces of a Southern drawl. After graduating from Maroochydore High School, she had gone to America for a break before starting a degree in social work at USC. Jack and Carol now had their two children living at home. Josh, twenty-four and single, worked as an accountant in Stan Mullins's hardware business. We rarely saw him. His work days in Nambour were long, at weekends he tinkered with his Ford Mustang and, in the warmer weather, he went surfing. He did not attend SCIF. According to Jack, Josh felt five days of Stan Mullins was enough. I wondered if SCIF as a whole, not just Stan, made him a victim of the Pied Piper's revenge—or was SCIF the victim?

Lauren, eighteen, attractive and vivacious, loved to socialize with people of all ages. With her dark hair and smooth olive complexion, her youthful beauty contrasted starkly with the average SCIF member. How long before she followed her brother? Or would Anna Zimmerman prevent her departure from SCIF?

When Lauren insisted on going to the airport to welcome the Zimmermans, Jack and Carol felt their Land Rover would not accommodate seven people plus luggage so I offered to take our Toyota Camry to help with passengers. I was rather surprised when Josh, on annual leave, asked to come along. Meeting strangers at an airport didn't sound like a fun thing for a surfer on holidays. I wondered if his sister's description of Anna Zimmerman lay behind his request.

The QANTAS flight from Los Angeles arrived on time. We waited for thirty minutes before passengers began to dribble from the customs hall.

After a further ten minutes, Jack exploded: "Here they come!" Three Wilsons rushed toward trolleys piled so high with suitcases only one head was visible, Andy's. His "How y'all doin'?" was followed by excited shrieks (Lauren and Anna), hugs and kisses (Carol and Linda), and a handshake (Jack and Andy). Sam, was almost overlooked till Lauren drew him into the mix.

Josh held back with Charlotte and me till the shrieks subsided, then we slowly approached the unwinding mix for introductions. The Zimmermans looked quite as impressive in real life as in their photos. In spite of obvious sleep-deprivation from the thirteen-hour flight from Los Angeles, they related to us strangers with ease. Charlotte and I both commented later on how comfortable they made us feel. Andy noticed Josh standing back a little and greeted him: "You must be Josh. Glad to meet you. Lauren's said good things about you." Josh lit up like a sixty-watt bulb, a nice change from the usual flickering candle.

Jack and I managed to stack most of the Zimmermans' luggage on the roof-rack of the Land Rover and in the boot of the Camry. As I squeezed a guitar case next to Sam, who was on his own in the third row of the Land Rover, he asked, "Will we see any kangaroos on the way?"

"You might be lucky," I replied. "Keep a lookout to your right as you travel."

Carol and Linda sat in the middle row, Jack and Andy in the front seats. Jack drove off as I organized the seating in the Camry: Charlotte, Lauren, and Anna in the back, and Josh beside me in the front. Within minutes of leaving the airport, the chatter in the back seat was like feeding time on our bird table. I sensed Josh was content to listen to the chatter, not being in the habit of initiating conversation. He seemed particularly interested in the conversation behind when he heard the twang of Anna's voice. On one occasion he leaned in my direction to peep in the rear-vision mirror. I didn't think it was my wife or his sister he was hoping to see. If silence in the front seat was to be broken over the next sixty minutes, it was up to me.

"Fantastic January weather we're having, Josh. You must be enjoying your holidays."

"Yep."

"I see you driving with a surfboard on the roof of your car. Are you a keen surfer?"

"Yep."

"You drive a Mustang, don't you?"

"Yep."

Whether the repeated "yeps" reflected my poor questioning skills or Josh's limited conversational skills, to prevent further monosyllabic responses, I said, "I don't know much about Mustangs, Josh. Tell me about yours."

As if he were a CD player and I'd pressed the play button, he gave me a comprehensive history of the Mustang from its birth in the sixties to the sixth generation that included his 1991 GT model. Repainted in avocado green, it had a five-liter engine, sixteen-inch aluminum wheels (each with five spokes), front and rear anti-sway bars, ten-inch front brakes, and a host of other features whose technical descriptions embarrassed my vocabulary. The CD player did not switch off till we were passing the Ettamogah pub, an intentionally miss-shaped country-style hotel modeled on an Australian cartoon—only fifteen minutes from our destination. "I'd love to go for a spin in your Mustang, Josh."

The sixty-watt bulb lit up again: "How about tomorrow?" he beamed, as if anticipating the highlight of his holidays.

"Sounds good," I replied. Josh had a smile on his face for the rest of the journey.

After climbing the plateau, we drove along the ridge through the Buderim village and arrived at the manse not long after the Land Rover. Sam ran to me shouting, "I saw three kangaroos."

"Were they on the right-hand side of the road?" I asked.

"Yes, eating grass on the edge of the small airfield we passed. There were three of them, a daddy, a mummy, and a baby kangaroo that jumped out its mother's pouch."

I was pleased for him but, noticing Jack had already unloaded the roof-rack, I took Sam to the Land Rover and gave him the guitar to carry upstairs. Jack suggested he leave it on the veranda with the other cases and that when both vehicles were unloaded, we give the Zimmermans a tour of house and garden. As Anna struggled towards the stairs with a heavy case, Josh gallantly offered to help. Her appreciative smile was shyly reciprocated.

We began our tour from the luggage pile on the veranda. From there the view across the lush coastal plain to the surfing beaches of Maroochydore and Mooloolaba, with the lighthouse on Point Cartwright in the background, elicited a succession of awe-inspired noises from the Zimmermans. They seemed to be saying they liked the location of the manse so much they could live there whether we'd refurbished the house and garden or not. As we continued the tour, I sensed that the appreciative comments were more than polite, that they were thrilled with the house and garden. Carol led the tour of the house with comments from Jack about structural changes and innovative improvements he had supervised. Along the way, Andy selected a room for his study, Linda identified the ideal location for items of furniture yet to arrive in a shipping container, and Anna and Sam negotiated a deal over who would occupy bedrooms two and three.

Charlotte took us through the garden, giving both the botanical and popular names of native plants. I tried (humbly) to outdo Jack with comments on the struggles we'd had (under my supervision) to put boulders (large ones) in place for a retaining wall and to dig (all by hand) the "massive" holes on the western fence line for the mature foxtail palms we trucked in from Manawee Garden Centre in Buderim.

When Jack frowned and shook his head in the direction of the vehicles, I initially thought he'd had enough of my impersonation of a presenter on *Better Homes and Gardens*, but I quickly realized he felt we should withdraw to give the travel-weary Zimmermans time to rest and settle in. After variations on "See you Sunday," Jack rounded up his family, Josh gave a reluctant goodbye look in Anna's direction, and Charlotte and I drove home conversing positively about our impressions of the new pastor and his family. We both felt a new day was dawning for SCIF.

Charlotte took a nap after lunch while I checked emails. The first was from the arthritic widow of a Nigerian colonel who had left her a fortune from oil discovered in his backyard. She offered me twenty-million dollars to help invest her money in the west. I deleted her generous offer along with several outstanding real estate bargains and a chance to earn $2,000 a week working from home. Robyn Bradford emailed to recommend I listen to the latest Hal Lindsey Report with its update of events in the Middle East supportive of an any-minute rapture. I declined when I noticed an email from Luke Rodman. I thought I'd heard the last of him.

After introductory small talk and an apology for his delay in replying, Luke said he had given serious consideration to the unfulfilled prophecy I identified in Matthew 24:14 and had come to believe it *was* fulfilled. He asked me to read an attached file containing his response. I thought, "This guy won't admit defeat," and opened the attachment with a supercilious smile. Disdain turned to dismay and the smile disappeared as I read:

> Jesus said in Matthew 24:14, "And this gospel of the kingdom will be preached in the whole world as a testimony to all nations, and then the end will come." You said the whole world has not heard the gospel so the end can't have come. That's the common view but there are good reasons to question it.
>
> The generally accepted view needs to reconsider the significance of two phrases in the text: "the whole world" and "the end." In the New Testament it is not uncommon for apparently universal language to be used with a limited reference. For example, note the phrases I have italicized in the following texts:

> Luke 2:1 (KJV): "And it came to pass in those days, that there went out a decree from Caesar Augustus that *all the world* should be taxed"; Acts 2:5: "Now there were staying in Jerusalem God-fearing Jews from *every nation under heaven*"; Acts 17:6: "These men who have caused trouble *all over the world* have now come here." In none of these cases is the entire planet earth intended.
>
> "End" in Matthew 24:14 is likely to be the same "end" as in verse 3: "When will this happen and what will be the sign of your coming and of the end of the age?" These questions were asked in the context of Jesus' announcement of the destruction of the temple in Jerusalem. This happened in AD 70 and marked the end of an age, the age of the Jewish priesthood and sacrificial system, the age of the old covenant.
>
> You say, "But was the gospel preached to the whole world before AD 70?" Let Paul answer that question: In Romans 1:8 he said the faith of the Romans was known "*all over the world.*" In Colossians 1:6 he said, "*All over the world* this gospel is bearing fruit and growing"; and in verse 23 he wrote: "This is the gospel that you heard and that has been proclaimed to *every creature under heaven.*" Note the verb: "has been proclaimed," not "will be proclaimed."
>
> Just as these texts do not refer to the whole world as we know it, neither does Matthew 24:14. The disciples had asked for a sign of the end of the age they were living in, not the age we are living in. One of the signs Jesus gave was the widespread preaching of the gospel in their world, not ours. The sign was fulfilled.
>
> A radical confirmation of what I've just written comes from the great commission in Matthew 28:18–20. The disciples are commanded to disciple "all nations" (verse 19), the same words as in Matthew 24:14. Of course we have the same responsibility to evangelize our world, but Jesus' promise to be with them (the disciples) to the "end of the age" indicates that they are to fulfil their task, as he intended it, before the age they were living in came to an end.

Luke's response unsettled me. The issue I thought dead and buried had sprung to life. Luke's comments made a lot of sense and rebuked my exegetical sloppiness. What was I to do? I could walk away from the subject—after all, I was retired—or I could make an honest attempt to grapple with it. Neither option appealed. If I walked away from the issue, would the issue walk away from me? If I pursued the issue, where would it lead? It was as if Luke had shut me in the middle of a haunted house. I didn't want to stay but I feared to open every closed door.

12

An Unsettling Address

I awoke later than usual the following morning; rather, I was awakened by metallic sounds from next door accompanied by vigorous barking from Chuffey. I wasn't happy: I'd had a bad night, much of it spent fiercely debating Luke Rodman's shocking implication that Jesus might have returned in the first century. Charlotte was already up and watering the garden. I dragged myself to the window with negative thoughts towards a noisy neighbor to find Josh Wilson tinkering under the bonnet of an avocado green Mustang. I'd forgotten he was taking me for a spin. *He* hadn't. I needed to brighten up so took a cold shower, shaved, and dressed in my most contemporary shorts, a Billabong T-shirt and a baseball cap with a Nike tick on the front. I didn't want to embarrass Josh too much on the trip. A cup of strong coffee and a slice of toast and I was ready to go.

Josh's cheery grin and greeting at the sight of me said he was delighted I'd remembered our arrangement. I didn't disillusion him. "Where are we going?" I asked.

"I thought we might shoot up the Bruce Highway to Eumundi and cut across to Noosa."

"Sounds good to me." I'd always enjoyed Noosa, a beach resort near the mouth of the Noosa River at the northern end of the Sunshine Coast.

I leaned over the fence to wave to Charlotte who smiled indulgently as if I were a teenager leaving on his first date. The Mustang's engine revved impatiently so I hurriedly strapped myself in thinking a seatbelt might be a decided asset on such an occasion. Once on the road, I was flung against the back of the seat as Josh demonstrated the Mustang's powers of acceleration, accompanied by excessive exhaust noise. I pulled my cap down a little in case neighbors were watching.

Once on the highway, Josh seemed to be the victim of an obsessive compulsive disorder that forced him to overtake every vehicle ahead of him with little regard for speed signs. Surprisingly, we made it to Noosa without being pulled over by the police. Along the way, conversation was limited. Josh was absorbed in showing off his driving skills and I was in survival mode, praying for protection but unsure if such prayers were valid under the circumstances.

After Josh parked near a bakery on Hastings Street, I bought a couple of take-away cappuccinos and some slices of quiche and we walked the hundred meters to the waterfront. I was pleased to sit down at a vacant picnic table that was not travelling at 120 km per hour. We had a good view of the beach which was crowded with families on holiday and local surfers pleased at the size of the waves generated by a steady south-easterly.

Josh broke the silence: "I wish I'd brought my surfboard. Those waves are epic."

"It must take a lot of courage to ride two-meter waves," I said.

"It can get scary in the green room but that's where I get my stoke on."

"The green room?"

"It's a term for being in the barrel of a wave."

I suspected I'd only continue to show my surfing ignorance if I kept asking questions so I listened, with limited understanding, as Josh gave a commentary on the surfers' performance: "What a kook! He's always grubbing . . . She'd catch more waves if she went out to the impact zone . . . Did you see that 180 degree shove-it? Even Mick Fanning would be proud . . . If he keeps riding those shore breaks he'll snap his fin off."

As the tide went out, the surf subsided and the commentator had less to say. I saw an opportunity to change the subject so, after commending Josh for his extensive knowledge of surfing, I asked: "Josh, did you never consider taking over the family business?"

"Nah. I used to help out in the shop on Thursday nights and Saturday mornings but that was enough for me. I didn't have the people skills to be a good salesman and I didn't fancy putting in the hours Dad worked, always at the shop an hour before opening time and an hour after closing time. I'd rather be at the beach on a Saturday morning than trying to sell ginger tonics to old ladies. Dad was a bit disappointed when I decided to be an accountant because he'd worked so hard to build up the business and he hoped it would stay in the family. He accepted my decision but deep down I think he feels I've let him down."

"I don't want to be nosey," I said, "but I notice you don't attend church and I'm wondering if that's of greater disappointment to your dad than the issue of the shop."

"I used to be part of SCIF but increasingly lost interest. The music was old-fashioned, the sermons bland and irrelevant, and most of the members were old enough to be my grandparents. I haven't given up on God, only my link with the church."

"With Lauren home from overseas and the Zimmermans now part of the church, there's a fresh injection of younger blood."

"True," said Josh, "and I might even turn up to see what Andy Zimmerman is like."

"There's a welcome lunch for the Zimmermans this Sunday. Why not come along?"

"I'll think about it," he said. I didn't press the point but hoped he'd come. Perhaps Anna Zimmerman rather than her father would be the drawcard.

On the way back to Maroochydore, Josh drove with greater restraint. I didn't know whether he was repentant for having visibly aged me ten years on the forward journey; whether the frightening demonstration of his driving skills and the Mustang's capabilities required no further proof; or whether he was thinking over my invitation to come to SCIF on Sunday morning. Whatever the reason, I arrived home more relaxed than on the forward journey. I thanked Josh warmly (and sincerely) for the invigorating experience and he seemed pleased when I said (a little less sincerely) that we should do it again some time. I felt that the foundation of a friendship had been laid that would be easy to build on. Charlotte was pleased to see me alive and wanted a full report on the "teenager's first date."

When Charlotte and I arrived at SCIF on Sunday morning, the car park was unusually full though we were quite early. The hum of animated conversation before the service started was also unusual. We sat in our usual row, third from the back, and noticed faces we had not seen before. Were they former members who had returned to SCIF, disaffected members from other churches, or just curious visitors? One thing was certain: Stan Mullins's advertising campaign was paying off. He had written to all the churches in the district announcing the arrival of the Zimmermans, had put an advertisement (posing as a news item) in the local paper and had been interviewed on Radio Rhema, the local Christian station, with a promise that the interview would be replayed at intervals during the week. Charlotte looked across at me with a smile I interpreted as, "Aren't you glad you've stuck it out at SCIF?" I responded with a smile that she probably took as a "Yes" but that I intended as a "Let's wait and see."

The four Zimmermans were seated towards the front of the church with the addition of Lauren Wilson next to Anna Zimmerman. Josh Wilson had not shown up.

Stan Mullins welcomed visitors, especially the Zimmermans, to "this historic occasion on the verge of a new era for the Sunshine Coast Independent Fellowship." Andy Zimmerman tried to look humble as the catalyst of the new era; Jack Wilson looked disappointed that he received no credit for finding the catalyst; Stan beamed as if it was all his doing; and Lauren and Anna smiled at each other—just glad to be together.

During the opening hymn, "Be Thou My Vision," Mrs. Beecroft's overly-energetic thumping on the pedal organ was enough to trigger a stroke; the enthusiastic congregational singing made Charlotte's eyes glisten; and I felt a few goose bumps growing as Josh Wilson slipped in at the back on the other side of the aisle. I gave him a wink and an unobtrusive thumbs-up.

Before Andy gave his inaugural address, the Zimmerman family sang a Southern Gospel quartet to the accompaniment of a guitar played by Linda. Mrs. Beecroft looked relieved that no request was made to use the organ. I wondered how the syncopated beat and quick tempo of the song would go down with the locals after the steady rhythm of "Be Thou My Vision." It proved sufficiently unlike rock music to be enjoyed by all. Robyn Bradford tapped (gently) with one foot, several heads swayed (just a little), and Josh Wilson looked glad he came.

Andy began by saying, "Our family is delighted to be in Buderim at last. We've followed a very busy *skedule* to get here—I understand you say *shed-ule*. It must depend on which *shool* you went to." After the laughter subsided, Andy shared his sense of call to the church and thanked folk for their welcome and the work they had put into preparing such a comfortable home for the family. He then read Romans 13:11–12, in the King James Version:

> And that, knowing the time, that now it is high time to awake out of sleep: for now is our salvation nearer than when we believed. The night is far spent, the day is at hand: let us therefore cast off the works of darkness, and let us put on the armour of light.

Andy challenged us to be alert and active because the end was near. There was no room for lethargy because each day was bringing us one step nearer to the day of ultimate salvation at the soon-to-occur coming of Christ. With genuine passion he emphasized the urgency of the hour and committed himself to work diligently in reaching the community and in building up the church. He urged all of us to work with him in the short time left before that day arrived. I was quite moved and I sensed others were as well.

Following the benediction, the earlier buzz of conversation resumed, only a little louder. Some enthusiastically greeted people they hadn't seen for years; others welcomed strangers; and many spoke about the fine Zimmerman family and Andy's convicting message. I made a point of speaking with Jack and commending him for his role in initiating a pastoral appointment for SCIF. He was encouraged. Suddenly I heard a familiar rumble in the carpark, the exhaust of a Ford Mustang. I rushed out just in time to catch Josh Wilson. While he found the service a big improvement on his earlier experiences at SCIF, he felt a bit out of place, almost embarrassed to be with people who knew him but hadn't seen him in a long time. I tried to get him to stay for lunch. He thanked me for the invitation but declined. I could have pressed him further but felt it wiser to let him go, thankful he'd had the courage to come at all.

On my way back to the church I was pleased to see Sam Zimmerman happily chasing Mark Mullins's son around the church yard. Inside the church, well-wishers surrounded Andy and Linda Zimmerman; several of the elders were conversing excitedly, obviously satisfied with the decision to appoint Andy; Lauren and Anna were chatting to three teenagers whom I had not seen before; and in the hall behind the church, preparations were well in hand for lunch.

I was standing near the door into the hall when lunch was announced. I entered to see Charlotte sitting at a table talking to Linda. The two wives summoned their husbands and the Sutherlands and the Zimmermans sat down to lunch together. With the Zimmerman children eating with new friends at a separate table, the four of us began to chat. The conversation at one end of the table was about renovated houses and gardens. At the other end Andy and I gently probed each other's backgrounds. Andy took a particular interest in my role at AIMS and looked forward to interacting on theological matters in days to come. I found him to be very personable and noticeably humble: he asked if he could pick my brains if he got into difficulty when preparing his sermons. I asked about the pastorates he had served in and discovered that though each of them was conservative and independent like SCIF, they were far more contemporary. All of them had grown during his ministry. When he said that he hoped to help SCIF catch up, I was pleased that he planned to do it gradually and sensitively.

When Charlotte and Linda went to get desserts, I thanked Andy sincerely for his sermon and then said, "Andy, in your message you stressed the urgency of the hour and that the day is near. It almost seems that Paul got it wrong, that he thought the end was near in his day and here we are 2,000 years later saying the same thing. How do you handle it?"

"I understand your concern, Ed, and when preparing for this morning, I checked out what others have written on the matter and made some notes in an appendix to my sermon." He reached under the table and produced a loose-leaf notebook, opened it and said:

> The old commentary by Jamieson, Fausset and Brown said the passage was "in the line of all our Lord's teaching, which represents the decisive day of Christ's second appearing as at hand, to keep believers ever in the attitude of wakeful expectancy, but without reference to the chronological nearness or distance of that event."
>
> The *People's New Testament* commented: "Some have thought that Paul referred to the speedy second coming of the Lord. He did not know the time of that event, nor did any man, but it might be that he shared the hope of the early, suffering church, that it would be speedy."

Andy would have gone on but Charlotte and Linda had returned with generous helpings of Black Forest cake and Tiramisu. When Charlotte saw the notebook and sensed I was talking shop, her body language caused me to postpone my response to Andy's quotations and I resolved that the conversation for the rest of the meal would include everyone.

Although we knew about the Zimmermans from the pastoral appointment process, we extended our knowledge over coffee and dessert. We learnt that Linda met Andy at a college in Tennessee from which she graduated with a major in church music. She hoped to use her musical gifts at SCIF. As well as an interest in American football, Andy loved hiking and looked forward to exploring the Australian bush after he settled into his pastoral role. I agreed to show him some of the better walking tracks on the Blackall Range. Anna hoped to become a high school teacher and had already applied to USC to study science. She had never had a steady boyfriend. I thought Josh Wilson would be interested in that piece of information. Although Sam had completed a semester of year 6 in the States, he was quite content to begin year 6 again in ten days at the Buderim State School. Like his father, he loved sport and the outdoors. Andy and Linda shared their concern about Anna's health. At the age of six she had contracted nephritis. It had responded well to antibiotics but medical opinion could not guarantee it was gone for good.

So absorbed was I in getting to know the Zimmermans, I was oblivious of the sweeping and stacking going on around us and that we were at the last table to be put away. Any twinge of conscience at having left the clean-up to others was stifled by the pleasure of getting to know the Zimmermans and of feeling that in spite of possible theological differences, a new friendship had begun.

Our car was only one of three left in the car park. As we drove home, I found myself in full agreement with Charlotte's excited reflections on the morning and had to admit that the attitudinal gap that had existed between us over SCIF was narrowing.

Within twenty minutes of arriving home, Charlotte was asleep. I was tired but it was an hour before I dozed off because my mind was pursuing the conversation with Andy that had been interrupted by the arrival of the Black Forest cake and the Tiramisu. I felt Andy believed that what he'd read from his notebook had satisfied my concern but I was far from satisfied. If anything, his comments had only increased my concern.

13

At the Surf Club

While Charlotte and I ate scrambled eggs and croissants on the back veranda overlooking the poinciana tree, noisy parrots were having their breakfast on the bird table. The phone rang. It was Andy. I was pleasantly surprised when he said he was conscious that our conversation at the church luncheon had been cut short and asked if I wanted to catch up for coffee. I certainly had more to say in response to the points he had made and appreciated his sensitivity to my situation. We agreed to meet at the Mooloolaba Surf Club.

I arrived fifteen minutes early and selected a table near the window overlooking the beach. A couple of lifesavers were carrying an orange inflatable rescue boat up the beach from the water. I could not see the face of the powerfully built man at the near end of the boat but at the far end I recognized Josh Wilson. As they approached the clubhouse, I stood and waved to attract Josh's attention. He didn't recognize me at first, probably because he didn't expect to see someone from SCIF in the context of the Mooloolaba Surf Club. He waved back and I went to the foyer of the club to see if Andy had arrived. He wasn't there but within a couple of minutes Josh turned up.

"What are you doing here?" he asked.

"I'm a member," I said. He looked surprised. "And I'm meeting Andy Zimmerman for coffee."

"Is Anna coming with him?" he asked with a smile. I responded with a knowing look as I shook my head. "I quite enjoyed the service yesterday morning," he said, "particularly the song sung by the Zimmerman family. They're pretty talented and Andy's not a bad preacher though I must admit I've been bombarded a lot lately with second-coming stuff and could do with a break from it." I was about to ask where it was all coming from when Andy arrived and greeted him with, "Hi, Josh, good to see you, man." Josh seemed pleased that Andy had remembered his name and after a few pleasantries excused himself to finish putting the boathouse in order.

We took our coffees to the table I had reserved and after chatting about the inauguration service and making admiring comments about the view in front of us, Andy took out his Bible and notebook. It was a big King James Version Bible whose presence in the Mooloolaba Surf Club would have surprised Josh Wilson even more than my presence. Andy began: "Ed, you expressed concern that Paul anticipated the end in his day and yet 2,000 years later the end has still not come. Did the commentators I quoted help?"

"Not a lot," I said, rather euphemistically. "Why don't you read the Romans 13 passage again and I'll try to respond to the comments you read from your notebook. Andy read from his KJV:

> And that, knowing the time, that now it is high time to awake out of sleep: for now is our salvation nearer than when we believed. The night is far spent, the day is at hand: let us therefore cast off the works of darkness, and let us put on the armor of light.

"Andy", I said, "Paul clearly anticipated an imminent climactic event. The sources you quoted interpreted the event to include the second coming of Christ and on that point they may well be correct. My concern is with Paul's language. If after 2,000 years the event is still future, use of words such as 'high time,' 'far spent,' and 'at hand' seems intemperate. Quite frankly, I struggle to accept that something 2,000 years away is at hand."

Andy opened his notebook and read again the excerpt from the *People's New Testament*:

> Some have thought that Paul referred to the speedy second coming of the Lord. He did not know the time of that event, nor did any man, but it might be that he shared the hope of the early, suffering church, that it would be speedy.

Knowing that my response to Andy's quotation would be threatening, I paused before speaking to adopt a softly-softly approach: "Andy, on the face of it, your quotation is in line with the teaching of Jesus that no one knows the day or the hour and it says a lot for Paul's pastoral concern for his fellow suffering Christians. However, and be assured my major concern is to be true to the text, Paul says that rather than his *not* knowing the time, he *did* know the time. I'm not suggesting he knew the day or the hour—I've no desire to go against Jesus—but Paul *did* know that it was near, that it was at hand. When Linda found herself pregnant with Anna, she didn't know the day or the hour of Anna's arrival but she knew from the outset that it would be within about nine months and towards the end of that period, she certainly knew when it was 'high time' to leave for the hospital.

"Andy, what you just quoted sounds like wishful thinking on Paul's part, as if he *wanted* the end to be near to relieve the suffering of the church but he wasn't sure that his wish would be fulfilled. But Paul did not say he'd *like* it to be near but that it *was* near. I regard Paul as an inspired apostle, as do you, and I'm not happy to twist his words to fit our eschatological scheme. Either Paul got it wrong or we have misunderstood him. You can see my concern."

Andy may have *seen* my concern; I wasn't sure he *shared* it. What did the strained look on his face mean? Was he pastorally concerned for me in my struggle to know the truth or was he concerned that I was going off the orthodox rails? Was he concerned that his own eschatological position might be wrong or was he simply expressing strong opposition to what I had said? I suspected the latter. The last thing I wanted was to end a friendship that had hardly begun. I thought it best to change the subject so we could leave the Mooloolaba Surf Club as happily as we'd entered it. Andy clearly wanted to stick to the subject. With his head in his notebook he said, "Do you recall the comment by Jamieson, Fausset and Brown that Christ's return was expressed in terms of nearness 'to keep believers ever in the attitude of wakeful expectancy, but without reference to the chronological nearness or distance of that event?'"

"Yes, Andy, I do remember it because it worried me: it sounded like an attempt to make the text fit an existing framework rather than to listen to what the text actually said. If words mean anything, 'at hand' *does* have reference to 'chronological nearness or distance.' Paul's motive for misusing such words may be good but I'm not sure he was into justifying the end by the means."

Andy's mobile rang. Linda informed him of an urgent pastoral request so he apologized for having to leave early and stressed that he would like to continue the conversation on another occasion. I felt bad that I had made the final point in the discussion without his having the opportunity of rebuttal. One part of me thought my point was so strong that he wouldn't have had an answer even if he'd stayed; the better part of me wanted us to separate on a less confrontational note.

After Andy left, I walked past the boat shed and found Josh Wilson busily putting surfing equipment on racks along the walls. He saw me and beckoned me in. The only other person in the shed was the lifesaver I had seen helping Josh carry the inflatable dinghy from the beach. Although at that time I had only seen him from the back, I recognized him from his bronzed, well-built frame.

"Working hard, Josh? I thought you were on holidays."

"Beats accountancy any day. I'm back to work at Nambour on Monday so I'm making the most of it." He called to the other lifesaver, "Fitz, come and meet my neighbor, Ed Sutherland." Josh introduced Fitz as Paul Fitzgerald whose powerful physique matched the strength of his handshake. "Hi, Paul," I said, my smile a cover for my hurting hand. "Looks like you're as keen on surfing as Josh."

"Sure am. I joined the Nippers when I was seven and have been with the club ever since."

"What do you do when you're not surfing?" I asked.

"I've been working as a clerk for a finance company at Maroochydore but this year I'm going back to USC to do my MBA degree."

"Good on you," I said. "I wish you well."

"Thanks," he replied, and returned to the life jackets he was shelving. Not wanting to detain Josh, I simply reminded him of my desire to go driving with him again and left it to him to arrange a time. He seemed pleased but the self-conscious expression on his face suggested he felt overshadowed by the tall, strikingly handsome Paul. I felt a bit sorry for Josh. He may have been a bit of a loner but I liked him for his openness and humility.

14

Coffee Club and the Antichrist

As I buried some food scraps in our vegie garden one Saturday morning, I heard the Mustang roar into life next door. Thinking Josh was planning to stimulate my adrenalin glands with a further demonstration of his driving skills, I looked over the fence. Two attractive girls stood admiring the Mustang. Josh sat proudly at the controls pumping the accelerator and admiring one of the girls, Anna Zimmerman, who was visiting his sister.

Josh saw me, turned off the motor and came over to the fence. "Lauren and Anna want to go for a spin," he said. "You're welcome to join us."

"You wouldn't want an old fogy like me tagging along," I said.

"You'd help to balance the sexes," he said. "We'll put the girls in the back and you can keep me company in the front."

I was about to decline strongly for fear of playing gooseberry but I sensed Josh really *did* want me to come. Were the seating configurations with just the three of them too awkward or was he just plain shy? Lauren and Anna also urged me to come, and since they also seemed genuine, I relented and hurried to inform Charlotte. She tried to talk me out of going: "They're just being friendly," she said. "They don't want a baby boomer on board. Act your age, Edward." Charlotte only uses "Edward" when she feels very strongly about what I should or should not do so it took an unusual degree of self-assertiveness to go against her advice. As she pursed her lips and shook her head, I grabbed my baseball cap with the Nike tick on it, said I'd be home for lunch, gave her pursed lips a kiss, and headed for the Mustang.

Josh suggested we drive to Caloundra, at the southern end of the Sunshine Coast, via the Sunshine Motorway and the Bruce Highway. I suspected he preferred that route to the more direct route with its traffic lights and restricted speed limits so he could put the Mustang through its paces—perhaps to impress one of the back-seat passengers. If I thought he would expose them to the alarming speeds I had experienced on my previous trip with Josh, I was wrong. Surprisingly, he was a model of respect for the road rules, perhaps a better way to impress. As we drove, he kept looking in the rear view mirror and I knew he wasn't checking to see if the police were following. The conversations in the back and front seats were unrelated and only rarely did communication cross the divide.

Josh parked at Kings Beach in Caloundra and suggested we take the scenic boardwalk around the headland to Bulcock Beach on the channel separating the mainland from nearby Bribie Island. With two reserved men walking in front of two chattering women, it took the Coffee Club at Bulcock beach to convert the two groups into one. I flashed my membership card to the other three as we entered the club and said, "The drinks are on me." A table for four and Anna's open personality helped to unify the group.

"Josh," she said, "Lauren has told me a bit about you but I still don't know much. You're an accountant I believe." Josh affirmed her belief with a one-word answer but she drew him out with, "Tell me what that involves." For someone who was not excited about accountancy, Josh responded as if he'd been asked a question about surfing or Ford Mustangs. I was proud of him and could only put it down to the power of a beautiful woman to evoke conversational skills uncommon in a man of few words. Throughout the conversation, Anna maintained eye contact with Josh and gave the impression of being genuinely interested in him as a person.

When she appropriately ended the conversation with Josh and spoke of her plans to be a teacher, she asked me about my teaching career and, again, the same eye contact and genuine interest were evident. As she spoke, I glanced at Josh. His face shone like he'd just come down Mount Sinai with Moses rather than engaged in a discourse on accountancy. I was concerned. I feared he was interpreting Anna's genuine interest in people too narrowly. Did he not notice that the way she treated him was the same way she treated others? Did he think that by her body language she was reciprocating his interest in her? Was he aiming too high and heading for a painful tumble?

Lauren steered my thoughts in a different direction by initiating a new topic: "Robyn Bradford sends Mum a lot of scary emails and Mum forwards them on to Josh and me—and lots of other people. Sometimes there are two or three emails a week." Anna was not aware of the emails and although I was on Robyn's mailing list I generally deleted them unopened. I asked, "What are they about?"

"Sometimes about climate change or global economic disasters but mostly about end times. Last week she sent a link to a website that claimed the numbers representing the stripes on barcodes appear below the barcodes, except the numbers for the stripes at the beginning, middle and end of the barcode. The missing numbers are said to be 666. It's all supposed to have something to do with the mark of the beast and the approach of the great tribulation."

"I'm skeptical about such speculation," I said. "I think it's more likely that the antichrist was around in the first century than that he's to be found in the twenty-first century." Three mouths opened and three sets of eyebrows were raised.

After a prolonged pause, Josh turned to me and said: "Remember when I saw you at the Mooloolaba Surf Club that I said I'd been bombarded by second coming stuff and could do with a break from it?" I nodded to indicate that I remembered it well. He continued: "I had those emails in mind. There's something fascinating about them but they're all so depressing. They leave me thinking there's no news but bad news and that the world is about to end any day soon."

"I'm sorry to add to the onslaught," I said.

"No, no," said Josh. "I'm pleased to know that not everyone goes along with that doom-and-gloom stuff and that some of it at least may be in the distant past rather than the near future. I'd like to hear more."

"So would I," said Lauren. Anna said nothing.

"There's a lot I could say," I began, "but to go back to the antichrist, there are good reasons for thinking 666 has reference to the first century emperor Nero." Anna broke her silence: "Could you give us some of those reasons?"

"Sure," I said. "In Revelation 13, we are told that 666 is the number of the beast and that it is the number of a man. It was customary in ancient times to assign numerical values to the letters of the alphabet. You've all seen dates written in Roman notation where letters represent numbers: M=1000, C=100, X=10, and so on. One form of Nero's name in Latin and another form in Hebrew calculate to 666. You might notice in the footnote of your Bibles that some manuscripts have 616 instead of 666. Again, in both Latin and Hebrew there are forms of Nero's name that add up to 616, which could account for the alternative reading."

Anna spoke up again: "That's interesting, but calculations have been performed on many names over the years and come up with 666 again and again. If the man whose name equals 666 is also the beast of Revelation 13, haven't you got to show that Nero was the beast to prove your point?"

"A good question, Anna," I replied. "There is good reason to identify Nero as the beast. One of his contemporaries actually refers to him as a beast and his known behavior warrants the description. Wouldn't you regard someone as a beast who murdered his own parents and his own wife, not to mention many other people?"

"Certainly," said Anna, "but I'd call Stalin and Hitler beasts as well. They probably killed more people than Nero."

"I agree, but the original readers of Revelation are told to calculate the number of the beast. There's no way people living in the first century could calculate the number 666 in relation to Stalin or Hitler. But, Anna, there's more evidence to suggest Nero is intended. Revelation 13 says that the beast would persecute Christians for three and a half years. Nero began persecuting the church in mid-November, AD 64, and he committed suicide on June 8, AD 68, about three and a half years later."

"Ed, that's very interesting," said Josh, "but why didn't John just tell his readers that Nero was the antichrist and put an end to all the speculation in the many emails I've been getting?"

"Good question, Josh," I said. "It would certainly make the interpretation of Revelation easier if John had written without the use of symbols. However, I'm sure if you had lived during the persecution under Nero, to save your skin you wouldn't mention him by name in a negative way. You might rather resort to code language such as 'beast' and '666' which your mates would understand but not Nero."

I had gone on at length and our coffees were getting cold. I didn't know if I'd convinced the others but their previously open mouths were now shut, their eyebrows had dropped, and Josh and Lauren nodded and smiled as if to say, "It makes a lot of sense." Anna was less affirming but obviously reflective.

On the return journey there was more conversation in the front seat than in the back seat as Josh went over our discussion in the Coffee Club and thanked me for arming him against the next volley of end-of-the-world emails.

15

Apocalyptic Language

"I'm home," I shouted, as I breezed up the hallway towards the kitchen, thinking Charlotte would be there preparing lunch. Instead, she called out from the lounge, "We're in here." I didn't know who was included in the "we" but soon saw it was Carol Wilson and imagined two women had been talking about an old man going on a teenage excursion. Charlotte's first words were, "How was it, Ed?"

"We had a great time in Caloundra. Josh drove his Mustang as I would have."

"You mean he broke the speed limit," interposed Charlotte.

"Not at all," I said. "He drove so conservatively the Mustang must have felt someone else was behind the wheel."

"I'm glad to hear it," said Carol. "I get worried about my boy at times. When he's out in his car I fear I'll get a phone call to say he's had an accident, he drives so fast."

"Not on this occasion," I said. "I don't think *my* presence had anything to do with it but the presence of the passengers in the back seat might have. You had nothing to worry about, Carol."

"Speaking of the girls," said Carol, "how did Josh get on with them? He thinks a lot of his sister but with her being so friendly with Anna, I hope he's not feeling isolated. He's a bit of a loner, you know. Has never had a girlfriend and apart from Paul Fitzgerald at the surf club, he has no close male friends. That's another thing I worry about."

"I've sensed he's no extrovert," I said, "but I was impressed with the way he joined in the conversation when we stopped for coffee at Bulcock Beach. I think he's coming out of his shell."

"That *is* good news," said Carol. "What did you all talk about?"

"Josh talked about his work and I talked about mine and then we had a discussion about the book of Revelation."

"How interesting," said Carol. "That's my favorite Bible book. How did you steer the conversation in that direction?"

"I didn't start it," I said. "Lauren did. She asked us if we all got the end-times emails that originate with Robyn Bradford and told us about some recent ones concerning the beast of Revelation. From then on we talked about 666 and who the antichrist might be."

"How interesting," said Carol. "I wish I'd been there. It's a topic I think a lot about. Robyn and I are always exchanging emails about the signs of the times. Given the nearness of the Lord's return, I think we should all be getting the word out before it's too late."

I sensed Carol expected me to respond but I applied "Be swift to hear, slow to speak," and said no more. Charlotte came to my rescue: "Jack and Carol have invited us over for a barbecue with the Zimmermans on Saturday night."

"Sounds good," I said. "I'll look forward to it."

After Carol left and we had eaten lunch, Charlotte had a nap and I went to the office to write to Luke Rodman. In our debate over Matthew 24, I had yet to respond to his point that the gospel *had* been preached in the entire world as "world" was understood in the first century. The Scriptures he quoted surprised me. To be honest they stunned me. I wasn't beaten yet and I wasn't about to let on that I was rather bruised. After saying his email had given me something to chew on, I fired another unfulfilled prophecy at him from Matthew 24:29–30:

> Immediately after the distress of those days "the sun will be darkened, and the moon will not give its light; the stars will fall from the sky, and the heavenly bodies will be shaken." At that time the sign of the Son of Man will appear in the sky, and all the nations of the earth will mourn. They will see the Son of Man coming on the clouds of the sky, with power and great glory.

"Luke," I wrote, "these verses speak of astronomical disasters that must occur before the return of Christ. They haven't occurred as yet so Christ cannot have returned." I heard myself speaking in the tone Alex Symons had used when having a go at me during my lecture at AIMS. Even so, I sent off the email hoping Luke would reel under it. He must have been sitting at his computer because I got a reply before Charlotte woke from her nap:

> Dr. Sutherland,
>
> You said the astronomical disasters of the verses you quoted have certainly not occurred, presumably because the stars are still in

the sky. There are good reasons to question this view. As you know, Matthew 24 has rightly been called the *Little Apocalypse*. That's not surprising given that it contains apocalyptic language. You also know that apocalyptic literature makes heavy use of symbolism. One such use of symbols is to describe disasters on earth under the figure of disasters in the heavens.

Consider Isaiah 13:10: "The stars of heaven and their constellations will not show their light. The rising sun will be darkened and the moon will not give its light." The context (verse 1) shows that the prophecy concerns ancient Babylon. Commotions did not literally occur in the heavens but disaster did occur on earth for Babylon.

The same sort of language is used in Isaiah 34:4: "All the stars in the sky will be dissolved and the sky rolled up like a scroll; all the starry host will fall like withered leaves from the vine, like shriveled figs from the fig tree." The context concerns God's judgment on earthly nations, including the ancient nation of Edom (verse 5). The devastation on earth is described under the figure of astronomical disturbances.

Failure to recognize the nature of apocalyptic language and its presence in Matthew 24 has led many to take literally what Jesus did not intend should be taken literally. The disciples were familiar with the Old Testament and would have understood his intention.

I remember your telling us at AIMS, "When interpreting the Bible, it is not a sound rule to take everything literally that *can* be taken literally but to take literally what was *intended* to be taken literally." I don't believe Jesus intended us to take the astronomical disturbances literally. He was speaking to Jews who knew their Old Testaments and who understood the nature of apocalyptic language.

Ouch! Another bruise. Luke was right and I knew it. I was behaving in retirement as if I'd forgotten all I knew and had taught for years. Or was I using arguments that deep down I knew to be without merit hoping that Luke would be fooled by them and would leave me alone? I felt a twinge of guilt at being disingenuous and a need for deliverance from "the laziness that shrinks from new truth" as in the ancient Hebrew prayer. I still had a couple of unfulfilled prophecies in Matthew 24 but decided to delay firing them at Luke till my wounds healed, just in case "unfulfilled" was too strong a word.

16

Conflict at a Barbecue

On Saturday afternoon, I gave Jack Wilson a hand to set up for the barbecue. We wired the large mango tree in his backyard with temporary lighting and erected three folding tables for the guests and one for food. The guests began arriving about five o'clock, among them Josh Wilson's friend, Paul Fitzgerald, whom I had not expected. Jack fired up the barbecue and began cooking steaks, sausages and sliced onion, eager to demonstrate that his ability warranted the white apron and chef's hat he was wearing.

Young and old mixed freely as they helped themselves to drinks and crackers but once Jack had served the meat and they had added extras from the buffet table, they formed into distinct groups, wives at one table, husbands at another, young people at the third. Sam Zimmerman did not fit into any of the three groups so amused himself by playing with Chuffey who, attracted by the smell of steaks and sausages, had crawled through a hole in the fence. Sam's generosity ensured Chuffey got more than a smell but like another Dickens character he constantly barked, "Please, Sam, I want some more." To put an end to his barking, I excused myself from the men at my table who were talking about the history of Buderim, Andy asking all the questions and Jack and Arthur providing all the answers. After threatening Chuffey with going back home the way he'd come if he didn't shut up, I gave Sam a stick to throw for Chuffey to fetch. The barking stopped but instead of returning to the history of Buderim, I headed for the young people's table where Paul was impressing his audience of three with tales of his surfing prowess. He acknowledged my presence with a brief glance in my direction and continued:

"Last year I came third in my division of the Coolangatta Gold competition. It involves swimming and surf-skiing, paddleboarding and running, forty-six kilometers in all. I'm training four mornings a week for this year's competition. I have a good chance of winning, don't you think, Josh?" Josh gave a short nod. I recalled my recent view of Paul's fine physique at the Mooloolaba Surf Club and felt he might well be a winner but I would have preferred less hubris and more humility. Lauren and Anna did not share my preference: they leaned forward with chins in hands and eyes wide open. Josh seemed caught between the pleasure of glory by association and concern that Anna was showing too much interest in Paul. I broke the spell he had over the girls by asking a question during a brief pause in the recital:

"Were you in last year's competition, Josh?"

"I was," he replied, "but I was just part of the pack that wasn't placed."

"Hold on, Josh," I said, "it's commendable that you had a go." I felt a bit mean for dampening the ardor of Paul and his female admirers but continued my meanness by changing the direction of the conversation even further.

"Girls," I said, "how are your studies going at USC?"

"I'm struggling a bit," said Anna, "getting used to Queensland's education system and its Aussie accent. Lauren's a big help. We have some classes in common and act as study buddies to each other."

"You're doing very well, Anna," encouraged Lauren. "Come the end of the semester, I'm sure your grades will outshine mine."

Paul was not to be left out of the conversation: "I'm doing a post-graduate course in business administration. It's a cinch. If either of you girls wants some private coaching, I'm your man."

Paul's pride prompted another diversionary question: "Does USC have a student Christian group?" I asked.

"A Real Life group meets weekly on campus," said Lauren. "Anna and I enjoy going and we've made a number of new friends."

"You'd be welcome to attend, Paul," said Anna. "Midday on Mondays."

"It's not really my cup of tea," he said, with a shrug of his shoulders. "Our family's not really into that stuff. My father's Dr. Max Fitzgerald, philosophy lecturer at USC and chairman of the Humanist Association. I attend meetings he organizes on campus."

My diversionary tactic had caused a cone of silence to descend on the group so, thinking it time to withdraw, I thanked them for letting me chat and made my way back to an unfinished plate of cold steak and chips.

My return did not distract my friends from their continuing discussion on the history of Buderim. It was interrupted, however, by an announcement from Carol Wilson that it was Robyn Bradford's birthday. We moved our chairs into a circle, Robyn cut a cake, we sang "Happy Birthday" and then someone called "Speech!" Not given to reticence, Robyn responded as if she'd spent the week rehearsing for the occasion, which made me wonder at the sincerity of her opening sentence:

"My, this is an unexpected surprise. I should have let you all know about my birthday in advance and then you could have brought presents." Robyn paused till the laughter subsided then continued: "When I reminded Arthur about my birthday, he said, 'How do you expect me to remember your birthday when you never look any older?' I accepted his kind excuse for forgetting my birthday but knew it wasn't true. Just the other night I looked in the mirror and remarked to Arthur, 'I've got wrinkles on my forehead, bags under my eyes, flab under my arms, and an oversized stomach.' Arthur was silent so I turned to him and said, a little crossly, 'Well, say something positive, Arthur.' He replied, 'There's nothing wrong with your eyesight.'" More laughter. When all was quiet, she became more serious: "When I was a child, the time between one birthday and another seemed like an age; now they come around all too quickly. However, I don't know whether I'll be here this time next year." One or two in the circle, Paul Fitzgerald in particular, may have thought Robyn had an incurable disease and a short life expectancy. Those who knew her better anticipated how her speech would continue.

"Should the Lord tarry, I may have another birthday but my conviction that the coming of the Lord will occur very soon has intensified this past week. On Monday, a severe earthquake rocked western Turkey; on Tuesday, there was an outbreak of war in the Sudan; on Thursday, another earthquake, this time in Chile; and only yesterday, on a morning TV talk show, a Queensland man was interviewed who claimed to be Jesus and to have more than 3,000 disciples. You'd have to be blind not to see the connection between these events and the signs Jesus gave of his second coming. Brothers and sisters, we are in the last days of the last days and that is why I expect to be taken out of this rotten old world at the rapture, before my next birthday."

Robyn's speech had become very impassioned. I was not particularly moved by it but was pleased that her excessive emotion prevented her from continuing. She sat down next to Arthur who put his arm around her shoulders and whispered sweetness in her ear. During the prevailing silence, I looked around the circle to see affirming nods from the older adults, a tear or two in some eyes, and thoughtful uncertainty in the faces of the young people, except Paul's which showed an obvious skepticism.

As everyone collected cake and coffee, the circle broke up and the previous age groups re-formed. The history of Buderim was not revisited in my group. Arthur and Jack reflected at one side of the table on Robyn's speech. Andy and I sat quietly for a few moments before he took up the same topic. "Ed, what Robyn said reminded me of something I wanted to say when we were chatting at Mooloolaba. You'll remember how our conversation about my inaugural sermon on Romans 13 was interrupted by an urgent pastoral call."

"Of course," I replied. "I must admit I was a bit concerned that your sudden departure, in the context of my overly forceful responses to your position may have strained our relationship."

"Not at all. I know you want to be honest to the text of Scripture. I think you're wrong," he said with a smile, "but I respect you all the same."

"Thanks, Andy."

"At Mooloolaba," said Andy, "we didn't fully explore the words in Romans 13:11, 'Now is our salvation nearer than when we believed.' You'd have to agree that each day beyond our conversion is a step closer to the end. Paul used the word 'nearer' and Robyn is simply saying that what was nearer then is near now."

"Andy," I said, "Paul's statement, 'Now is our salvation nearer than when we believed,' was true five minutes after their conversion and is so obvious that it hardly needed to be said. Why did Paul say it then? Because he had just said, 'It is high time to awake out of sleep.' He proceeded to tell them why it was time to wake up: because their salvation was nearer than when they believed. There is a note of urgency not present if there are 2,000 years before the end. Permit me to use an illustration.

"Let's suppose you and your family are driving from Buderim to Sydney. It's about 1,000 kilometers. You can say twenty kilometers from Buderim, 'Now is Sydney nearer than when we left home.' But you can't say to the kids who are sleeping in the back seat, 'It is high time to awake out of sleep because now is Sydney nearer than when we left home.' Not with over 900 kilometers to go. You could say it if you have only ten kilometers to go before you see the Sydney Harbor bridge."

The look on Andy's face was thoughtful but not hostile, even though he did not agree with the implications of what I was saying. Jack and Arthur had stopped talking with each other and were listening quietly to Andy and me. In an attempt to keep the conversation calm, I said, "Andy, I want to stress that I have no interest in being controversial for love of an argument. My concern is to understand and respond appropriately to the text as Paul intended it."

Andy was silent but I could almost hear his mental cogs whirring. Arthur broke the silence: "I'm not sure I follow you, Ed, but I agree with what Robyn was saying that this age is quickly coming to an end because the signs Jesus gave of the end are being fulfilled in our day before our very eyes." It was Jack's turn to speak.

"I'm with you, Arthur." He then turned to me and asked, "Ed, what's your take on the earthquakes, wars and false prophets that are regular features of the daily newspapers?"

My interaction with Luke Rodman over Matthew 24 had prepared me to answer the question but I knew it wouldn't go over well with my three friends. Was it courage or folly that caused me to say, "Arthur, what Robyn shared is a widely-held view and appears to fit with the words of Jesus in passages like Matthew 24. I've been studying that chapter a good deal lately and while I used to follow the common view, I think I was wrong. When I listen to the words of Jesus in the context that gave rise to them, I believe the earthquakes, wars, and false prophets referred to events in the first century, within the Roman world and not in Chile or Queensland."

"What caused you to change your mind?" asked Jack.

"One significant reason was that Jesus expected his disciples to experience the signs, not people living in the twenty-first century on the Sunshine Coast."

"Please explain," said Jack.

"Well, when some of his disciples asked when the temple would be destroyed and for a sign of the second coming and the end of the age, Jesus said, "*You*, the disciples, not us, will hear of wars and rumors of wars." He warned *them*, the disciples, against being deceived by false Christs. He said *they*, the disciples, would be persecuted and killed, experiences that were to occur *after* the earthquakes and wars."

If hostility had not shown on *Andy's* face earlier in the evening, it began to show now on the faces of Jack and Arthur. I feared folly, not courage, had prompted my answer to Arthur's question and I regretted it, not the content of what I said but the timing. I had been thinking about these matters for months; it was like a bombshell to them. Years earlier I had been given a three-point check before speaking: "Is it true? Is it kind? Is it necessary?" In hindsight, I felt that at best I'd only passed the first check-point and my friends questioned even that. I felt bad, but worse was to come.

17

In Big Trouble

The temporary lighting in the mango tree went off and on a couple of times. It was not a fault in our wiring efforts before the barbecue but Carol Wilson on the veranda flicking the extension lead switch to signal that it was time to go. So engrossed were we men in our discussion that we failed to notice that the tables around us had been cleared and the young people were stacking chairs and folding tables. We got the message and lent a hand. After the others had gone, I stayed back to help Jack carry tables and chairs under his house. He seemed a bit distant. I didn't need a lot of discernment to know why and I didn't need to ask because he came out with it.

"Ed, the conversation at the table tonight quite upset me."

"I'm sorry, Jack, I . . . "

"Hear me out, Ed. After Robyn's speech, Arthur and I chatted on one side of the table while you and Andy chatted on the other side. Arthur did most of the talking and I listened, not so much to him but to you as you implied that Andy's inaugural address was wrong and that Robyn's position was wrong. Robyn's position is the position that our church has held as long as I can remember. It's the position heard on the Christian radio stations we listen to and it's the position of many of the well-known authors in our local Christian bookstore. You're the odd man out, Ed, and if you're going to be part of SCIF, you need to know what we believe and you need to affirm it."

"Jack, I really am sorry. I . . . "

"I haven't finished yet, Ed. The other day you went to Caloundra with my kids and Anna Zimmerman. That evening at the dinner table, Lauren reported on the conversation you had at the Caloundra Coffee Club. I thought at the time that your view of the antichrist did not agree with mine but dismissed it till tonight when I realized that it was not an isolated issue. Now that I know more of your views, I'm angry that you are sowing false teaching among our young people, that you are critical of our pastor, of the beliefs of our church, and of respected biblical scholars."

I was about to respond when he interrupted again: "Furthermore, my son Josh has been struggling with his faith for some time. Since the Zimmermans' arrival, he has been coming to church and Carol and I have been greatly encouraged. Now that you've come out with your off-beat views, I'm concerned he's going to be so confused that what has *begun* will be *undone*. Ed, I'm sorry to have to say this, but I think I'll have to take the whole matter to the eldership meeting for their decision about where we go from here."

I was reeling under the blows Jack had socked at me. My folly had boomeranged. I didn't feel like responding. It was late, Jack was not in the right mood to listen to me and, to be honest, I understood why he felt so strongly and even sympathized with him.

I gave Jack a third apology for upsetting him, this time uninterrupted, thanked him for his hospitality, and said goodnight.

Charlotte was already asleep when I got home. I was glad. She would have read on my face that all was not well and I did not relish an explanation. Sleep did not come easily, mainly because I kept kicking myself for thoughtlessly blurting out my ideas before people whom I knew would be upset. "What an idiot!" I told myself. I knew what the church stood for and how entrenched their views were. Why did I have to be so insensitive—and at my neighbor's house? I'd unnecessarily destroyed a good friendship with little hope of repair.

I imagined what Jack would report to Carol, what Arthur would report to Robyn, what Robyn would put in her next email, and what those on her contact list would put in *their* emails. And what about the next elders' meeting? No wonder I couldn't sleep. There was not much of the night left when I finally dozed off.

I woke, later than usual, to the unwelcome realization that it was Sunday morning. Never had I felt less like going to church. I was tempted to concoct an excuse for not going but knew Charlotte would see through it and the story of last night would come out. I wasn't ready for that so I decided to go, again unsure whether to label it courage or stupidity.

Arriving at the church late was uncharacteristic, but not unwelcome on this occasion. We slipped in during the singing of the first song. I felt uncomfortable throughout the service but was unsure whether the feeling was just self-inflicted punishment for my outspokenness of the night before, or a reaction to real or imagined negative vibes from church members. When the announcements were given, I winced as Andy reminded the elders that their monthly meeting was on Tuesday night. I knew one item that would be on the agenda.

After the service, I stayed close to Charlotte during morning tea, feeling like a shy child attached to his mother's apron strings. Linda Zimmerman approached us and reflected on the barbecue. She included me in the conversation quite normally so I thought Andy had not had time to tell her about my weird ideas. He joined us a few minutes later and said, "Ed, could I speak with you for a minute?" We broke away from our wives and stepped into a side room that Andy had set up as a church office. I now felt like a schoolboy summoned to the principal's office for misbehavior.

"I really enjoyed the barbecue last night," he said. I was a bit surprised by his friendliness but when he said, "I had a call from Jack Wilson late last night," I thought, "Here it comes."

"I'm sure you know why he phoned. He told me rather heatedly what he'd said to you last night. Because I knew some of your ideas from previous conversations, I was not as affected as Jack. I don't agree with those ideas but I recognize you are on a journey and want only to be true to the Scriptures, as I do. In time, I hope we can work through our differences. Meanwhile, I pleaded with Jack to promote harmony and not discord within the fellowship and to urge Arthur to do the same. He was insistent that the matter be raised at the elders' meeting on Tuesday. I agreed and that's where we left it. I'll get back to you after the meeting. Ed, I'd appreciate if you too would take to heart what I said about harmony."

"I'll lie low with respect to my eschatology, Andy, and do my best to relieve any strain I may have caused in my relationship with Jack and Arthur." We shook hands and rejoined our wives.

On the way home, Charlotte asked, "What did Andy want to talk about?"

Prevarication was out of the question. I told her how I had upset Jack and Arthur, what Andy had said to me, and about the consequences I feared from gossip and the outcome of the elders' meeting on Tuesday night. I expected her first word would be "Edward." It wasn't.

"Linda has kept me informed about your theological conversations with Andy since their inauguration so it doesn't come as a surprise to me. You mentioned the word 'gossip.' Thankfully, Linda and Andy are not gossips so you can be assured they will not feed the grapevine. I can't speak for Robyn Bradford. I'm very happy at SCIF, Ed, and would be very disappointed if what has happened were to threaten our continuance there."

For what seemed a long time I said nothing. I had felt bad about how my lack of discernment had affected my friendship with Jack and Arthur and potentially threatened the unity of the church; I now saw how it could affect Charlotte. Over the years I have discovered that when my wife is happy, I am happy, the dog next door is happy, the whole world is happy. I had begun to think my views on eschatology were of the utmost importance but realized afresh that relationships are right up near the top of the list of important things. I determined to keep them there.

"Charlotte, I want to assure you that I am committed to you and to SCIF. I love you and I have come to appreciate the people at our church as well. I am going to put my agenda aside and work towards SCIF's becoming a united and growing fellowship."

Given my fears about emails flying off in all directions and an elders' meeting that might want to excommunicate me, I may have been overly optimistic, but I was resolved nevertheless.

On Monday mornings I always went fishing with Jack but late Sunday night he sent me a text message to say he couldn't make it. I thought I knew why and my thoughts bothered me throughout the day. On Tuesday, my thoughts had not improved knowing that the elders would soon be discussing my case. If Jack and Arthur had primed the chairman, Stan Mullins, about my views, my fate was sealed.

I was still in my pajamas when the phone rang on Wednesday morning. Charlotte answered it. I listened to her side of the conversation.

"Good morning, Andy . . . That *was* a late meeting. I'm surprised you are up so early . . . I guess you'll have to postpone the other agenda items till the next meeting . . . Yes, he's here. I'll get him for you."

Andy asked if he could drop by after breakfast. I wanted him to say more on the phone but he preferred to speak face to face. I feared the worst.

18

A Statement of Faith Proposed

Apprehensive about Andy's feedback from the elders' meeting, I was inclined to chat privately with Andy in my office but, on reflection, I felt it would be simpler if Charlotte heard the report first hand. Whatever the elders' decision, it concerned her as much as me. The three of us sat on the veranda. Sunk in the low-slung canvas of my deck chair, a cold drink in the hole at the end of the wide wooden armrest, my outwardly relaxed appearance belied the state of my inner self which was still standing up.

Andy's preliminary conversation about pelicans and parrots did not help me relax. I wanted him to get to the point of his visit but the more he talked, the more I felt he was only delaying the opening sentence of his report which would be, "Do you want the bad news or the bad news?" He began differently:

"To date I am only an ex officio member of the board without voting rights. The church is not used to having a pastor so it may be some time before my status at the meetings changes. I've only been to a few elders' meetings and on no occasion have I seen the agenda prior to the meeting. Last night was no exception. I went to the meeting fearing acrimonious discussion and a call for your instant dismissal from the church on the grounds of false teaching—the last thing I wanted."

"The last thing we want too," said Charlotte.

"Excellent," said Andy. "To my surprise, Ed's name was not on the agenda. Then I noticed an unexpected item, 'Statement of Faith for SCIF,' and I knew it was relevant to your case. Stan Mullins introduced the topic by saying Jack Wilson had phoned him early on Sunday morning, concerned about the unorthodox views of a newcomer to SCIF and wishing to address his concerns in the context of a Statement of Faith."

"Tick the boxes or you're out!" I said.

"Hold your fire, Ed," said Andy. "Jack began by recalling my recent appointment as pastor and his role in recruiting me in anticipation of church growth. He said that some of the growth could come through transfers from churches that hold views different from our own, views that could cause problems. That's when your name was mentioned, Ed. Although Jack had cooled down since the barbecue, he was still quite forceful in his account of Saturday night: your reaction to Robyn's speech, your interaction with me, and your chat at Caloundra with Josh, Lauren, and Anna."

"How did the others react?" I asked.

"Arthur said, 'I share Jack's concerns.' Stan Mullins said, 'He's got to go.' Dr. Mark Mullins, Stan's son, said, 'Hang on, one minute we're talking about additions to the church and now we're talking about subtractions. There's got to be a better way round this problem.' I was about to speak in an effort to curb the rising tension when Jack spoke up. He said he'd given a lot of thought to the problem and believed the way forward was to draft a Statement of Faith for SCIF that made clear not only our stance on the basic doctrines of Christianity but also our position on issues where churches differ."

"Like eschatology," I said.

"That and other matters," Andy replied, conscious that I had interrupted. "I asked Jack if people like Ed Sutherland would have to affirm total agreement with the Statement of Faith to be part of SCIF. He thought it would be counter-productive to growth to exclude from the fellowship people from other churches who didn't see eye-to-eye with us at every point. However, he felt the Statement of Faith would serve the church in three ways. One: it would alert potential members to our views and help them decide if they wanted to be part of SCIF; two: it would be a criterion for leadership appointments in the church; and three: it would set boundaries for the teaching ministry of the church on doctrinal matters."

I interrupted Andy again: "You mentioned the word 'members.' I didn't know SCIF embraced the concept of formal membership. Am I wrong or is the Statement of Faith to be a catalyst in that direction?"

"You're right," said Andy. "SCIF does not have an official list of members. Over the years people who have regularly been involved in the church have been regarded as part of the church."

"Is that about to change?" I asked.

"A matter yet to be decided."

"Did anyone else have concerns about the Statement of Faith?" Charlotte asked.

"Mark Mullins made an interesting point," said Andy. "He was concerned that a Statement of Faith could become an authority on a par with the Scriptures and that it could prevent us from being open to new insights into the Scriptures. He reminded us of the commendation given in Acts 17 to the Bereans who checked Paul's teaching against the Scriptures before embracing it."

"Mark has a point there," I said.

"I agree," said Andy. "I told the elders the Statement of Faith would represent what we as a church stand for, that it would contain truths that all Christians regard as essentials, and other elements that are not common to all."

"Ed, what are those lines about essentials and non-essentials you often quote?" asked Charlotte.

"It's a quote from seventeenth-century Germany: 'In essentials unity, in non-essentials liberty, in all things charity,'" I replied.

"I like that," said Andy. "If a Statement of Faith is adopted for the church, we'll use that quote when we launch it."

"You say 'if,' Andy. Is there uncertainty about it?" I asked.

"By the time we discussed Jack's recommendation for a Statement of Faith, it was quite late. Stan called for an extraordinary meeting in two weeks' time and asked that I prepare a draft Statement of Faith for the elders to critique. They will then decide if it should become the official doctrinal statement for the church. If accepted, Jack asked that the elders also decide whether it will be used as a criterion for church membership. Stan Mullins reluctantly agreed to put it on the agenda. That's about all I have to report at this stage. Perhaps I should say, 'See you same time, same place, in two weeks.'"

"Thanks for coming, Andy," I said, "and for filling us in on the current state of play. I wish I could say I'm relieved but, to be honest, I feel the problem has only been deferred, not resolved."

After Andy left, Charlotte and I sat in silence on the veranda. If she was angry with me for unsettling the security she'd begun to enjoy at SCIF, it didn't show. I was certainly angry with myself and full of questions. Was my friendship with Jack Wilson recoverable? Did he introduce the concept of a Statement of Faith in relation to membership to put pressure on me to leave the church? Was I destined at best to be a second-class citizen with no hope of being involved in leadership or even of preaching? As far as my view of end times was concerned, it was not even strongly in place. I was lost in a thicket with as many doubts about where I'd come from as about where I was heading. Was it worth the price to keep going? Why not admit that the jury was out on the case for the ultimate eschatology and agree with the Statement of Faith, pending a clear verdict?

19

Reconciliation

The winter whiting were running but no invitations to fish came from Jack Wilson. I thought I knew why. I spent more time in my office, straightening books, shuffling papers, indulging in self-talk, unable to settle to serious work. A touch of winter had crept into my soul. I mulled regretfully over the offence I had given to good people in the church from whom I felt increasingly isolated. A sense of foreboding hung over me as I thought about the future. An email from David Barnes seemed to justify my apprehension. He wrote:

> Luke Rodman regularly drops into my office claiming new insights that confirm his eschatological tendencies. Yesterday he shared some of the correspondence he's had with you and I was appalled to sense that your efforts to correct his errors had so far failed. What's more, he's beginning to talk with other students who think he's onto something. The faculty here at AIMS are worried about the reputation of the college if this leaks out. In short, Ed, we are disappointed that you have not pulled Luke into line.

Paradoxically, while the content of David's email was discouraging, the fact that I was in touch with a person other than myself, even if only in cyberspace, warmed me just a little. I did not feel like replying to David—anything I said would only add to his worries. If only I could prove to Luke that parts of Matthew 24 awaited fulfilment, particularly the second coming of Christ, I could then write to David and ease his concerns. To date, Luke countered my arguments fairly convincingly. I had not even responded to his treatment of apocalyptic language in Matthew 24 and did not intend to, mainly because I knew he was right and I wanted to unsettle him, not encourage him. Instead, I wrote to him as follows:

> Further to our discussions on Matthew 24, I would add the following objection to your view that Christ came in AD 70. Note verses 30 and 31: "At that time the sign of the Son of Man will appear in the sky, and all the nations of the earth will mourn. They will see the Son of Man coming on the clouds of the sky, with power and great glory. [31]And he will send his angels with a loud trumpet call, and they will gather his elect from the four winds, from one end of the heavens to the other."
>
> Christ has not been seen coming on the clouds, there has been no multinational mourning, no trumpet blast or angelic roundup of the elect. Your association of the destruction of Jerusalem with the second coming is plainly wrong in the light of this text and I urge you to return to the consensus view of the Christian church that holds to a still-future second coming.

"I've got him this time," I said out loud.

"Who have you got?" said Charlotte who had quietly entered my office with a welcome cup of coffee.

When I explained the background to my outburst, she said, "Leave it alone, Ed. Luke Rodman is not your concern. I thought we left AIMS behind when we moved here to the coast but it seems you haven't left it behind. Give up on this controversy over the second coming. Stick to what you've always believed for your own peace of mind and for the sake of unity in the church."

I nodded as if to say, "You're right, Charlotte."

"But what are you going to do about it?" she asked.

"I'm confused about it all, anyway, so I'll be happier if I put it behind me. As for unity in the church, I'll seek reconciliation with those I've offended and will avoid controversial matters that create discord."

The thanks she whispered in my ear as she hugged me made me realize afresh that being part of SCIF meant a lot to her. I had to avoid any action that would put her relationship to the church at risk although I feared I may have passed the point of no return.

Who better to begin reconciliation with than Jack Wilson? My earlier attempts at an apology had almost been forced from me at the barbecue by Jack's heated criticism. Now I felt truly sorry. As I climbed the Wilsons' back stairs the following morning, I thought how easier it was to apologize when you didn't feel sorry than when you did. Carol Wilson opened the door in response to my gentle knock. Her opening words surprised me.

"Ed, come on in. You're just in time for a cuppa. The kettle's boiling." She then called down the passage, "Jack, morning tea's ready and Ed's joined us."

Jack was quite as warm as Carol in his greeting and even apologized for not having been fishing of late. "We've been tied up with the passing of an elderly uncle of mine," said Jack. "He lived alone in Brisbane and we've had to make funeral arrangements and help settle his affairs. That's behind us now so how about we chase some winter whiting tomorrow morning?"

The cheery atmosphere in the Wilsons' kitchen seemed to make my intended apology inappropriate but that's why I'd come and I determined to proceed.

"Jack, I'd love to go fishing with you tomorrow. To be honest, I thought I'd lost a fishing mate by upsetting you at the barbecue two weeks ago when I expressed views at variance with those held by the church. The reason I've come over this morning is to ask for your forgiveness and, if possible, to renew our friendship. Charlotte and I really appreciate you both and would hate for anything to come between us."

The pained look on Jack's face suggested I was hurting him now more than at the barbecue. It was a long few seconds before he spoke. "Ed, I didn't agree with your views and I gave you an earbashing which, unfortunately, is my way of making a point. I'm sorry for being so forceful. Be assured, however, that I still respect you as a good friend and will not let the differences in our beliefs separate us."

"Thanks for that, Jack," I said, "your friendship means a lot to me."

"I'm still learning how to handle people I disagree with," he said. "I need to listen more and be less blunt when I speak. The other day I read something helpful on the internet. It was part of an essay called 'On Liberty,' by John Stuart Mill, written in 1859. He mentions three benefits of arguing a case with someone who see things differently. One person might be wrong and the other person right. As they discuss, the person who is wrong might come to see the truth. On the other hand, one person might have only half the truth and the other person might have the other half. Through discussion, each might get the half he didn't have and both end up with the whole truth. But the most important benefit is that through discussion the two parties discover whether the rationale for their beliefs is sound."

I was seeing another side to Jack. I had never thought of him as a reader of much beyond his King James Version, let alone John Stuart Mill. "Some good points there," I said. "I particularly like the last one. I'm realizing that some of my beliefs have been inherited with too little examination of their validity. Now when those beliefs are under attack, I discover that their foundation is shaky. I need people like you to challenge me so I can be sure my views are soundly based. At my stage of life, you'd think I'd have everything worked out but I've a long way to go, Jack, and would appreciate your patience with me and your help in working through issues I struggle with."

Jack gave me a hug that pleased me far more than if he had responded in words. I was glad he didn't ask me to be specific about my struggles and I was glad for the assurance the hug gave me that we were still friends. We all need a hug a day but when I went home and reported to Charlotte, I got a second hug.

20

The Rationale for Our Beliefs

Rugged up against a cold pre-dawn south-westerly, Jack and I looked like a couple of crooks in a James Bond movie with our collars turned up and our beanies pulled down. Jack steered the dinghy to the middle of the river, cut the motor and allowed us to drift quietly towards a sandbank popular for winter whiting. As we waited for the first bite, Jack said, "Ed, at the barbecue I told you how pleased Carol and I are that Josh has returned to church. However, I implied that your influence over Josh might jeopardize his return. I spoke hastily, I regret it, and I'm sorry." Before I could respond, he continued, "Josh respects you as someone who can relate across the generations and as a thinking Christian who expresses himself clearly. He told me he wishes there were more like you at SCIF."

"I appreciate your kind words, Jack. I'm also pleased to see Josh in church on Sunday mornings." I resisted the temptation to say that Anna Zimmerman might be the bait luring him there and simply added, "Your efforts to get Andy appointed as pastor will be repaid for he will be one of the factors in Josh's ongoing commitment to SCIF. Andy will gradually move the church in the direction of its being more relevant to people like Josh and I expect we'll see other young people attending as well. For my part, Jack, I will try to be a positive influence on Josh's spiritual development."

"He'll listen to you, Ed, because you're like him in wanting to think things through. Over the years, Josh has found SCIF to be too rigid, even legalistic. He would ask questions about why we believed or acted in a particular way only to be told, "God says it; that settles it."

"That sort of a reply may have left Josh thinking proof texts were being used that didn't mean what they were assumed to mean," I said.

"Can you give me an example?" asked Jack.

"I can," I said, "but I'm afraid to give the example that comes to mind for fear of re-igniting the controversy that spoilt our friendship a fortnight ago."

"John Stuart Mill has made me more willing to listen to things I may not agree with," said Jack. "Here's your chance to challenge the rationale for what I believe. Besides, our friendship is not very strong if a mere difference of opinion can tear it apart."

Only yesterday I'd told Charlotte I'd put controversy behind me. What to do? I reasoned in favor of using the example I had in mind because Jack wanted me to and I could not see it leading to discord. "Jack," I said, "I was thinking of Matthew 24:37–41." I took out a pocket New Testament and read:

> As it was in the days of Noah, so it will be at the coming of the Son of Man. [38]For in the days before the flood, people were eating and drinking, marrying and giving in marriage, up to the day Noah entered the ark; [39]and they knew nothing about what would happen until the flood came and took them all away. That is how it will be at the coming of the Son of Man. [40]Two men will be in the field; one will be taken and the other left. [41]Two women will be grinding with a hand mill; one will be taken and the other left.

"I know it well," said Jack. "It compares the days of Noah and the coming of Christ and makes mention of the rapture. Do you think we've assumed something here that was not intended, Ed?"

"It's true that the days of Noah are compared with the coming of Christ but the point of comparison is not as is sometimes represented. I have heard preachers emphasize the wickedness preceding the second coming as like that preceding the flood on the grounds that 'eating and drinking, marrying and giving in marriage' referred to gluttony, drunkenness and immorality."

"I've heard that sort of preaching too," said Jack. "What do *you* think it means?"

"The phrase 'eating and drinking, marrying and giving in marriage' refers to everyday events not wicked events. The flood struck as neighbors ate snags at a backyard barbecue and a happy couple repeated their vows at a nearby wedding service. Jesus was saying that as people did not expect the flood, so they would not expect his coming which would catch them unprepared."

"That makes more sense," Jack said. "Is there anything else in the passage that we may have got wrong?"

"The phrase, 'one will be taken,' has generally been applied to the rapture, the removal without dying of the godly, on the basis of 1 Thessalonians 4:16–17. However, the immediate context of Matthew 24 should take precedence over a remote text in Thessalonians. The previous verse says that in Noah's day the flood 'took them all away.' Those taken away in the flood were not the godly but the ungodly, so the ones taken away in verses 40 and 41 may also be the ungodly who were taken away in the judgment that fell on Jerusalem in AD 70, in contrast to the ones that were left, namely, spared that judgment."

"Mm. That's pretty radical, Ed." At that moment Jack got a bite and reeled in a large whiting. Between us we caught nine more before Jack resumed the conversation.

"Ed, I don't go along with all you've said but I'll chew it over, and even if I don't come round to your view of things, it won't come between us."

After we'd cleaned and filleted our catch, I went home with a greater appreciation for Jack Wilson and less apprehension about the outcome of the elders' meeting to discuss the Statement of Faith for SCIF. I felt confident that it would not be used as a tool to get rid of me.

21

Still Tangled in the *Little Apocalypse*

Charlotte was pleased with our haul of whiting and promised fish and chips for lunch. She was also pleased to see me happier than I'd been of late. I went to my office pleased that she was pleased. Luke Rodman's name on a new email entitled "Matthew 24:30–31" took the edge off my pleasure. I opened it with mixed feelings. I had told Charlotte I was putting controversy behind me and Luke Rodman was keeping it in front of me. The email was Luke's response to my I've-got-him-this-time email so I hoped to read, "You've got me there, Dr. Sutherland," but such hopes in the past had been unfulfilled. What if this email was more of the same? Luke began by quoting the text:

> "At that time the sign of the Son of Man will appear in the sky, and all the nations of the earth will mourn. They will see the Son of Man coming on the clouds of the sky, with power and great glory. And he will send his angels with a loud trumpet call, and they will gather his elect from the four winds, from one end of the heavens to the other."

> Dr. Sutherland, you said Matthew 24:30–31 had not been fulfilled because Christ hasn't appeared on the clouds, there has been no multinational mourning, no trumpet blast, or angelic roundup of the elect. It's a difficult passage, and I don't profess to have the last word on it, but a number of considerations caution against a literal approach to every phrase in this text: "All the nations of the earth will mourn" draws on Zechariah 12:11–14 and is to be understood in the sense of "all the tribes of the land." The King James Version has "all the tribes of the earth" but the Greek word for "earth" is also the Greek word for "land." This is a local reference not a universal one.

Clouds, trumpet, and angels are typical of apocalyptic language. This needs to be kept in mind to avoid being too literalistic. Clouds are associated with judgment. Isaiah 19:1 describes God's coming in judgment on Egypt: "An oracle concerning Egypt: See, the LORD rides on a swift cloud and is coming to Egypt."

"The Son of Man coming on the clouds" draws on Daniel 7:13 in the context of the coming of the kingdom which Jesus said would occur in conjunction with angels before some of his disciples had died (Matthew 16:27–28). He also said the kingdom would not come "with your careful observation" (Luke 17:20).

Milton Terry sums up the passage: "It may safely be affirmed, therefore, that this language concerning the coming of the Son of man in the clouds means no more on the lips of Jesus than in the writings of Daniel. It denotes in both places a sublime and glorious reality, the grandest event in human history, but not a visible display in the heavens of such a nature as to be a matter of scenic observation. The Son of man came in heavenly power to supplant Judaism by a better covenant, and to make the kingdoms of the world his own, and that parousia [coming] dates from the fall of Judaism and its temple."

Luke's email left me thoughtful and I hadn't finished reading it. He had shown the influence of the Old Testament in the teaching of Jesus. His Jewish audience would have been familiar with that background but many of today's readers of Matthew 24 were not. Were our interpretations at fault because of such ignorance? Luke concluded his email by saying:

> Dr. Sutherland, I understand that you may not agree with my responses to the problems you have raised in your emails but I want you to know that I have throughout tried to respect three over-riding considerations that should, I am convinced, govern any interpretation of Matthew 24:
>
> 1. The context in which the discussion took place: Jesus' shock announcement about the destruction of Jerusalem.
>
> 2. The time frame in which the events of the chapter were to occur: the generation in which they were living. He said, "I tell you the truth, this generation will certainly not pass away until all these things have happened" (verse 34).
>
> 3. The danger of presuppositions: reading the text through the lenses of an assumed interpretation that distorts the intended meaning.

> Failure to observe these interpretative criteria casts doubt on our exegetical integrity. What I have written fits better with the criteria than did my previous views but, if I'm wrong at any point, I welcome correction.

I was encouraged to see that Luke was open to change but, having determined to leave these matters behind, I was not going to make further attempts to correct him. Our chats were at an end. It was time to log off. I wrote commending him for his desire to be true to the text; I wished him well in his eschatological explorations; and I urged him to cling at all costs to the tenets of orthodoxy. I sent a copy of my email to David Barnes and hoped my plea to Luke to adhere to the generally agreed beliefs of Christians throughout the ages would help restore my reputation. From the tone of David's last email to me, I was not hopeful. In checking my inbox, I noticed an unexpected email from Lauren Wilson:

> Dear Dr. Sutherland,
>
> The Real Life committee at USC plans to run a debate on campus entitled, "God does not exist." Dr. Max Fitzgerald, Paul's father, philosophy lecturer, and chairman of the Humanist Association, has been asked to affirm the non-existence of God. I suggested you as a suitable speaker to oppose him and was asked by the committee to invite you to participate in the debate on the first Monday in August. It will be held in B Block, Room 15, between 12 noon and 1:00 p.m. We expect it to be well-attended and to be a good opportunity to present the case for God.
>
> I look forward to your reply.
> Lauren Wilson.

I'd never seen myself as an apologist and I knew the risk if Max Fitzgerald made a stronger case. However, I decided to accept the invitation: I felt I owed it to the young people from SCIF, not to mention the opportunity to fly the flag for faith. The next few weeks would be busy but at least my mind would be off matters eschatological.

The worst part of preparing for the debate was not knowing what line of attack Max Fitzgerald would take. Putting an argument for the existence of God was less daunting than answering unexpected questions from a committed atheist. I had to read widely and hope that on the day my resources would be adequate to rebut his position.

My study on Wednesday morning was interrupted by a knock on the office door. Andy Zimmerman had come to report on the elders' meeting of the night before. I was glad to lay aside *Dawkins' GOD: Genes, Memes, and the Meaning of Life* by Alister McGrath to hear where I stood with SCIF.

After a minimum of small talk, Andy handed me a two-page document headed, "Doctrinal Statement of the Sunshine Coast Independent Fellowship."

"Has it been officially approved?" I asked.

"Unanimously."

"Did the elders make any changes to your original draft?" I asked.

"They tinkered with the wording of several statements but when it came to the doctrine that precipitated a Statement of Faith, they wanted more detail."

"Thanks to me," I said.

Andy smiled and said, "If you turn to page two, clause 24, you'll see the statement about things to come." He read from his copy:

> We believe that we are in the last days and that at any moment Christ could come to rapture his church. Those left behind will experience seven years of tribulation that will end with the personal and visible return of the Lord Jesus Christ with his saints to usher in the kingdom of God, a literal 1,000-year reign by Christ on earth. The resurrection and judgment of the wicked and the creation of a new heaven and earth will follow.

"That covers most of the bases," I said.

"Not enough according to some. Had I not observed that we were formulating a statement not writing a thesis, it would have included the return of the Jews to Palestine, the antichrist, the 144,000, and mystery Babylon, to mention just a few."

"Where to from here?" I asked.

"As you know, the issue of membership was on the agenda. Jack proposed that those who endorsed the Statement of Faith be regarded as members and that those who agreed with the essentials but not all of the non-essentials be regarded as associate members. Mark Mullins thought a two-tiered system would draw attention to differences and create suspicions and disunity."

"What did Stan Mullins think?" I asked.

"He was opposed to using the Statement of Faith to separate members from non-members."

"I'm surprised," I said. "I thought Stan would be all for withholding membership from those who can't sign it."

"I've only been here a short while," said Andy, "but I think I understand his concern. Here at SCIF, decisions are made by the elders and I think Stan fears that formal membership will be the first step towards congregational meetings where decisions are made by a vote of members."

"I understand," I said. I was fully aware of the different forms of church government that existed in the denominations: the Anglicans and Catholics had their hierarchical form of government; the Baptists allowed their members to vote; and the Presbyterians were like SCIF, the local church being ruled by a body of elders. Was Stan Mullins afraid of losing power if members made decisions? I didn't voice the question but suspected Andy was asking it without my help.

"So is SCIF about to have a membership roll?" I asked.

"No, Stan won the day. He argued that the modern concept of membership was unbiblical on the grounds that in the early church a person was automatically regarded as a member on profession of faith, that to be a member of Christ was to be a member of the church."

I didn't agree with Stan that the church could only implement practices taught or modeled in the New Testament but, in my present circumstances, I felt Stan was an ally. At least I wasn't about to be excommunicated because I couldn't tick all the boxes. Nevertheless, all was not clear so I said to Andy, "Given that the Statement of Faith, particularly clause 24, was written with me in mind, where do I stand in relation to SCIF?"

"Be assured," said Andy, "that you are not being pressured to leave the church. We want the church to grow not decline."

"I take it I can't be a leader if I don't agree with clause 24, but can I preach?"

"You're right that leaders must agree with the whole document but you can still preach. Your preaching should not be at variance with the Statement of Faith but since you agree with most of it, you should not be short of preaching material."

"You're right," I said, "and I'll do my best to observe what you're saying. By the way, what happens to the Statement of Faith now? Does it get put in a bottom drawer until the next controversial issue surfaces?"

"I've been asked to present it next Sunday as part of the sermon. I hope we can all move on together in peace and unity even if at some points we disagree."

After Andy left, I felt pleased that I would not be asked to sign the Statement of Faith. Why did I feel pleased after earlier being willing to agree with the church's view of eschatology on the grounds that it was not an open-and-shut case? I now realized that I was pleased because deep down I knew I could not sign it in good conscience. I was almost 100 percent sure we were not in the last days in the biblical sense since they were the last days of the old covenant. I was also unhappy to relegate the kingdom of God to the millennium. Was it not here already and growing from the smallness of a mustard seed towards the bigness of a bush in which birds could nest? Although I had signed off in my correspondence with Luke Rodman, his ideas were lodged in my mind like a hibernating bear in a cave. I chose not to think too deeply about them for fear the bear might awake.

I looked forward to Andy's presentation on Sunday and wondered whether the Statement of Faith would have positive or negative consequences for the church.

22

A Statement of Faith Adopted

As we entered the foyer of the church on Sunday morning, Arthur handed us our red Sankey's *Sacred Songs and Solos* with a two-page document inserted. Did I detect a smug look on his face as he did so? He also handed me a sealed envelope.

Inside the church, the usual buzz of conversation was replaced by a quiet reading of the hymn-book insert. Did I detect an occasional look in my direction by people who had reached clause 24 in the document?

After a doxology and invocatory prayer, Stan Mullins announced, "At a meeting on Tuesday night, the elders and our pastor unanimously approved a Statement of Faith representing the doctrinal position of our church. This morning it is being presented to the congregation and the pastor will focus on its role during his sermon." Stan announced the opening hymn and while Mrs. Beecroft adjusted the clothes pegs on the music book, he read the first verse:

> How firm a foundation, ye saints of the Lord,
> Is laid for your faith in His excellent Word!
> What more can He say than to you He hath said,
> You, who unto Jesus for refuge have fled?

The aged organ was in danger of a seizure as, with all stops out, Mrs. Beecroft pumped its pedals like Cadel Evans on a hill climb in the *Tour de France*. The volume of the congregational singing more than matched her efforts and seemed to come from people convinced that their new doctrinal statement was a very firm foundation.

Stan offered a pastoral prayer and then read the first verse of the second hymn:

> Faith of our fathers, living still,
> In spite of dungeon, fire and sword;
> O how our hearts beat high with joy
> Whene'er we hear that glorious Word!

I was beginning to think the hymns were aimed at me and that I had undermined the firm foundation and forsaken the faith of our fathers. I felt slightly comforted with the possibility that many in the congregation may have understood "our fathers" to refer to the Buderim farmers who founded SCIF and that had they known what the fathers further back in history believed, they may have been reading a different clause 24.

During the third hymn, I opened the sealed envelope and found a brief note from Andy: "Thanks for the quote that forms an important part of this morning's message. Copy enclosed."

Andy read Acts 2:42 in the King James Version as the text for his sermon:

> And they continued steadfastly in the apostles' doctrine and fellowship, and in breaking of bread, and in prayers.

He began by saying, "You all received a copy of the Statement of Faith when you arrived this morning. Please resist the temptation to read it during the sermon, boring as that may be, but do read it carefully when you go home."

Those who had already fallen into temptation rustled their papers out of sight as Andy continued: "Some of you will be asking, 'Why do we need a Statement of Faith? We've got the Bible, what more do we need?'" A number of heads nodded. Andy seemed to be on track. "Good questions," he said. "To help answer them, I want to consider some of the benefits of the Statement of Faith.

1. "The Statement of Faith is a summary of what we believe. Paul Little wrote a book with an excellent title: *Know What You Believe*. Many Christians are not sure what they believe. The early Christians knew what they believed and they adhered to it. You can't continue steadfastly in the apostles' doctrine, or teaching, if you don't know what it is.

2. "The Statement of Faith will help you when people ask, for example, 'What does your church believe about creation, Christ, or the second coming?' If you are familiar with the Statement of Faith, you will be able to answer them with confidence. Some of you know your Bible well and you may be right in asking, 'What more do we need?' but

there are young people and new Christians who do not have your depth of knowledge. The Statement of Faith will help them.

3. "The Statement of Faith will help people who move into our community, and are looking for a church, to know whether our church believes what they believe; whether they are likely to feel at home in our church.

4. "The Statement of Faith will be a guide for the elders in determining the suitability of future leaders for the church.

5. "The Statement of Faith will set the boundaries for the teaching ministry of the church. Visiting speakers and members of our own congregation who preach from time to time will know what we stand for and will be expected to respect our doctrinal position.

"Yes, there are a number of benefits in having a Statement of Faith but there are also some dangers. Please bear with me as I sound a couple of cautionary notes.

1. "The Statement of Faith is a human document and must never be given the same authority as the Scriptures. Over the centuries, churches have produced creeds and confessions such as the Apostles' Creed, the Nicene Creed, the Westminster Confession, and so on. None of these is on a par with the Bible. They have served to maintain orthodox Christianity over the centuries but they are not infallible and must always be subject to the scrutiny of Scripture. The same is true for our Statement of Faith.

2. "The Statement of Faith contains some doctrines that are essential beliefs for all who call themselves Christians; for example, that God is creator, that Christ is God, that salvation is by grace not works. But it also contains beliefs about which good Christians disagree; for example, the frequency for celebration of the Lord's Supper, the proper mode of baptism, whether the church goes through the tribulation, and so on. It is very important that we learn to distinguish these two types of beliefs."

At this point in his message, Andy made me feel uncomfortable. He said, "Last week I was speaking with Ed Sutherland and he shared a helpful quotation, attributed to Rupertus Meldenius, that I would like to pass on to you." On the one hand, I was pleased that he publicly associated himself with me in a positive way; on the other hand, I was concerned that those who might wish to distance themselves from me might begin to distance themselves from Andy. The last thing I wanted was to be the cause of division in the church. I hoped people would realize that Andy, having agreed with the Statement of Faith at the leadership meeting, was not my ally in an eschatological revolution. I also hoped they would respect and emulate his willingness to fellowship with someone with whom he did not agree at every point.

The data projector (a recent innovation of Andy's) displayed the quotation:

> In essentials unity,
>
> In non-essentials liberty,
>
> In all things charity.

I was glad Andy had checked out the source of the quotation and that my name did not appear on the screen. He continued: "Let me unpack these lines to ensure that we all understand them. The doctrines classified as 'essentials' are non-negotiable. We must be united in upholding them. Regarding the doctrines classified as 'non-essentials,' we must allow others the freedom to have their own convictions. The last line of the quotation is all-important: we must love those who disagree with us whether the difference is over an essential or a non-essential."

I tried to read the thoughtful expressions on the faces of Andy's listeners and imagined some of them thinking, "Is clause 24 an essential or a non-essential?" It even crossed my mind that some were thinking, "Do we really have to love someone who disagrees with clause 24?"

Good communicators anticipate the questions in the minds of their hearers and Andy was a good communicator. He said, "Another good question that some of you are asking is, 'How do we distinguish the essentials from the non-essentials?' I have found it helpful to ask two questions. First, I ask, 'Is the doctrine a salvation-related issue?' The deity of Christ is a salvation-related matter about which we must agree. If Jesus is not God he cannot be the mediator between God and man. He needs to be both God and man to reconcile the two. If he is not God, he is not adequate to the task. In other words, the person of Christ affects the work of Christ, which affects our salvation. As the old children's hymn says:

> There was no other good enough
>
> To pay the price of sin.
>
> He only could unlock the gate
>
> Of heaven and let us in.

"Whether I celebrate the Lord's Supper once a week or once a month is unrelated to salvation so the frequency of communion is a non-essential.

That doesn't mean it is unimportant. Many non-essentials are very important but they do not affect one's salvation. I personally believe that the church does not go through the tribulation; I personally believe the millennium is a literal 1,000 years, but neither of these beliefs is essential to salvation. Many think differently about these matters but I must love them nevertheless."

Andy was drawing on clause 24 to illustrate his point. I would not have been surprised if heads had turned in my direction at the mention of many who believed differently, but Andy's "I must love them nevertheless" prevented their turning. He continued with the issue of distinguishing the essentials from the non-essentials: "Here is the other question I ask: 'Is the doctrine a foundational doctrine?' In other words, 'Would the superstructure of Christianity collapse if the doctrine were removed?' If you take the deity or resurrection of Christ out of Christianity, you will destroy it. If you change your view on the frequency of communion or the nature of the millennium, Christianity will not collapse."

In concluding his sermon, Andy referred back to the text in Acts 2:42: "The early church was committed to four things: apostolic doctrine, fellowship, breaking of bread, and prayers. Our Statement of Faith is about doctrine. Doctrine will be divisive if our fellowship is on the basis of non-essentials. It will not be divisive if we keep Christ and his cross central through the breaking of bread and if we pray for one another."

After the service, I got a coffee and moved around the hall eavesdropping on the small groups engaged in noisy conversation. Andy's sermon and the Statement of Faith dominated. Many were impressed by the balance in Andy's sermon; few were critical.

As I passed the Wilsons and Bradfords, I overheard Robyn Bradford say, "While more could have been written about end times, the statement does at least identify our church as committed to a pre-tribulation rapture and a pre-millennial, visible return of Christ." She spotted me and broke away from the group to say excitedly, "Ed, what a great day for our church! No one can be in any doubt about where we stand doctrinally with such a clear Statement of Faith. What did you think of it?"

I assumed Arthur had informed her about the views I expressed at the barbecue so I felt she could be luring me into an argument over clause 24. I replied innocuously, "The elders are to be commended for having expressed the church's doctrinal position so clearly."

Robyn was not to be put off so easily: "So you'd give all the clauses an affirming tick?"

I now had no doubt that my earlier assumption was true: she knew what I'd said at the barbecue but I was not even going to nibble at the bait. "A big tick for all the essentials," I said.

"What about the non-essentials?"

With a smile, I said, "I glory in having liberty to embrace them in so far as they tally with my understanding of Scripture."

"And what if that understanding is wrong?" she asked, without a smile.

"I will gladly alter my view."

Robyn returned to the group less excited than when she left it. I congratulated myself for the outstanding restraint I had exercised throughout the conversation and believed any impartial judge would acknowledge my having won the day.

But I didn't feel like a winner.

23

A Debate with an Atheist

For several weeks, Lauren Wilson kept me informed about preparations for the debate. Members of Real Life had displayed posters advertising the event on courtyard pillars, in the campus refectory, and on lecture-room notice boards. They had handed leaflets to fellow students and inserted them in student magazines. They were excited. Max Fitzgerald and his fellow humanists had also been busy advertising the debate. They were excited. I was nervous. I had worked hard at my preparation but the uncertainty about the direction the debate would take and the certainty that a large section of the audience would be unsympathetic, even hostile, meant I had to work particularly hard at hiding my nervousness on the day.

On arrival at the lecture theatre, Lauren introduced me to Dr. Martin Forbes, Senior Lecturer in Physics at the University, a Christian and a strong supporter of Real Life. He was to chair the debate. After checking that the comments he planned to make when introducing me to the audience were correct, he reminded me of the format of the debate. The hour would be divided into three twenty-minute segments. The first two would involve uninterrupted presentations by the speakers, beginning with Dr. Fitzgerald as spokesman for the affirmative. In the last twenty minutes, the two of us would respond to questions from the floor.

My nervousness increased as I was introduced to Max Fitzgerald. A big man with a big voice, he was dressed in a black academic gown complete with doctoral colors. I presumed he felt it enhanced his authority. He greeted me pleasantly enough although the curl in his smile held a touch of cynicism that suggested I was a loser and that he was saying, "Are you sure you want to go ahead with this?"

Five minutes before starting time there was standing room only. Noisy supporters of Max Fitzgerald, including his son Paul, were on one side and spilling over to the other side where the quieter Real Life members were sitting. A few of them were huddled together praying. I needed it. I noticed Josh Wilson sitting near the front and hoped he hadn't phoned in sick to his boss, Stan Mullins. His nod and a wink encouraged me.

Martin Forbes welcomed the crowd and the protagonists. I imagined he might begin by saying, "In one corner we have Dr. Max Fitzgerald" at which the larger section of the crowd would out-yell the response to his "In the other corner..." While I did hear comments like, "Sock it to him, Max," both sides generously applauded both speakers. I hoped that the postmodern tendency to respect the opinions of others would prevail throughout the debate. Martin outlined the structure of the meeting and called on Max to give his presentation.

I feared he would lift an unfamiliar atheistic rabbit out of the hat but it was an old, well-known one. He began: "Christians say that God is all-loving and all-powerful. Was he all-loving when he allowed this child to be born?" He then projected the image of a girl with an oversized head and ghastly facial disfigurations. The horror elicited audible groans across the audience. Max had everyone's attention. He continued: "Perhaps God loved this girl but he did not have the power to avert the tragedy. In other words, he is not all-powerful." Using this line of argument, he showed graphic images of emaciated children in the Sudan, victims of a tsunami in Japan, of a suicide bomb in Afghanistan, of a mudslide in the Philippines, and of teenage prostitution in Asia. In each case, he asked, "Did God love these people? Perhaps he did but he was just too weak to do anything about it. Perhaps he could have prevented the tragedies but he just didn't care." Max concluded his presentation by saying, "The bottom line is that history and human experience demonstrate that an all-loving, all-powerful God does not exist. Dr. Sutherland will try to convince you that he does exist but the facts show that the God he believes in does not exist."

Max's supporters whistled, shouted and stamped their feet as he finished his presentation. Paul Fitzgerald stood and thrust an energetic high-five in his father's direction. The Real Life group was subdued. So was I. It was my turn. How should I handle it? Should I give my prepared speech or put it aside and respond to the specifics of Max's speech? He had been cunning: logic combined with an emotional appeal; a single point reinforced by visuals; anecdotes rather than statistics. My material was too diverse and much of it did not follow on from Max's point. Taking a huge risk, I laid aside my notes and, with a silent telegram prayer for help, began.

"I was moved, even to tears, by Dr. Fitzgerald's presentation and I thank him for his vivid reminder of the dark and painful realities of our world. I recalled the occasion when my wife and I lost our much-loved four-year-old daughter to meningococcal disease. We did not understand why it happened—and we still don't—but in our grief we did not reject God. Were we ignorant of Dr. Fitzgerald's argument? Not at all! It just did not deal with the deeper issues at stake. No one believes that the frightful occurrences identified by Dr. Fitzgerald are problem free but God is not so easily dismissed.

"Behind Dr. Fitzgerald's argument is a technical term, 'theodicy.' The term was first introduced by the eighteenth-century German philosopher Leibniz. In simple terms, it tries to answer questions such as, 'If God is so good and strong, how come there's so much evil in the world?' Attempts at answering such questions go back many centuries before Leibniz. One book in the Bible, the book of Job in the Old Testament, is devoted to the problem. Job loses all ten of his children, his flocks, his herds, and even his health. Readers of the book know why his suffering occurs but Job is never told. At the end of the book, God puts Job in the dock. The scores of questions put to Job leave him open-mouthed and humbled, but with a strong conviction of God's awesome power and providence. Job may not understand what's going on but he knows he can safely leave his cause in the hands of such a God.

"The Nazi extermination of six million Jews raised the question, 'Where was God?' A Jewish response I heard on a recent radio program was, 'He spoke: he said, "You shall not kill."' You say, 'What's the point?' It is that suffering in our world is used as an argument for rejecting God but the truth is that much suffering in our world is *caused* by our rejection of God. If the Nazis had listened to the God of the Jews they would not have killed the Jews.

"God says, 'Husbands love your wives,' but some husbands disregard this and abuse their wives and when we see a picture of a bruised and bloodied wife, we say, 'There is no God.' But, you say, 'Why didn't God intervene?' What would you like God to do in such a case? Force the bad husband to be a good husband against his will? You'd be the first to complain. Strike the husband dead? If he did, you would add his death to your argument against the existence of God. God is damned if he does and damned if he doesn't.

"God is expected to act when really bad things happen but where do we draw the line? We want to put Hitler above the line but well-fed westerners who let Sudanese children starve to death below the line. We want to put the pimps who kidnap young girls for prostitution above the line but those who indulge in internet pornography below the line. We've heard today that God is thought to be all-loving and all-powerful. There's more: God is all-holy. If he were to intervene to punish evil, none of us would escape. There's no 'above the line' and 'below the line' with a holy God. His holiness reacts not only to mass murder but to selfishness, lust, greed, and hypocrisy.

"Dr. Fitzgerald has argued, on the one hand, that there is much evil in our world and, on the other hand, that the God of Christians is either indifferent or incompetent to deal with the evil. Be sure of this: God *has* done something about it. Two thousand years ago, God entered human history in the person of Jesus Christ. We call it the incarnation. The very best of men suffered unimaginably as long iron nails were hammered into his hands and feet, and as he pressed on those pierced feet to enable his suspended body to take each excruciating breath. His death was undeserved; his death was a voluntary act of supreme love; his death was the divine solution to the greatest problem of our world, a problem within the human heart.

"I said earlier that Dr. Fitzgerald's argument does not deal with the deeper issues. It ignores the fact that many intelligent Christians have experienced the kinds of tragedies he portrayed but have not given up on God. Countless Christian martyrs have been burnt alive, boiled in oil, or been eaten by lions. They did not give up on God. Above all, his argument ignores the central historical events of the Christian faith: the incarnation, a demonstration that God exists; the crucifixion, a demonstration that God is loving; the resurrection, a demonstration that God is powerful."

As I stepped away from the lectern to make way for Martin Forbes, the Real Life group gave enthusiastic applause, Josh Wilson punched the air with his thumb up; a few of Max's supporters gave polite applause but most were disapprovingly mute, no doubt waiting their turn to put me on the spot during the open question time. There was no high-five from Paul Fitzgerald but, unlike the others, he appeared more thoughtful than sullen.

24

Question Time at the Debate

Hand-held microphones were given to Max and me as we sat on either side of Martin who remained standing at the lectern to coordinate the question time. He asked that questions be addressed alternately to the two of us and that responses not exceed two minutes. A cynical student began by asking me a worn-out question: "Can God make a rock he cannot lift?"

I replied, "The form of your question calls for a Yes/No answer but you have asked me to give a single answer to a double question—hardly fair. Let's separate your questions: on the one hand, you've asked about God's rock-*making* ability; on the other hand, you've asked about his rock-*lifting* ability. Can God make a very big rock? Yes. Can God lift a very heavy rock? Yes."

A more thoughtful student asked Max, "Dr. Sutherland heaped blame on unbelievers for suffering in the world, but are there not accounts in history of suffering caused by believers?"

"Indeed there are," said Max. He then gave graphic descriptions of the torture methods used by the inquisition in Spain, of the slaughter of Muslims during the crusades, of the burning of heretics under Queen Mary of Britain, and of the 1572 Saint Bartholomew's Day massacre in France—"all of this," he said, "in the name of God."

Paul Fitzgerald continued his father's line by asking me, "How do Christians respond to the accounts of suffering that we have just heard?"

"Dr. Fitzgerald is right," I said. "The events he described were atrocious and inexcusable. The Muslims deserve a public apology for the atrocities committed against them. The crimes of the inquisition call for public repentance." Paul smiled. "However," I said, "the nature of the crimes is in such contrast to the nature of God that there are no grounds for using his name in connection with them. He was more grieved by them than we are. The founder of Christianity said we should love our enemies and that we should treat others as we would like to be treated. What Dr. Fitzgerald described was *not* Christian behavior. He has a strong case against misguided and even wicked people but not against God." The smile disappeared from Paul's face and he resumed the thoughtful mien I had noticed earlier.

The next question addressed to Max took up a different topic: "Hasn't science eliminated the need for God?"

"God was a useful resource in a pre-scientific age to explain the inexplicable," replied Max, "but as science answers more and more questions about the universe, believers will begin to realize that God was merely a human fabrication in an age of ignorance."

Martin Forbes was itching to respond but as the chairman he declined. He was, however, visibly relieved when Josh Wilson asked, "Dr. Sutherland, has your faith diminished with each advancement in science?"

"Not at all," I said. "If anything, science increasingly confirms that the universe and everything in it owe their origin to an intelligent designer. Humanistic scientists would have us believe that no self-respecting scientist believes in God. No one would say that Isaac Newton, Michael Faraday, Robert Boyle, and James Maxwell were not respected scientists. They were also firm believers in God and saw no contradiction between their scientific outlook and their faith. The situation is no different in the present: our chairman today, Dr. Martin Forbes, is a respected scientist and a believer. Alister McGrath, author of *The Dawkins Delusion,* has earned doctorates from Oxford University in molecular biophysics as well as divinity. Dr. Francis Collins, a geneticist and leader in the Human Genome Project, is a firm believer in God. A Christian in the scientific community today is not a rarity. God will not be debunked by science because, contrary to the assertion that he is just a gap filler pending a scientific explanation, Christians believe he is at all times involved in every aspect of the material universe, responsible not only for its existence but also its maintenance."

My two minutes were almost up but I felt I should pick up on a phrase used by Max: "Dr. Fitzgerald referred to God as 'a human fabrication in an age of ignorance.' In keeping with this thought are the words of a philosopher I heard recently. He referred to the Ten Commandments as the invention of ignorant goat-herds in the desert. Dr. Fitzgerald would have us believe that God and ethical values are the result of a bottom-up rather than a top-down process, but neither God nor ethical values are of human origin. If we had invented God we would have invented a far less demanding being: one whose standards were more achievable and whose expectations pandered to our desires—certainly not a God who puts restrictions on our sexual behavior even to the point of forbidding lustful thoughts, who commands us to love our enemies, and who requires absolute submission to his will. Dr. Fitzgerald implies that before God was fabricated everyone was an atheist. Now atheists don't like the God they created."

Martin was pointing to his watch so I lowered my microphone and he took another question. "Dr. Fitzgerald, were you always an atheist?" a student asked.

"No," he said. "I was brought up in a religious family and went to church services every Sunday. I was even an altar boy. Three things influenced my switch from Christianity to atheism: One, I found the ritual in the church irrelevant to my everyday life. Two, my studies at university steered me towards atheism: science showed me that evolution dismissed the need for God and philosophy offered me rational arguments for atheism. The third influence towards change was the hypocrisy I witnessed within the church and in our home. A prominent leader in the church was well-known in the community as an unscrupulous businessman and my own father, who had insisted I go to church with him every week, had an affair with a woman in the church resulting in the breakup of our family."

"Dr. Sutherland," said the next student, "you must admit that there are plenty of hypocrites around. Do they not argue strongly against your position?"

"I meet plenty of hypocrites," I replied, "not only in church but also on the roads as I drive my car. I regularly see drivers who ignore the rules of the road and whose behavior endangers the lives of others. These reckless drivers are hypocrites: they have a driver's license that acknowledges them as knowing the rules of the road and as competent to drive a vehicle but their behavior says otherwise. When I see these drivers, do I say, 'With so many hypocrites on the road, I am going to park my car in the garage and never drive again?' Of course not; yet many say, 'I'll never go to church again because there are too many hypocrites there.' A hypocrite is a counterfeit. We should no more dismiss Christianity because of the phonies than we should burn our twenty-dollar bills on hearing that counterfeits are in circulation. Why are there counterfeit twenty-dollar bills but no counterfeit ten-cent coins? Because a ten-cent coin is virtually worthless. It's only valuable things that get counterfeited. If there are counterfeit Christians it's because Christianity is so important."

A member of Real Life said to Max, "Dr. Fitzgerald, is it possible that your rejection of Christianity in favor of atheism was due to your having been inoculated against true Christianity through the church experiences of your youth?"

"Would you care to unpack your question?" said Max.

"Inoculation involves a minimal exposure to a disease, not enough to catch the disease, only enough to build up an immunity against it. A person can similarly be exposed to a form of Christianity that does not lead to an experience of the real thing, only a resistance to it."

"That is possible," said Max. I was surprised by his answer and expected him to say more. If he intended to, he paused too long because Anna began to ask me a question.

"Dr. Sutherland," she said, "what advice would you give to a sincere atheist who was an honest seeker after truth?"

"An American evangelist called Reuben Torrey addressed that question well. He recommended that such a person take a copy of the Gospel of John and begin by praying along these lines: 'God, if there is a God, as I read this book, show me if it is true. If you do, I pledge to believe it.' Torrey maintains that an atheist who is unwilling to do this is not an honest seeker after truth. It is worth noting that John's purpose in writing the Gospel was that through it people might come to faith in Christ and experience life through him."

I wish the question time had finished on that note but unfortunately Martin said, "There is time for one more question." A well-meaning member of Real Life asked Max a question Jesus once asked: "What do you think about the Christ?"

"I think he was only a man and not God." Adopting a philosophical style, he continued: "If A does not exist but B claims that C is A, then B is wrong. In other words, the deity of Jesus stands or falls on the outcome of the case for the existence of God. As an atheist, I have established to my satisfaction that there is no God. Consequently, whenever others say that Jesus is God, in my view they're wrong. In support of his not being God, consider the failure of some of his prophecies to be fulfilled. He said he would return before some of his hearers died. Because this didn't happen, Bertrand Russell wrote in *Why I Am Not a Christian*, that Christ's teaching was defective. Christ said in Mark 13:30 that all the earlier predictions in the chapter, including his second coming, would be fulfilled before that generation expired. C. S. Lewis called the text 'the most embarrassing verse in the Bible.' Well-known biblical scholars, Oscar Cullmann and Joachim Jeremias, both maintain that Jesus erred in predicting his soon return. What do I think of Christ? I think he was a man capable of error."

The debate was over. If the volume of the applause from the two factions in the audience was any indication, the case for God was foundering, not helped by the negative note on which it had ended. I was disappointed; the smirk on Max's face said he was not.

25

Changes in the Church

The following Monday, Martin Forbes phoned to give some feedback on the debate. He began by saying, "Ed, I'm sorry the question time ended as it did. I would have preferred it to finish with the challenge to read John's gospel but, having stressed that questions should alternate between you and Max, the first question having gone to you, it was fair that Max receive the last question. To have done otherwise would have given the impression we had rigged the debate to our own ends."

"I understand," I said. "How did the Real Life group think the debate went?"

"They were encouraged. Their hard work in promoting the event paid off with a greater-than-expected attendance and they were particularly pleased that there were newcomers at today's Real Life meeting. And guess who was among the newcomers," he said.

"I give up."

"Paul Fitzgerald," said Martin.

"Dad won't be too happy about that," I said.

"I guess not. And what's more," said Martin, "Paul asked Anna for a copy of John's gospel so he could read it as you suggested."

I was sure Josh Wilson would gladly have given Paul a copy of John's gospel and wondered why he had approached Anna. Anyway, it was good news.

"And there's more," said Martin. "A number of students were so impressed with the way you handled Max and the questions put to you that they want you to give a series of three studies at our Monday lunchtime meetings."

"Do they have a topic in mind?"

"They'd like you to talk about the kingdom of God. In order to tap into the interest generated by the debate, they would like the series to begin sooner rather than later, in a fortnight's time. I know it's short notice but that would allow us to finish the series before the mid-semester break. Exam pressures after the break would greatly reduce numbers. Once we know if you're available, the students will advertise it on campus."

"I'm happy to fit in with those dates," I said, "and with the topic. The kingdom of God is of great interest to me and I hope I can enthuse the students about it as well. Is there anything else I need to know?"

"There is one more thing," he said. "Given the unfortunate conclusion to the debate and the impression left on the listeners that Jesus' teaching was defective, the students would like you to clear up that point before you launch into the topic." I agreed to do so and told Martin I looked forward to seeing him soon.

As I put the receiver down, I thought it ironic that while opportunities to share my eschatological thoughts at SCIF were shrinking, I was invited to address two controversial eschatological issues at Real Life: Jesus' prediction of his coming within a generation, and the kingdom of God. I did have a twinge of concern that the daughters of Jack Wilson and Andy Zimmerman were members of Real Life but I refused to allow SCIF to control my wider teaching opportunities.

Next morning, Jack and I dropped anchor at the Cod Hole as an orange sun tinged the clouds on the eastern horizon. Catching fish was secondary to the colors of dawn, the quietness of the river, and the company of Jack. He broke the silence by telling me how delighted Lauren was with the crowd that attended the debate and how pleased Josh was to hear that his friend Paul was showing interest in the gospel.

"Josh invited Paul to come to SCIF this Sunday morning and, believe it or not, he's agreed. Josh has arranged to pick him up. I told Andy about Paul," said Jack. "He's going to look out for him and keep him in mind as he preaches."

"You know his father's the atheist I debated with?"

"I do," said Jack. "If Paul is converted, it won't go down well with his father or the Humanist Association."

"That's for sure. Speaking of Sunday mornings, I'm enjoying the services under Andy's leadership. He's slowly making changes for the better don't you think?"

"I agree," said Jack. "He's introducing new songs, is involving members of the congregation in the program, and his preaching is regularly attracting newcomers, including young people. I'm very encouraged but there are some who feel that guitars and data projectors mean the world is creeping into the church."

"The pace of change is all-important," I said. "When there is no change over many years, the gap between where the church is and where it ought to be becomes so great that to bridge the gap in a hurry is disastrous. Older people in particular become unsettled with rapid change. They don't know what to expect next. They feel insecure. An element of predictability is not a bad thing."

"I understand perfectly," said Jack. "I'm part of the old school that for years resisted change but my attitude has altered in recent days. I used to think change was synonymous with compromise and I criticized other churches when they differed from ours. Now I have come to see that it's possible to make adjustments in the interests of growth without sacrificing truth. The few changes we've recently made have already led to growth. I used to pride myself that I was part of the faithful remnant upholding the truth and I attributed lack of growth to the hardness of people's hearts in the last days. I now know that we were not growing because we were isolated from our community and irrelevant to its needs. I used to hark back to 'the good old days'; now I look forward to good new days."

On Sunday morning, as Charlotte and I walked from our car to the church foyer, a rather noisy Mustang screeched into the car park and braked suddenly beside Stan Mullins's car which had just arrived. As Stan emerged from a cloud of dust, he aimed a disapproving frown at both the driver of the Mustang and the visitor dressed in T-shirt, board shorts, and thongs.

Paul was clearly a novelty for most of the SCIF members whose curious glances in his direction prior to the commencement of the service led to whispered conversations and even a smile or two, probably a reaction to the words on his T-shirt: "665: Guess who lives next door to me."

Under the influence of Andy's measured attempts at innovation, the service began with a contemporary Southern Gospel song accompanied by Linda Zimmerman on the guitar. Paul didn't know the song but his body language synchronized with its rhythm and his smile showed he was making an effort to fit in. Using a PowerPoint presentation, Mark Mullins led the reading of a Psalm with alternate lines read by the congregation; then, following another of Andy's innovations, he asked the members of the congregation to move about the room and greet one another, particularly newcomers. Lauren, Anna, and several other young people surrounded Paul and were still chatting with him after everyone else had settled down. He reveled in the attention.

When the Zimmerman family sang "He's Got the Whole World in His Hands," I wasn't sure if Paul was rapt by the music or a particular member of the quartet. The same doubt crossed my mind when I looked at the beatific expression on Josh's face. After Stan Mullins gave the announcements, the service reverted to a more traditional mode as Mrs. Beecroft mounted the organ stool to play "Abide with Me." At that point the mood of some members of the congregation switched from apprehension to approval, in contrast to a switch by others from enjoyment to acquiescence. SCIF's transition into the twenty-first century was going to require the application of "in all things charity" not only to doctrinal differences but also to worship styles.

Andy announced that he was commencing a series of messages on the book of Hebrews. He read the opening verses of the first chapter in the King James Version:

> God, who at sundry times and in divers manners spake in time past unto the fathers by the prophets, ²Hath in these last days spoken unto us by his Son, whom he hath appointed heir of all things, by whom also he made the worlds. ³Who being the brightness of his glory, and the express image of his person, and upholding all things by the word of his power, when he had by himself purged our sins, sat down on the right hand of the Majesty on high: ⁴Being made so much better than the angels, as he hath by inheritance obtained a more excellent name than they.

While I appreciated the beauty of the language, the passage seemed rather heavy for someone like Paul so I hoped Andy had remembered to keep him in mind when he prepared his sermon. I also hoped he was not going to neglect the gospel in preference to a dissertation on the last days. I was not disappointed.

In simple language, he made much of Christ as Son of God and superior to the angels; and he stressed his work at creation and at the cross. The same thoughtful look I had seen on Paul's face at the debate was maintained throughout the message. In his conclusion, Andy invited the congregation to follow him in a silent prayer of commitment, seeking forgiveness at the cross and yielding to Christ as king. The arrogant and skeptical Paul I had seen at the barbecue bowed his head in prayer, perhaps for the first time in his life. What transaction took place within, only time would tell.

After the service, I was pleased that Josh did not rush home as he usually did but invited Paul to stay for morning tea. My pleasure was dampened when Robyn Bradford zeroed in on Paul as he entered the hall. I suspected she had been lying in wait to buttonhole him about the wording on his

T-shirt. I caught snippets of the conversation that confirmed my fears: "perilous times . . . antichrist . . . tribulation . . . should the Lord tarry." Lauren and Anna arrived excitedly and rescued Paul from an extended eschatological harangue. As we drove home later, I said to Charlotte: "I wonder if the culture shock experienced by the son of an avowed atheist on his first visit to SCIF will make it his last."

26

The Integrity of Jesus

Martin Forbes's introduction on the first day of the series on the kingdom of God was hardly necessary since most of the Real Life group had met me at the debate. The contrast with that event was noticeable and pleasing. Instead of the formality of a tiered lecture hall and podium, there was the intimacy of a seminar room and a chair for me to sit on while I spoke. Instead of a largely hostile audience, there were twenty-five or so enthusiastic students sitting with Bibles in hand and smiles on faces. Instead of Paul Fitzgerald sitting with the skeptics, there was Paul Fitzgerald sitting with Lauren and Anna, and holding what looked like a copy of John's gospel.

Martin announced that before launching into the topic, I would give a brief response to Max Fitzgerald's argument at the debate that Jesus was not God because his prediction that he would return within a generation was not fulfilled.

"I'm delighted to be here," I said. "As Dr. Forbes mentioned, I am to begin with the question of Jesus' integrity. Was he deceptive? Was he in error when he announced his return within a generation of his speaking? I am reminded of the story about a student who, when asked a question by his lecturer, replied hesitantly, 'I think . . . ' but was interrupted by the lecturer who, in a loud, emphatic voice, said, 'I don't *think*—I *know*.' The student then said, "I don't think I know either, Sir."

The laughter that followed the story made it easier for me to tackle what I knew to be a controversial issue. I continued: "Our mind has been likened to a parachute: it works better when it's open. Some of you are thinking that I'm dodging the issue raised by Dr. Fitzgerald; that like the student in the story, I don't think I know. I *do* think I know but my answer will not please all of you so I plead for open minds."

I asked the students to turn in their Bibles to Matthew 24. A little confused, Paul opened *his* "Bible" and, finding only twenty-one chapters in it, moved closer to Anna to share *her* Bible. I read verse 34:

> I tell you the truth, this generation will certainly not pass away until all these things have happened.

"We believe Jesus always told the truth so why does he say on this and other occasions, 'I tell you the truth'? Certainly not because sometimes he *didn't* tell the truth but on this occasion he *was* telling the truth. The reason is that he knew his disciples would find it hard to believe what he was about to say. In other words, he was saying, 'What I'm about to tell you will seem untrue but it really is true. You are going to find it hard to swallow but it's true nevertheless.' The same words occur at the beginning of the chapter in verse 2. What he announced there was so unbelievable that he needed to emphasize it was true. The disciples were drawing Jesus' attention to the magnificent temple in Jerusalem. According to the Jewish historian Josephus, some of the white stones in it were fifty feet long, twenty-four feet wide, and sixteen feet thick. Imagine the shock when Jesus announced that it was all to be destroyed. They naturally wanted to know when it would happen. Part of his answer is here in verse 34: 'before this generation passes away.' The plain meaning of this is that some people who were alive when Jesus spoke would live to see the demolition of the temple. And they did. About forty years after Jesus made his astonishing prediction, in the year AD 70, the Roman general Titus destroyed Jerusalem and its temple."

I paused because one of the students wanted to ask a question. I noticed from the tag he was wearing that his name was John. He said, "I don't have a problem with the occurrence of the destruction of Jerusalem within that generation. My problem is with the words 'all these things.' They include worldwide proclamation of the gospel, catastrophic astronomical disturbances, and the second coming of Christ. These things haven't occurred yet so doesn't Dr. Fitzgerald have a case?" I wondered if John was an infiltrator from the Humanist Association sent to disrupt the meeting but his respectful attitude and the sense that his question represented honest concern made me dismiss the thought. I wished other Christians were as open to share their concerns and that there was always within the Christian community an atmosphere that facilitated such frankness.

"You're throwing me in deep water before I've paddled far from the shore, John, but you've asked an excellent question. You've correctly perceived the heart of the problem. I'll need time to offer a solution to it and some of you are thinking we'll never get to the topic of the kingdom of God but, cheer up. I hope to show that the problem before us is related to the kingdom of God and while not all of you will agree with me, I urge again that you keep an open mind. Let's make sure we all understand the problem. If 'this generation' refers to the people living in the days of Jesus and 'all these things' includes the matters John raised, as he and many others understand them, then Jesus got it wrong and Dr. Fitzgerald has a point." Paul smiled and several sets of pursed lips indicated that at least some of the students saw the implications of the problem. I waited in case others wished to ask for clarification. No one did so I continued.

"None of us is happy to concede the point that Jesus was wrong, so what are our options? One option is to adopt a different understanding for 'generation.' Some want to translate the Greek word behind 'generation' as 'race,' meaning the Jewish race, or unbelievers generally, but there is a commonly used word for 'race' that could have been used had this been Jesus' intention. Besides, 'I tell you the truth' hardly seems necessary in that case. Some regard the word as referring to a generation in the future that would experience the signs Jesus gave of his second coming. Years ago I saw an example of this thinking in the magazine *Christianity Today*. A full-page advertisement promoted a 1998 jubilee celebration of the founding of the modern state of Israel fifty years earlier, in 1948. In the corner of the ad were these words: "Jesus said the generation that sees this will not pass away before his return." You don't have to be good at math to work out that that generation is rather grey-haired. If they insist on this interpretation, they run the risk within a very short time of making Jesus a false prophet. Let's hope that before then they admit that their interpretation of 'generation' is false.

"The most obvious meaning of the phrase 'this generation' is the most obvious meaning—the meaning that any sensible person would normally give it. In the gospels it consistently refers to the people living at that time and there is no sound reason for thinking it means something different here."

John had another question, probably because he felt I was getting nowhere. "Dr. Sutherland, we seem to be running out of options. You mentioned that the problem of Matthew 24:34 was related to the kingdom of God. Does that connection offer a way forward?"

"I think it does, John," I said. "Let's go back a little in Matthew's gospel to chapter 16, verses 27 and 28." I read the verses:

> "For the Son of Man is going to come in his Father's glory with his angels, and then he will reward each person according to what he has done. [28]I tell you the truth, some who are standing here will not taste death before they see the Son of Man coming in his kingdom."

"Several matters claim our attention in these verses: the coming of Jesus and the coming of the kingdom are connected; both are to occur before some of the people then living have died; and this is so unbelievable that Jesus again includes the words, 'I tell you the truth.' Jesus could have put it this way, 'This generation will not pass away before I come and usher in the kingdom of God.'

"Some think Jesus was referring to his transfiguration, which is described in chapter 17 as occurring within a matter of days, but it is inappropriate for Jesus to say, in effect, 'Some of you are not going to die before next Saturday.' More importantly, the transfiguration was not a coming of Jesus, nor a coming of the kingdom, nor associated with the presence of angels or the distribution of rewards.

"Jesus' prediction that the kingdom of God would come within that generation is consistent with his teaching elsewhere and also with the preaching of John the Baptist. Both of them announced the nearness of the kingdom of God."

I was aware that most of my time had been spent on wrapping up the debate and I wasn't sure that I'd done that well, given the puzzled looks on many faces. I decided to conclude and invite questions. "I am saying that the best way to answer the critics who say Jesus was mistaken in expecting his second coming within a generation, is to say, 'Jesus got it right; we've got it wrong.' All the things he predicted in Matthew 24 were fulfilled in that generation but we have misunderstood those things and complicated his plain statement in an effort to safeguard his integrity and our preconceptions. Does anyone have a question?" A dozen hands went up.

27

This Generation

With a forest of hands raised before me, I didn't know where to start. I seemed to have created more questions than answers. John had a question but I avoided him in preference to a demure young lady with a sweet smile whose name tag read "Elizabeth" and whose question I expected to be innocuous.

"Dr. Sutherland," she said, "the second coming of Christ is mentioned before verse 34 so it would appear to be one of the 'all things' Jesus said would occur within that generation. Dr. Fitzgerald said it didn't occur so the failure discredits Jesus. Are you saying that Jesus *did* return within that generation? If so, have we no hope of a future coming of Jesus?"

If only I'd known what lay behind that sweet smile. Of course, the question was sure to come sometime but how to answer it? I could not publicly deny a future return of Christ. Word would very smartly get back to SCIF through Lauren and Anna and I would be held in serious breach of clause 24. I'd face instant excommunication. Should I prevaricate? I wouldn't fool naive-looking Elizabeth for a moment. I had to be honest but what did "honest" mean in the context of my theological meanderings? If I was really honest with myself, I was by no means clear about the future. I believed some references to *a* coming of Christ were fulfilled in the first century but I was not in a position to say that every biblical reference to a return of Christ had been fulfilled. For all I knew there could be a future coming to wrap up human history, in addition to the coming he predicted within that generation. Elizabeth was waiting for an answer and so was everyone else judging by the anxious expectation that pervaded the room.

"Your question is a very important one, Elizabeth," I finally said. "I wish I could give you a definitive answer to both parts of it. I do believe that the coming Jesus predicted as occurring within a generation did occur. We have seen that there was to be a coming before some of the disciples died. Attempts to make the words of Jesus in Matthew 24 fit with a future coming are unconvincing and only confirm the skeptics' view that Jesus got it wrong. I will say categorically that Jesus came in AD 70 in judgement on decadent Israel and that this upholds the integrity of Jesus and fulfils some of the second coming predictions in the New Testament. I am not in a position to say whether or not other predictions of a coming refer to a still-future event. Much study remains to be done on the question. I can say that my wholehearted commitment to the authority of Scripture leaves me no option but to accept the verdict of that study when it becomes clear." Elizabeth was still smiling—on the outside at least—but the forest of hands had grown.

Lauren had a question: "Dr. Sutherland," she said, "I have heard it said that prophecies have a double fulfilment. Is it not possible that the words of Jesus have an application both to the destruction of Jerusalem and to events future to us?"

"Lauren, many commentators and popular preachers resort to that approach as an attractive option to resolve their difficulties. Along with others, I have doubts about the double-sense view of prophecy and I would caution against it. Jesus did not say, 'What I am predicting about the destruction of Jerusalem will have one fulfilment within this generation and another fulfilment centuries later?' What could be clearer than verse 34? 'I tell you the truth, this generation will certainly not pass away until all these things have happened.' Adherents of the double-sense view are not willing to take Jesus' words at face value. They want to change the meaning of 'this generation' to make Jesus' prediction fit their paradigm. Jesus said that his clear statement was the truth. We need to accept it as such. It may be astounding; it may cut across all we have been taught about end times; it may put us at odds with our favorite authors or preachers, but it is true.

"Lauren, if this prophecy has a double sense, what about other prophecies? Who decides which ones have a single fulfilment and which ones have a second—and why not a third fulfilment? And since the extra fulfilments are not stated by Jesus, who decides what they are and when they happen? No wonder we have so many conflicting views of the future when it's left to us to make these decisions.

"The double-sense approach to prophecy shifts authority from the text of Scripture to the interpreter of Scripture. It is popular because it allows people to adhere to their prophetical school of thought and to avoid the humbling experience of having to admit they're wrong and should reject their end-time scheme because it is contrary to the plain sense of Scripture."

I took a question from Martin Forbes hoping it was representative of many: "The second coming was not the only prediction Jesus gave that appears not to have been fulfilled. How do you account for the non-fulfilment of worldwide proclamation of the gospel and the astronomical disturbances he spoke of?" I knew John would be interested in my answer since he had raised these matters in his first question.

As I prepared to answer Martin, I mentally expressed gratitude for Luke Rodman. For several months he'd been my email opponent but now he was my ally. My use of his material in answering Martin was an admission that he'd made a strong case when I had put to him the same issues Martin was putting to me. In responding to the issue of worldwide evangelism, I shared examples of universal language that referred only to the known world, and I read Paul's statement in Colossians 1:23 that the gospel "has been proclaimed to every creature under heaven."

Using examples from the Old Testament I showed how apocalyptic literature described disturbances on earth under the figure of disturbances in the heavens. I stressed that the astronomical catastrophes were never intended to be taken literally and that the Jews of Jesus' day, familiar as they were with the Old Testament usage, would not have felt obliged to understand Jesus' statements literally. Martin seemed satisfied with my answer and the reduction in the number of raised hands suggested that the questions of others had also been answered.

"We have time for one more question," announced Martin. Anna's hand had been one of the first raised so I invited her to speak.

"Dr. Sutherland, your emphasis on the fulfilment of Jesus' prediction in that generation seems at variance with his words later in the chapter that no one knows the day or the hour when he will come."

"A very good question, Anna," I said. "Those words of Jesus have certainly been ignored by the date-setters who tell us that Jesus is coming on May 21 or October 15. However, there is no contradiction between 'this generation' and 'no one knows about that day or hour.' Suppose your lecturer in biology announces at the beginning of the semester that the assessment will include a class test worth 20 percent. Unfortunately, he does not give you the date of the test. He merely tells you that the test will be some time after Week 2 and before the end of semester. You do not know the date of the test but you do know that it will be within the semester. It will not be next semester, or next year, or 2,000 years from now. If Week 8 has passed, you know that the test is not far off. You still don't know the date but if you have not done any preparation for it, wisdom would urge you to get cracking. Similarly, Anna, Jesus told his disciples that the events he foretold would certainly occur within that generation, before some of them died, but the actual date was not known. That is why they were urged to watch and to be ready."

I concluded by stressing briefly that atheists like Bertrand Russell had no grounds for attributing error to Jesus. They at least understood the predicted *time* of fulfilment but misunderstood the *nature* of the predicted events. Sadly, many well-meaning Christians were wrong on both scores.

I apologized for having said so little about the kingdom of God and promised to make up for it next week. Martin closed the meeting with a note of thanks and a further plug for the rest of the series. Students who had classes quickly dispersed. Those who remained approached me. Some were shaking their heads and breathing out "phew" and "wow." I interpreted these visible and audible reactions not as accusations of heresy but, from other body language, as expressions of enlightenment, gratitude, and even relief. Elizabeth encouraged me by saying, "Books and sermons about end times have often left me confused, even frightened, but your talk today made a lot of sense and left me more at ease. I still have questions but I'm going to go back to the Scriptures and begin to listen to what they're saying instead of trying to reconcile them with what the books and preachers are saying, as if their take on these things is like a sixty-seventh book in the Bible."

When the last of the students had gone, Martin thanked me again for coming and said, "I found your talk on eschatology very stimulating and would like to catch up for coffee some time to pursue these matters." We agreed to meet in the university refectory after next week's session.

I left the seminar room with mixed feelings. On the one hand, I had enjoyed being back in a classroom with freedom to talk about matters of personal interest to students eager to learn; on the other hand, I was apprehensive. My talk was largely a response to Max Fitzgerald. Paul had left the meeting as soon as it finished. What sort of a report would he give his father? Would Max incite the Humanist Association against me? Lauren and Anna had also left promptly so were not part of the "wow" group. Did they have to rush off to a lecture or were they upset by what I'd said? With memories of what I'd stirred up at the barbecue and a vision of Robyn Bradford crouching in the background, ready to pounce with clause 24 in hand, I didn't know what to expect in coming days.

28

The Kingdom of God

Paul Fitzgerald did survive his first Sunday at SCIF. The following Sunday he arrived in Josh's Mustang with the addition of two extra passengers in the back—Lauren and Anna. He was still wearing shorts and thongs but his T-shirt showed he was a member of the Mooloolaba Surf Lifesaving Club rather than a neighbor of the antichrist. Charlotte and I followed the four of them into the church. Lauren and Anna sat in their usual seats halfway down on the left-hand side. Josh was about to enter a row towards the back on the other side of the church when he felt a tug on his sleeve. He turned to see Paul jerking his head in the direction of the girls and followed meekly as Paul crossed the aisle and sat next to Anna. A faint smile between increasingly pink cheeks showed she was not totally opposed to his move. There was no smile on Josh's face.

My fear that Lauren and Anna had been upset by my talk at the Real Life meeting proved to be unfounded. I had no sooner arrived in the hall for morning tea than I was surrounded by all four occupants of the Mustang, three of whom enthusiastically spoke of the Real Life meeting. Anna began by saying, "Your talk made a lot of sense. It opened my mind to a school of thought other than the one I inherited. I always thought my view of end times was the only view of the future but you've broadened my thinking."

Paul didn't wait for me to respond to Anna. He interrupted with, "I told Dad you'd addressed the point he made at the debate about Jesus' failed prophecy. I gave him a brief summary of your talk which he dismissed with a backhanded wave, but I could tell it made him think."

I was about to comment on Max's reaction when Lauren burst out with, "Your position on Matthew 24 was a bit of a shocker. It was quite different from what I learnt at college in Tennessee but, remembering that my mind is to be like a parachute, I'll keep it open."

Josh was silent—and slightly sullen—but cheered up when Anna said, "I'm sorry you couldn't be at the Real Life meeting, Josh. You'd have enjoyed it. There are two more sessions on the kingdom of God. We'll keep you posted."

A stickler for clause 24 seeing me at the center of a group of SCIF young people and overhearing bits of the conversation might well have thought I was blatantly undermining the publicly-affirmed doctrinal position of the church. I said little and hoped no such people were within earshot. I excused myself from the group to join Charlotte who was chatting with Mark and Cathy Mullins.

"How does an old guy like you get to be so popular with the youth?" asked Mark.

"Must be my irresistible charm," I replied.

"Be sensible, Edward," said Charlotte.

"Josh Wilson is my neighbor," I said, "and I'm the co-driver of his Mustang." Another "Edward!" from Charlotte. "The other three are students at USC where I've been speaking at the Real Life meeting recently."

"That's interesting," said Cathy. "I did my education degree at USC and was a member of Real Life. What were you talking about?"

"I had a debate on the existence of God with the philosophy lecturer at USC a few weeks ago. I'm currently giving a series on the kingdom of God."

"You debated Max Fitzgerald?" interposed Mark. "He's a tough nut."

"You know him?" I asked.

"We're both members of the local Lions Club. He's always pushing his Humanist Association and takes every opportunity to disparage anything Christian. I've had one or two vigorous interactions with him. How did the debate go?"

"I thought it went reasonably well until the final moments. He was the last to speak so I didn't have a chance to rebut his claim that Jesus was in error in predicting his second coming within a generation. Mark, at your next Lions Club meeting, why don't you tell him you heard about the debate and ask him how it went? It might lead to another vigorous interaction."

"I'd feel like Daniel confronting a Lion called Max," said Mark with a smile. "I'm not much of a debater."

"If God could shut a lion's mouth in Daniel's day, he can open a Lion's mouth in our day," I said. Charlotte sensed I was beginning to get preachy so said it was time we were going. Before we left, the Mullins invited us to lunch the following Sunday.

On Monday, I arrived early at the seminar room for the second session on the kingdom of God. To my surprise, all the seats with desks were taken and the extra chairs at the back and sides of the room were beginning to fill. Paul, Anna, and Lauren were seated near the front—in that order. I greeted them and then moved around the room making good use of the name tags that the regulars were wearing. John and Elizabeth were sitting together. They were grateful for my responses to their questions the previous Monday and John said that during the week they'd met several times over lunch to discuss the issues further. The light in Elizabeth's eyes as John spoke seemed to say the lunch-time discussions were delightful for more than eschatological reasons. Had I inadvertently become a matchmaker?

After some introductory words from Martin, I began my talk: "My aim in this series is that we will all become kingdom-minded people. Kingdom-minded people are open-minded people. With respect to the kingdom of God, we need to be open-minded about the nature of the kingdom. What is it? What do we mean when we talk about the kingdom of God? Is it a place like the kingdom of Denmark located on the Jutland Peninsula? Is it a visible, political kingdom such as the first century Jews expected, a kingdom involving the reinstatement of the Davidic throne in Jerusalem and the overthrow of the occupying Roman government?

"In Luke 17:20–21, the Pharisees asked Jesus when the kingdom of God would come. Imagine their disappointment when he replied, 'The kingdom of God does not come with your careful observation, nor will people say, "Here it is," or "There it is," because the kingdom of God is within [or among] you.' In Luke 18:17, Jesus said, 'I tell you the truth, anyone who will not receive the kingdom of God like a little child will never enter it.' You can't receive a peninsula or a political system but you can allow God to take charge of your life. The kingdom of God is the reign of God; it is God ruling; it is a spiritual kingdom. Paul emphasizes the spiritual nature of the kingdom in Romans 14. He says in verse 17, 'For the kingdom of God is not a matter of eating and drinking, but of righteousness, peace and joy in the Holy Spirit.'"

A puzzled look on Lauren's face and an unobtrusively raised index finger prompted me to say: "Lauren, I think you have a question."

"Yes," she said. "Doesn't the visible reign of Christ on a throne in Jerusalem for 1,000 years, as described in Revelation 20, represent more than a spiritual kingdom?"

"A very good question, Lauren. I'm not sure I have a very good answer because, without doubt, Revelation 20 is one of the most disputed chapters in the Bible, with a range of interpretations each supported by respectable biblical scholars. Premillennialists, for example, believe the second coming of Christ *precedes* a literal reign of Christ on earth for 1,000 years. Postmillennialists, on the other hand, believe the second coming of Christ occurs *after* the millennium which they regard as a long period during which the world is largely Christianized. For the postmillennialist, the 1,000 years is not necessarily literal and Christ does not visibly reign from Jerusalem.

"The reason I mention these views—and there are others—is to point out the wide differences that exist among Christians and to stress that our preconceived millennial view should not determine our interpretation of Revelation 20. In examining the chapter, it is important to remember that since the book of Revelation is apocalyptic literature, it makes considerable use of symbolism. Knowing which parts of it are intended to be taken literally and which parts figuratively, is not easy. In Revelation 20, Satan is said to be bound with a great chain for 1,000 years. A literal chain could not bind a spiritual being so it is reasonable to think the chain is not a literal chain. If the chain is figurative, perhaps the 1,000 years are also figurative, like other numbers in the book of Revelation."

"But doesn't the chapter speak of Christians reigning with Christ for 1,000 years?" asked Lauren.

"It is clear from the chapter that certain martyrs will reign with Christ but there is no reference to Jerusalem and it is not even clear that the reign takes place on earth. I know that silence is not an argument but interpretations that lack clear Scriptural support should be held with an open hand."

Behind Lauren's question was a view of the millennium she had been taught at SCIF and in Tennessee. I was therefore not surprised that her body language said she was not entirely happy with my response. My aim was not to undermine what she believed but to ensure it was well-grounded.

I continued by telling the students that we needed an open mind not only about the nature of the kingdom but also its timing. I revisited Matthew 16:28: "I tell you the truth, some who are standing here will not taste death before they see the Son of Man coming in his kingdom." I then read the parallel text in Mark 9:1: "I tell you the truth, some who are standing here will not taste death before they see the kingdom of God come with power." I pointed out that if the kingdom of God came in power before some of Jesus' disciples died, then we were in the kingdom of God now. I stressed that if there was a future aspect to the kingdom of God we must not neglect its present aspect nor treat it as a mere curtain raiser to the main event. The words "with power" needed to be taken seriously.

"Let me briefly sum up what we have seen so far," I said. "The Scriptures are clear that there was a return before some of his disciples died. This return brought judgment on Jerusalem but, most importantly for us, it inaugurated the kingdom of God in power. There may be Scriptures that refer to a future coming and to a future millennial kingdom but if we are going to be kingdom-minded Christians here and now, we must embrace the kingdom as a present reality and participate in it enthusiastically, by welcoming the King to reign in us, and by working to extend his rule in the world. Kingdom-minded people are not only open-minded but also single-minded people who seek first God's kingdom (Matthew 6:33)."

After answering several questions from students who stayed behind, Martin took me to the student refectory where, over cappuccinos and do-nuts, we got to know one another through potted versions of our life stories. Martin ended his account with a transition to the purpose of our meeting: "I became a Christian a mere four years ago through the influence of my wife, Angela, so I'm a relatively new Christian. Many of the students in the Real Life group have been Christians longer and know more about the Bible than I do. Angela and I attend a conservative church—perhaps 'traditional' would be a better word—where we rarely hear sermons on the second coming of Christ and related matters. The only references to eschatology are in our weekly recital of the Nicene Creed when we rattle off, 'He will come again in glory to judge the living and the dead, and his kingdom will have no end . . . we look for the resurrection of the dead, and the life of the world to come. Amen.' The 'amen' seems to say, 'That just about covers it; no need to elaborate on such controversial matters'—and we don't. What bothers me, Ed, is that, as I read the New Testament, I discover references to the kingdom of God, the return of Christ, resurrection and judgment, at every turn. Just the other day, I noticed that every chapter in both First and Second Thessalonians mentions the return of Christ. Now, here's my point: we're supposed to be living nearer to eschatological fulfilment than the New Testament Christians yet, in our church at least, it's hardly mentioned."

"In contrast," I said, "to some churches where they talk about little else."

"Where's the balance?" asked Martin.

"We're on pretty safe ground when we give topics a similar emphasis in our own study and teaching to the emphasis found in Scripture. Christ is everywhere in the Bible so you can't say too much about him; the gospel and Christian discipleship are key issues that we cannot over-emphasize. On the subject of eschatology, you are right that it is not an isolated issue and churches should give it due regard. It's not the whole story but it is an important part of the story."

"Ed, you've stimulated my interest in the subject but where do I begin? What books should I read?"

I was tempted to suggest Milton Terry's book, *Biblical Hermeneutics*, J.S. Russell's book, *The Parousia*, or *The Last Days According to Jesus* by R.C. Sproul but I thought better of it. I was critical of Christians who got their eschatology from books other than the Bible but didn't observe what the Bible itself was saying. I didn't want Martin going down that track so I said, "Martin, you have an advantage in coming to the subject of eschatology with a relatively clean slate. I know many who have been so schooled from childhood in a dogmatic view of eschatology that it's difficult for them to consider alternatives. They feel the Bible confirms their belief at every point, but only because their brain-washed minds superimpose their eschatology on the Bible instead of listening to what it actually says. You, however, are able to listen to the Bible with fewer inhibiting preconceptions. I don't think the Nicene Creed will unduly hinder your studies.

"Begin with the Bible. Let it speak for itself. Don't make it fit yours or someone else's scheme of things. Interpret what is unclear in the light of what is clear and ask good questions of the text if you want good answers."

"Give me some examples of questions to ask?" said Martin.

"They will vary according to the passage studied but some good general questions are: Who is being addressed here? How would the original readers have understood the passage? How do the immediate and the more remote contexts influence the text? What is the *intended* sense of the passage?"

"Ed," said Martin, "you're talking to me as if I were a biblical scholar. If only I knew as much about theology and the Bible as I know about science. I'm not sure I'm up to your expectations of me."

"In the words of J.H. Jowett, Martin, 'Reverently believe in your own uniqueness.' Believe that with the help of the Holy Spirit you can discover truth from the Bible without having to make other people's views your first port of call."

"Are you saying there's no place for commentaries?" asked Martin.

"Not at all. Just as there is a place for good teachers in church and college, so there is a place for good teachers in books. Consulting a good commentary is like being in a class with a good teacher. However, before you rush off to the commentaries, try to determine the meaning of a Bible passage by following principles such as I mentioned a moment ago. It's exciting to make unaided discoveries. When you do read commentaries, don't read them uncritically. They are not infallible."

"I'll give it my best shot," said Martin.

"And I'll look forward to hearing about your exegetical discoveries."

"Don't expect too much uniqueness," he said.

29

The Doctor and the Atheist

After the service the following Sunday, Charlotte and I followed a black BMW convertible to the home of Mark and Cathy Mullins for our lunch engagement. The aroma of a baked dinner met us as we entered the front door of their triple-storied home, nestled in the north-easterly face of the Buderim plateau. While Cathy put finishing touches to the meal, Mark served us drinks in the living room as we expressed our admiration of the magnificent views of Mount Coolum and the adjacent coast and hinterland.

"There's a more easterly view from my office window," said Mark. We followed him through a family room where two Mullins children were setting up a game of Snakes and Ladders on the floor. Mark introduced them as Ryan, the older of the two, and Lisa. He then opened the door of his study. The far wall was all glass and framed an extended view of the Pacific coastline. As Charlotte commented on coastal features she recognized and asked about ones she didn't, I looked at the office walls lined with medical text books, journals and academic awards reflecting Mark's credentials. I noted that in addition to his basic medical training he was a Fellow of the Royal Australasian College of Physicians.

"Excuse me, Dad," said a voice from the door, "Mum said lunch is ready."

"Thanks, Ryan. Tell her we're on our way," Mark responded.

In between mouthfuls of roast pork with crackling and apple sauce, we answered questions about the Sutherland family, about Charlotte's work as an architect, my teaching work at AIMS, and how we came to be living on the Sunshine Coast. When the focus shifted to the Mullins, Cathy mentioned that she taught Grade 6 at the Buderim Mountain State School. Ryan added, "I'm in her class and so is Sam Zimmerman. He's my best mate." Not to be left out, Lisa informed us that she was in Grade 3 and had a friend called Suzy.

Mark talked about his medical practice in the heart of Buderim and said he also consulted in Maroochydore and Caloundra. I had yet to find a doctor I had confidence in. I'd been to several for minor complaints since retiring but had not been impressed with the bedside manner of any of them. Perhaps my local GP was sitting in front of me. Mark struck me as someone I could relate to and with his FRACP, I felt I could trust his advice. I hoped he had room for new patients but was not about to talk shop over lunch even though the conversation at the table was occasionally punctuated by silences. Charlotte revived it by asking Cathy, "How did you and Mark meet?"

"Our relationship developed through church," she said. "You know Mark is the son of Stan and Yvonne Mullins. I am the daughter of Arthur and Robyn Bradford. Both families have a long association with SCIF so Mark and I have known each other from childhood."

"Well I never," said Charlotte. "We had lunch with your parents the first Sunday we attended SCIF and I'm only discovering now that you were a Bradford."

I then opened my big mouth and said, "I get regular emails from your mother." Charlotte frowned at me as if suspecting where the conversation might go.

"Don't tell me about it!" said Mark. "We're on the end-times mailing list along with many others. The other day Robyn sent an article listing more than a dozen criteria for identifying the antichrist. The author of the article mentioned a candidate, without naming him, who fits all the criteria. He was described, among other things, as an English-speaking prince who has two sons, who lacked desire for the very beautiful and famous woman he married, and whose name in English and Hebrew has the numerical value of 666. We were asked to buy the author's book to find his name, hardly necessary because it was so obvious that Prince Charles was in mind. The article stressed the point that because the proposed antichrist was over sixty, the end of the age could soon be upon us.

"Ed, as long as I can remember," said Mark, "I've been bombarded with speculation about potential antichrists all of whom die without taking office and are replaced by other candidates who, one suspects, will suffer the same fate. In each case the speculation has been coupled with warnings that, unless the Lord tarries, the end is near."

"I don't like to criticize my mother," said Cathy, "but sometimes I find the constant barrage of doomsday predictions depressing. What are your thoughts on the antichrist Ed?"

I felt I was back in the Caloundra Coffee Club where the same topic had been discussed with Josh, Lauren and Anna. It didn't seem wise to pursue the matter with a family related to Robyn Bradford. The last thing I wanted was to be known as the guest who created family division on his first visit. Charlotte's frown and skewed mouth sent me the same message. I had no sooner determined to change the subject than Mark told Ryan and Lisa they could go to the family room and continue their game.

When they left, Mark said, "Ed, I've been reading through Second Thessalonians recently. In fact, I read chapter 2 the same day the Prince Charles email arrived. The chapter mentions that the man of sin, whom I take to be the antichrist, will only be revealed when the one who restrains him is removed. I've been taught that the restraining influence is the Holy Spirit who will be removed at the rapture and then the antichrist will take center stage. Is that how you see it, Ed?"

Charlotte winced but since my hosts had initiated the topic, I felt some obligation to respond and was glad that my recent reading of J.S. Russel's *The Parousia* had given me relevant material to share.

"Mark, we need to interpret the chapter in the context of the first century situation in Thessalonica. You may recall that Paul tells the Thessalonians that what he is writing about he had earlier told them face to face. The tense of the verb 'told' is a continuous tense that is rightly translated 'used to tell.' They were not hearing about the man of sin for the first time. Paul clearly regarded the issue of the man of sin to be of relevance to them. He stated that the lawlessness already at work was being restrained but when the restraining influence was removed, the lawless one, or the man of sin, would be revealed. This does not fit well with a fulfilment 2,000 or more years later which none of the Thessalonians would experience.

"You asked for my view of all this. Here it is: The man of sin is not someone we are waiting for but someone in the first century against whom the Thessalonians needed to be warned and about whom Paul spoke repeatedly. The best candidate is Nero, a beast of a man whose wickedness was restrained by the emperor Claudius, his step-father. It would not be long before Claudius would be poisoned by his wife Agrippina, and so 'taken out of the way.' With all restraints gone, Nero's blasphemous claim to deity, his unbridled debauchery, and ferocious cruelty prevailed. Before he died, he authorized the war against the Jews which culminated in the destruction of Jerusalem.

"If the one who restrains was the Holy Spirit, Paul would have mentioned him by name without fear of reprisals. But to mention in writing Claudius or Nero by name would certainly have endangered his life. He may have mentioned their names when speaking privately with the Thessalonians but in a public document he needed to be cryptic. The Jews at Thessalonica would gladly have reported Paul to the Roman authorities for sedition, a capital offence. We are far removed from the circumstances they faced and in an effort to interpret the document at such a distance have succeeded in distorting a communication that to the original readers was perfectly plain."

"You'd be a brave man to preach that at SCIF," said Mark.

"You think I'd need to be a bit cryptic to avoid a public lynching?" I replied.

"You're dead right."

"I think what Ed has shared makes a lot of sense," said Cathy. "I find it far less depressing than the doom-and-gloom scenarios I've been exposed to."

"So do I," said Mark. "Ed, you've given me a lot to think about and I hope we can explore these issues further on another occasion."

Charlotte looked relieved that I was about to dismount from what she regarded as my hobby horse and even more relieved when Cathy said, "Who's for pecan pie and ice-cream?"

When we retired to the living room for coffee, Mark said, "We had our monthly Lions meeting on Thursday night. Over supper I made a point of speaking with Max Fitzgerald. I told him I'd heard about the debate and, following your suggestion, asked him how it went."

"And what did he say?" I asked, fully expecting the answer would not be flattering. I was not wrong.

"He said, 'That idiot'—he inserted a word before 'idiot' that is better left unsaid—'could no more prove the existence of God than the existence of the tooth fairy. As the latter does not exist neither does the former.'"

"And what did you say?" I asked.

"The finality with which Max made his point was intended to signal that the conversation was at an end. Normally I would have left it there but I recalled your words last Sunday that God could open a Lion's mouth so I sent a quick prayer to heaven for help."

"And did you get it?"

"I'll let you be the judge. Our conversation went like this:

> "Max, I'm a specialist physician and, like you, I try to keep up to date by reading professional literature. Imagine I read an account in a medical journal of a clinical trial involving a drug developed to help war veterans from Afghanistan who suffer from post-traumatic stress disorder. The trial included a control group that was given a placebo. The results encouraged the scientists because while the placebo had negligible effect, the trial drug was associated with a 70 percent improvement in sufferers."
>
> "I have never been to Afghanistan and I don't suffer from PTSD so I don't know why you're telling me this," said Max.

"Bear with me please, Max. Suppose the results had been minimal for the drug and 70 percent for the placebo, would you object to the ongoing use of placebos by physicians when treating PTSD patients?"

"I guess not," said Max, "but I still don't know where you're going with this."

"Max, many people claim that their faith in God has transformed their lives with addictions cured, divorce averted, bitterness replaced by forgiveness, despair by hope. In your view, these benefits have nothing to do with a God who exists because God is no more than a placebo."

"That is my view," said Max.

"A moment ago you approved the use of beneficial placebos yet you campaign stridently against the use of a placebo-God from whom so many receive help."

"Placebos are all very well in clinical trials," said Max, "but if a drug doesn't measure up in a trial, a better drug should be developed that works so that patients can have the full benefit of a genuine product rather than the minimal benefit of a placebo. My job is to promote the better product."

"Max, you say 'minimal,' but we are not talking about a handful of believers but millions. In some cases whole people groups would describe the dramatic change God has brought as a change from darkness to light. If I created a placebo to help my patients and found it was as effective on the same scale, I would seriously consider it might not be a placebo at all. You claim that atheism is a better product than theism. For every atheist who claims a transformed life through *his* faith, I will show you ten thousand whose change is attributed to God, so many people that you really need to consider that he may not be a placebo-God at all."

Max sniffed and tossed his head but I continued: "Atheism has a very poor record when it comes to improving the lives of individuals and nations. Dictators like Joseph Stalin, Nicolae Ceaușescu, Enver Hoxha, Erich Honecker, and Kim Jong-il hardly left legacies worthy of atheistic canonization. You say you have a better product. Why then did atheistic communism have to lock its patients in with a Berlin wall which, at risk of life, many tried to scale to get away from your better product? It doesn't add up, Max."

Max gave a dismissive grunt and I continued. "Am I correct in thinking you believe that there are no more grounds for believing in God than believing in the tooth fairy?"

"Correct," said Max.

"So you believe that God is just a human construct with no more objective reality than Santa Claus or the man in the moon?"

"Correct again," said Max. "You're smarter than I thought."

"There are many very intelligent people who disagree with you, Max, but I think there is something you could do to prove them wrong."

"I'm all ears," he said.

"Just as people have invented stories about a tooth fairy or a man in the moon, you could create a fictitious story about a phony god. Let's call him Pluto because he lives on the far side of the planet of that name. Such a god would have no more credibility that the man in the moon or, in your opinion, the God of Christians."

"What's your point?" asked Max in an irritable tone.

"Well," I said, "Christians have convinced millions of people, including intelligent ones, that their God exists. All you need to do is to convince millions to believe in Pluto even to the point that they, like the many Christian martyrs, are prepared to suffer excruciating deaths rather than deny Pluto. That would be quite a challenge, wouldn't it, Max."

"I suppose so," he said reluctantly.

"There's more, Max. You have to demonstrate the life-changing power of Pluto and produce thousands of people who can testify to the transformation that occurred in their lives through faith in Pluto—all sorts of people including drug dealers, pimps, child molesters, self-righteous prigs, and even atheists. Furthermore, you must produce followers of Pluto who end their lives in sure and certain hope of living forever in bliss with Pluto on Pluto. A big ask, Max.

"There's more: followers of Pluto must be motivated to go to isolated parts of the world where Pluto is not known and proclaim him so that war-mongering cannibals are converted to belief in Pluto and become peace-loving vegetarians."

"I wouldn't waste my time on such a ridiculous exercise," Max shouted angrily.

"I wouldn't either," I said, "because it would be fruitless as you well know. The god Pluto doesn't exist so the outcomes we have postulated are unlikely. However, those outcomes do exist in the case of those who believe in God which suggests that he just might exist after all."

"Rubbish," he spat.

"Yes, the Pluto exercise would be fruitless but there's another reason for not pursuing it."

"O yeh?" said Max sullenly.

"You might have to get yourself crucified and three days later rise from the dead in order to launch your Pluto religion."

"Max stormed off twirling a forefinger at the side of his head implying my brain cells were suffering from severe atrophy," said Mark, twirling *his* forefinger as he spoke.

"What do you make of him?" I asked.

"I've known Max for five years and I've never known him to run away from an argument. He's always had an answer, but on Thursday night he did run away and he didn't have an answer. I believe his theatrics were a cover for his pride: he won't admit that he might be wrong and he can't afford to lose face before his humanist friends."

Cathy had not previously heard the full account of Mark's encounter with Max. She leaned over to him and said, "You did well, dear," and gave him a kiss. She then said to me, "Ed, how is your series at Real Life on the kingdom of God going?"

"I'm encouraged," I said. "Student numbers are increasing; they listen attentively and they ask intelligent questions. I'm looking forward to tomorrow's meeting when we will speak about the future of the kingdom."

Mark was about to speak and I feared he was going to start a conversation about the millennium. Fortunately, Cathy spoke before her husband, "Who's looking after the Real Life group these days, Ed?"

"Dr. Martin Forbes," I said.

"I know that name," she said. "I had a physics lecturer at USC called Forbes."

"The very same," I said.

"He's a Christian?" she asked skeptically.

"He sure is."

"He wasn't when I was a student at USC. Anything but, more like an atheist, and a pretty crude one at that," said Cathy.

"Maybe there's hope for Max Fitzgerald yet," said Mark.

30

The Growth of the Kingdom

Early Monday morning, bleary-eyed and carrying a cup of coffee, I went down to the office to put the finishing touches to the third talk on the kingdom of God. I was side-tracked from my intentions by a "You've-got-mail" message on my computer. The cup of coffee was not needed to offset the bleariness: the sight of Max Fitzgerald's name on the email created instant alertness. It read:

> Quit proselytizing my son Paul. I brought him up as a rationalist and consequently he rejected the mindless claims of religion. Now I find that he not only meets with Christians on campus but attends some fundamentalist—"no fun and mental"—group at Buderim. The other day I found him reading a booklet I discovered was part of the Bible.
>
> My investigations show that you are a common element in all these influences: you are a speaker at the campus meeting where you induced him to read the Bible and you are part of the narrow-minded group at Buderim.
>
> I won't have my years of wise parenting undermined by your manipulative promulgation of outmoded, medieval nonsense. Just lay off!
>
> Dr. Max Fitzgerald.
>
> (Senior Lecturer in Philosophy, USC)

The vitriolic tone of the message throttled fresh thoughts for my lunchtime talk about the kingdom of God. If Max expected the email would induce guilt, it failed. I hadn't asked Paul to attend Real Life, I hadn't given him a copy of John's gospel, and I certainly hadn't invited him to SCIF. My reaction to the email was ambivalent. On the one hand, I felt misjudged but fought valiantly against the impulse to dash off an angry, self-justifying reply. On the other hand, I was rather pleased. It sounded as if Max Fitzgerald, the well-known president of the Humanist Association, was peeved at losing ground—even within his own family—and I was only the scapegoat. I could live with that. Max's resort to an ad hominem attack reflected badly on his powers of rational persuasion and raised the possibility that the bitter tone of the email was an attempt to stifle incipient doubt about his atheism.

I wondered if Paul was a victim of Max's violent outbursts and whether they would stifle his fledgling interest in Christianity. Anna might be a help there, I thought. I didn't respond to Max's email but I did forward it to Mark and Cathy Mullins. Coming so soon after our visit to their home and the conversation Mark had had with Max at the Lions Club, it was sure to be of interest to them.

My coffee was cold when I finally settled my mind on the Real Life meeting due to start in a few hours. I wondered if Paul would turn up or, perish the thought, even Max. My undisciplined imagination pictured him bursting through the doors of the seminar room at the head of a fanatical horde of humanists, hell-bent on disruption, and on snatching one of their own from the perverse promulgations of a medieval moron.

When I arrived at the meeting, Martin met me with the news that he'd had an email from Cathy Mullins who was encouraged to hear that he'd become a Christian since her student days in his class. I told Martin about our lunch with the Mullinses, Mark's encounter with Max, and the subsequent email. I didn't upset him by warning of a possible humanist invasion.

After Martin introduced me, I took a few moments to look over the standing-room-only crowd. There was no sign of Max—so far. Lauren and Anna were sitting near the front but Paul was not next to her. I had no time to ponder the possible reason for his absence so began my talk: "Movies often depict church services with drones in the pulpits and crones in the pews. Those who think this typifies Christianity should read the book *God is Back* by Micklethwait and Wooldridge. The authors tell of more Christians in China than members of the communist party; of a Methodist church in Chile that seats 18,000, and of Presbyterian churches in Ghana with more people in attendance than Scottish Presbyterian churches. The kingdom of God is growing in fulfilment of biblical prophecy. Consider two short parables of Jesus in Matthew 13:31–33:

> He told them another parable: "The kingdom of heaven is like a mustard seed, which a man took and planted in his field. [32]Though it is the smallest of all your seeds, yet when it grows,

it is the largest of garden plants and becomes a tree, so that the birds of the air come and perch in its branches."

³³He told them still another parable: "The kingdom of heaven is like yeast that a woman took and mixed into a large amount of flour until it worked all through the dough."

"Both parables make a similar point: the kingdom of God begins small and becomes large." A quizzical look on John's face and a raised index finger induced me to take his question: "Dr. Sutherland, the text you read says 'kingdom of heaven' yet you speak of 'the kingdom of God.' Are they the same?"

Though unhappy at the interruption so early in my talk, I did my best not to show it and replied, "Good question, John. Some argue for a difference but I'm sure they're wrong. You have correctly noticed that Matthew's account of the mustard seed parable is told in relation to the kingdom of heaven but in Mark 4 the same parable is told in relation to the kingdom of God. Furthermore, at the beginning of Jesus' public ministry Matthew says he preached that the kingdom of *heaven* was near but in Mark's account he is said to have preached that the kingdom of *God* was near. Clearly the two terms are interchangeable. Jews not uncommonly used the word 'heaven' when referring to God. You may recall the words of the prodigal son when he returned home: 'Father, I have sinned against heaven and against you.' He meant, of course, that he had sinned against God and his father."

John seemed satisfied with my answer and Elizabeth's adjacent smile showed she was happy too. I tried to get back on track by returning to the main point of the two parables: "A very small seed becomes a very large bush; a small piece of yeast permeates a large amount of flour. It is clear from the two parables that we should expect growth in the kingdom of God and that we have every reason to be optimistic about the future of Christianity."

Lauren interrupted with "I have a question." I looked at Martin hoping he would postpone all questions till the end of the session but he had turned towards Lauren and seemed more interested to hear her question than I was.

"Dr. Sutherland," said Lauren, "recently I read an article in a magazine called *Last Days Bulletin* that leads me to believe the two parables may be making quite a different point from the one you identified."

The prospect of controversy stimulated interest in Lauren's question beyond Martin to the whole group. I may not have liked the interruption but I was pleased to have a very attentive audience. "Please continue, Lauren," I said, fully anticipating what she would say.

"In both parables there are symbols of evil: the birds in the first parable and the yeast in the second parable. Earlier in the chapter, Jesus spoke of birds in the parable of the sower as representing the devil and it's not uncommon in Scripture for yeast to represent evil as illustrated in its removal at the time of Passover and Jesus' reference to the hypocrisy of the Pharisees as yeast."

"What then would be the point of the two parables?" I asked.

"While the parables do speak of growth," said Lauren, "they refer to the growth of a kingdom mixed with evil such as unethical behavior, false teaching, and imposters. Big is not always beautiful." I was about to correct her interpretation of the parables but she was on a roll listing grounds for believing the statistics I had quoted did not represent the growth of the true kingdom of God. Her grounds included the use of modern Bible versions that contaminated God's word (by which she meant the King James Version), the substitution of psychotherapy for pastoral care, and the use of contemporary music in place of hymns based on sound theology. The pastors of large churches came under fire for compromising the gospel to make it more palatable to unbelievers. Such methods, she said, certainly built large churches but churches containing plenty of "birds" and plenty of "yeast." She finished by quoting the words of Jesus: "When the Son of man cometh, shall he find faith on the earth?" implying that the kind of growth I had been speaking of was not to be expected.

If I thought Lauren's overly vehement speech with its old-fashioned content and hermeneutical errors meant the youthful audience would be totally on my side as I responded, I was wrong, judging by the nods of approval and affirming amens as she sat down. Sensing the need for caution, I refrained from urging her to read reliable commentaries rather than the *Last Days Bulletin* and said that her question was an important one because it forced us to choose between an optimistic and a pessimistic mindset with regard to the future.

I continued by saying, "To help us decide between these alternatives, we should consider some important principles for handling the parables of Jesus. We should look for the central idea in a parable and be wary of overinterpreting by attaching hidden meanings to details that are only included in the parable to support the central idea. With respect to the details in a parable we should ask, first, if they need to be interpreted at all; second, if they *do* need to be interpreted, whether they bear the same meaning in one parable as they do in another.

"In the parable of the mustard seed, the kingdom of God is likened to something that at first is very small, a seed, but which in time becomes very big, a bush. What about the birds? Lauren is correct when she says that birds represent the devil in the parable of the sower but we cannot assume that the meaning of birds in that parable is transferable to this parable. For example, the seed in the parable of the sower represents the word of God but in the parable of the weeds—both parables are in Matthew 13—seed represents people. Jesus gave the interpretation of the birds in the parable of the sower but he said nothing about their meaning in the parable of the mustard seed. He didn't need to because they did not need to be interpreted. They are just birds. Why are they there? To show how big the bush is. Birds don't nest in a parsley plant but they do nest in a mustard bush. The very small mustard seed becomes a very large bush, large enough for birds to nest in. The growth is enormous.

"As for the yeast in the other parable, we cannot assume that the significance of yeast in the story of the Passover is intended here. Given that the parable closely follows the parable of the mustard seed which speaks of phenomenal growth, we should focus on the expansive power of the yeast not on the idea of evil, whatever it may mean elsewhere in the Bible.

"The two parables give every reason to be optimistic about the growth of the kingdom of God. We are seeing in our generation the kind of growth Jesus announced. For example, the protestant church in South Korea, according to *God is Back*, has grown from 2.4 percent of the population in 1950 to almost 20 percent so that five of the world's largest churches are found there, one of them claiming a membership of 830,000. We are on the winning side. Instead of a remnant mentality, let's expect kingdom growth and believe with Isaiah 11:9 that 'the earth shall be full of the knowledge of the Lord, as the waters cover the sea.'"

I was encouraged to hear a few amens, not as many as Lauren had received but, with a tinge of Schadenfreude, I noticed one or two of her supporters had joined my cheer squad. I also noticed that Martin was looking at his watch so I begged a minute to bring closure to the series.

"My aim in the three sessions we've had together has been to encourage the cultivation of a kingdom mindset. Kingdom-minded people see themselves as part of a spiritual kingdom that is present and growing; they think big because they are optimistically-minded; they walk tall because they are children of the King; and they get involved because they want to work with the King to extend his reign."

After Martin expressed thanks for my talks, the student applause was louder than I expected. I put it down to politeness but when five or six students, including some I did not know, personally thanked me for expanding their thinking and motivating them to be kingdom-minded, I was particularly gratified. The last to speak with me was a subdued Lauren who apologized for the length of her question which, she confessed, was more a diatribe than a question.

"Lauren," I said, "you sparked a lot of interest in the group and gave me the opportunity to talk about biblical interpretation, so thank you."

"Ed,"—I had previously told Lauren and her friends from SCIF to use my first name—"your treatment of the kingdom parables made a lot of sense and I learnt something about interpreting parables but, more importantly, about myself. Here I am at the university using my mind to evaluate the opinions of lecturers, fellow students, and peer-reviewed journal articles, but when it comes to my faith, I abdicate my intellectual responsibility and dogmatically mouth untested, second-hand views I've read in an unscholarly magazine as if they're absolutes."

"That's some lesson you've learnt, Lauren. By the way, I noticed Paul wasn't here today. Any idea where he is?"

"No idea. Anna doesn't know either. Normally he would have sent a text message if he couldn't make it. She's a bit concerned. I'm sorry, Ed, but I have to rush: I'm late for class."

Martin didn't have a lecture so asked if I'd like to join him for a coffee in the faculty club. Twenty minutes later, ensconced in leather tub chairs and waiting for a steward to bring our cappuccinos and carrot cake, he said, "Last time we met for coffee, you shared some tips for understanding the Bible. I've been putting them into practice. You also said you'd look forward to hearing how I was going."

"I remember it well," I said. "I'm all ears."

"I've been reading the book of Daniel."

"Starting at the deep end, eh?" I interjected.

"So far it's pretty plain sailing with nostalgic reminders of Sunday School stories about fiery furnaces and lions with lost appetites. What I wanted to chat about was, to use your words, an 'exegetical discovery' I made from Daniel 2 that fits well with what you were saying today."

"Now I'm really listening."

"I don't need to remind you about Nebuchadnezzar's dream of the statue with head of gold, chest of silver, belly of bronze, legs of iron, and feet of iron and clay. Even I recalled seeing pictures of the image as a child. What the pictures didn't show was the rock cut out of the mountain that smashed the image and grew till it filled the earth; but that seems to be the most important part of the story."

"I think you're right," I said. "Well done. So what was the significance of the rock?"

"Daniel said it referred to the kingdom of God that would defeat the kingdoms of the world and would last forever. What made me think of Daniel 2 as you spoke was that the rock that began as part of a mountain became so large it encompassed the globe. Not unlike the contrast between a small seed and a bush with nesting birds in it."

"Spot on," I said. "You must share that with the students at your next meeting. What else did you discover?"

"Not so much a discovery as an experience," said Martin.

Our drinks had arrived. Martin took a sip and a mouthful of carrot cake. I did the same but was more interested in hearing the rest of his story so urged him to continue.

"You spoke today of optimism versus pessimism. Though by nature I'm not a pessimist, recently I've been concerned about the world my kids and grandkids are going to inherit from us. Our papers regularly warn of climate chaos and economic collapse, report terrorist attacks, political uprisings, violent suppression of dissidents, racial tension, and religious persecution. Even here on the Sunshine Coast there seems to be an increase in violent crime."

"You mentioned you'd had an experience," I said.

"When I read in Daniel that God's kingdom will overthrow the world's kingdoms and that God's kingdom has a bright future, it was as if the pessimism that had begun to seep darkly into my soul suddenly changed to a delightful optimism. Hope for the future has replaced my fears for the future."

"You can see why the New Testament speaks again and again about the good news of the kingdom of God," I said. "You've experienced the good news, another thing to share with the students."

"By the way," said Martin, "I was pleased to hear your response to Lauren Wilson's criticism of 'big is beautiful.' For a moment there I thought my experience was baseless."

31

A Three-fold Package

We were running late for church the following Sunday and had difficulty finding a car park, evidence of the growth in attendance since Andy had become pastor. I noticed a car I had not seen before, a copper-red Mazda Miata, and pointed it out to Charlotte.

"More new members?" she asked.

"Could be, and by the look of that convertible, they could be young people."

Our late entry was made less conspicuous because the congregation was standing and totally absorbed in singing "O for a thousand tongues to sing." The enthusiastic singing, matched by Mrs. Beecroft's vigorous pumping on the organ, sounded as if the request for multiple tongues had been answered. When we sat down, I nudged Charlotte and nodded my head in the direction of Lauren, Anna, and Paul.

"Josh isn't there," whispered Charlotte.

"No," I whispered back, "but there are two newcomers next to Lauren."

"Do you know them?"

"John and Elizabeth, students at USC and members of the Real Life group."

From the row in front of us, a stern-faced Matthew Beecroft turned, his body language declaring loudly that our whispering disturbed him. I hoped he lip-read my "Sorry" before I put an open palm across my mouth.

The warmth of Stan Mullins's welcome to regulars and newcomers contrasted with his prosaic performance prior to Andy Zimmerman's appointment. He was so excited, I was tempted to suspect he'd become a closet charismatic who couldn't contain himself. After he gave the usual announcements, he said, "Over the last three months, the elders have been discussing the introduction of home groups into the life of the church. Last Tuesday evening we agreed that they should begin in the first week of November. We realized there will be a break over Christmas but we felt it would help to kick off the new year strongly if we made a start this year. This week and next week, there will be sign-up sheets at morning tea on which you can express your interest. We would encourage as many as possible to be involved."

I looked at Charlotte, who was looking at me, and we both raised our eyebrows together. Stan continued: "Pastor Zimmerman has an important announcement to make." I thought to myself, "It's all happening at once. As if the announcement about home groups wasn't important enough, we are about to get another important announcement, perhaps more important since Stan has allowed Andy to make it."

"Recently," said Andy, "I had an email from Dr. Chuck Harmon, the senior pastor with whom I worked for seven years in Tennessee. He and his wife, Susan, are planning to visit Australia as part of their long service leave. They will travel widely but included in their tour will be a visit to the Sunshine Coast. Dr. Harmon offered to contribute to the life of our church while he is here. Knowing that he has a deep interest and expertise in biblical prophecy, particularly as it relates to end times, I asked if he would be willing to speak about such matters at a weekend conference. He responded enthusiastically and said the first weekend in December would suit his itinerary. The elders are delighted and have begun discussing ways to promote the conference widely. The weekend will be a challenge for us all, in more ways than one. Please lock in the dates and gear up for some rewarding hard work as we prepare for what will be a highlight in the life of our church."

My raised eyebrows again met Charlotte's. I wasn't sure if her eyebrows were saying the same thing as on the previous occasion; mine certainly weren't. I knew Chuck Harmon by name as the author of a widely read book, *Hurtling to Armageddon,* and as the voice of the weekly radio program, *God's Word for the Last* Days. I felt positive about the introduction of home groups but felt the conference would merely be an exercise in reinforcing clause 24 of the Statement of Faith. I was tempted to take a holiday in the first week of December.

Andy continued his sermon series on the book of Hebrews. He read from Hebrews 9:24–28 from the KJV. In my NIV it read:

> For Christ did not enter a man-made sanctuary that was only a copy of the true one; he entered heaven itself, now to appear for us in God's presence. [25]Nor did he enter heaven to offer himself again and again, the way the high priest enters the Most Holy Place every year with blood that is not his own. [26]Then Christ would have had to suffer many times since the creation of the

world. But now he has appeared once for all at the end of the ages to do away with sin by the sacrifice of himself. ²⁷Just as man is destined to die once, and after that to face judgment, ²⁸so Christ was sacrificed once to take away the sins of many people; and he will appear a second time, not to bear sin, but to bring salvation to those who are waiting for him.

Andy built his message around three clauses: Christ appeared in our world for us (verse 26); Christ now appears in heaven for us (verse 24); Christ will appear a second time for us (verse 28). He linked the three appearances respectively to what he called the three tenses of salvation: we have been saved from the penalty of sin; we are being saved from the power of sin; we shall be saved from the presence of sin.

Because I was familiar with such a treatment of the passage, it was rather predictable—though well done—and I found myself reflecting on two matters that Andy did not comment on. As he spoke from verse 26 about Christ appearing in our world for us, he said nothing about the phrase, "at the end of the ages." It couldn't mean the end of all the ages of human history. What did it mean? The phrase reminded me of the text of Andy's sermon on Hebrews 1 where God is said to have spoken "in these last days" through his Son. Andy could rightly have said that Christ appeared in our world in the last days, not the last days of human history but of the Jewish age that was soon to pass away.

As Andy spoke of Christ's appearing a second time, I reflected on the words in verse 28, "to those who are waiting for him," a phrase whose present tense seemed to include the early church. Was the author of Hebrews promising that the Christians waiting in his day would experience the second appearance of Christ? If so he seemed to have got it wrong and to have given them false hope. As I asked myself if the author had got it right and I'd got it wrong, I was jerked out of my reflective state onto the track of Andy's sermon when I heard him say, "I learnt something this week that excited me and I'd like to share it with you. In preparation for this morning's message, I was reading a commentary on Hebrews by P.E. Hughes which made a connection between our reading and an important event in the Jewish calendar."

I listened in anticipation as he continued: "Once a year, on the Day of Atonement, as described in Leviticus 16, the Jewish high priest performed a ritual in three stages relevant to our text. Stage 1: the high priest sacrificed a goat on the altar outside the tabernacle; stage 2: he took the blood of the sacrifice into the most holy place within the tabernacle; and stage 3: he emerged from the tabernacle having completed his role on the Day of Atonement."

I could see where Andy was going with this and felt he was onto something. He went on: "When Moses was building the tabernacle he was told to make sure it conformed to the blueprint God had given him. The three stages undertaken by the high priest in relation to the tabernacle on earth prefigured three stages that a greater High Priest would undertake on our behalf. The three appearances of Christ we have considered this morning parallel the three stages of the Day of Atonement. Stage 1 was fulfilled when Christ appeared for the purpose of sacrificing himself at Calvary; stage 2 is being fulfilled now as Christ appears in the presence of God for us in the heavenly counterpart of the most holy place; and stage 3 will be fulfilled when Christ appears from heaven for our salvation."

I liked what Andy was saying and it stimulated my imagination. If I had been a Jew on the Day of Atonement, the highlight for me would have been stage 3, the reappearance of the high priest from the most holy place. What a sense of relief, of freedom, of salvation consummated!

While I appreciated Andy's insight, I was puzzled by one major difference between the three stages on the Day of Atonement and the three stages in Hebrews 9. The three stages on the Day of Atonement were part of a salvation package that occurred together. Stage 3, in the case of Christ's work, according to Andy, had still not occurred after 2,000 years. That had always been my position but was it right? The author of Hebrews had held out the hope of salvation at the second coming of Christ to those who were waiting for him. Did he mean that his fellow Christians were like the expectant Jews on the Day of Atonement waiting for their High Priest to appear from the most holy place in heaven? If so, they must have been very disappointed and he seemed to deceive them.

I turned to other Scriptures that spoke of the future aspect of salvation and discovered that the salvation package was more tightly wrapped than was generally assumed. Months earlier Andy had preached on Romans 13:11–12 (KJV):

> And that, knowing the time, that now it is high time to awake out of sleep: for now is our salvation nearer than when we believed. [12]The night is far spent, the day is at hand: let us therefore cast off the works of darkness, and let us put on the armour of light.

I had followed up Andy's sermon with concerns about Paul's inappropriate use of words such as "high time"; "far spent"; and "at hand" if the second coming was 2,000 or more years away. During our discussion we had not focussed on the word "salvation" in the text but I now saw that it was very relevant to Hebrews 9 where Christ's appearing is to bring salvation. Paul's language in Romans 13 was akin to his saying, "It's high time to wake up because the High Priest is about to emerge from the most holy place to complete the package."

As I flipped through the pages of my Bible to the next future-salvation text, Charlotte frowned at me as if to say, "You're making too much noise and you should be listening to the sermon." I looked up at Andy and pretended to listen but surreptitiously made my way to 1 Peter, chapter 1, fearful that Matthew Beecroft might be the next person to express disapproval if I didn't do it silently. Peter describes his readers as those "who through faith are shielded by God's power until the coming of the salvation that is ready to be revealed in the last time" (verse 5). The word "ready" spoke of nearness and if "the last time" seemed not to, Peter corrects that impression in verse 20 where he refers to the first coming of Christ as occurring "in these last times." Peter believed he and his readers were living in the last times. Though his readers are suffering, Peter describes them as "filled with an inexpressible and glorious joy, for you are receiving the goal of your faith, the salvation of your souls" (verse 9). Such a heightened sense of joy in the midst of suffering made more sense if the salvation was "ready to be revealed" rather than postponed for 2,000 years.

Peter further stimulates his readers' hope by telling them that Old Testament prophets spoke about the salvation Peter was describing. However, they did not know to whom it applied until it was revealed that their prophecies referred to the Christians of Peter's generation (verses 10–12). No wonder they were joyful.

As Andy began to conclude his sermon, my mind was in Matthew 24 and its parallels, Mark 13 and Luke 21. In these chapters, Jesus is in private conversation with four of his disciples. They have asked him when the fall of Jerusalem will occur and for the sign of his second coming and the end of the age. In Luke's account, Jesus tells the disciples, "When these things begin to take place, stand up and lift up your heads, because your redemption is drawing near" (Luke 21:28). The word "your" refers to the four disciples. They will not only be alive when Jesus' predictions begin to be fulfilled but at that time their future redemption will be near—hardly 2,000 years away.

Andy had announced the closing hymn. He would be shocked to know what I was thinking about as he preached and I was not about to inform him, particularly in light of clause 24.

Before I could catch up with John and Elizabeth at morning tea, Robyn Bradford buttonholed me with, "Just imagine, our own end-times conference! This is the best thing that's ever happened at SCIF. Should the Lord tarry, it'll be a weekend and a half. Don't you agree, Ed?"

Her question called for a one-word answer and I felt like giving it, though not the one she wanted. Instead, I answered evasively, "I'm sure it will provide much food for thought, Robyn. Please excuse me. I must catch up with a couple of visitors who are here for the first time."

John and Elizabeth were chatting with Paul. As I approached them, I overheard Paul talking about a new car he'd bought and, though not a betting man, would have put my money on its being a copper-red Mazda convertible. I soon discovered I was not wrong. John and Elizabeth nodded to me in the background but couldn't get a word in as Paul went on about how the two-liter engine in his convertible could spin its alloy wheels from zero to 100 kilometers per hour in 6.4 seconds. He hadn't noticed me and I thought I'd better interrupt or I might remain on the outer long enough for Robyn Bradford to pick me off on her next promotional round for the end-times conference.

"John and Elizabeth, what a pleasant surprise to see you here. Just visiting or here for the long haul?"

"You could call it a reconnaissance mission," said John. "Elizabeth and I met through the Real Life meeting at USC. I discovered she was not happy at the church she attended in Caloundra and she discovered I was not happy at the church I attended in Nambour. We both felt the need for warmer fellowship and biblically-based teaching, not to mention that we also wanted a church between our home towns that we could attend together. We've been church hopping for some weeks now."

The word "together" triggered a sweet smile on Elizabeth's face as she said, "I can't speak for John, but I'd be very happy to get the kind of teaching I heard this morning each Sunday and I was interested to hear about the introduction of home groups. That's the kind of fellowship I've missed."

"You *were* speaking for me, Elizabeth," said John, "because I entirely agree with all you've said." John got a second sweet smile.

"We'd be delighted if you end up here," I said. "My wife and I are fairly new to the church ourselves but already we've made good friends and enjoy Pastor Zimmerman's preaching. SCIF—that's what the locals call the church—may be just what you're looking for. If so, we would certainly value your involvement in the life of the church."

"Elizabeth and I will chat about it during the week and if you see us here next Sunday, it will mean today is the last of our reconnaissance missions."

I told Paul we'd missed him at the Real Life meeting on Monday. He said he'd like to have been there but was asked at short notice by his academic advisor to visit a multinational company in Brisbane to learn firsthand about its administrative structures. I was pleased that his absence had not been caused by his father's antagonism but a bit disappointed, as I moved away, to hear him immediately recommence a monologue on the features of the Mazda convertible.

Charlotte was talking with the Wilsons at the home group sign-up table. I joined them as they were about to put pen to paper. There were three sheets: one for people wishing to join a group; another for those willing to open their homes to a group; and a third for those willing to be considered as home group leaders. After we all signed the first sheet, we had a vigorous discussion about homes and leadership. Charlotte conceded that the Wilsons' lounge was larger than ours and Jack conceded that I would be a better leader than he. Pages two and three were filled out accordingly.

While Charlotte and Carol talked presumptuously about supper arrangements at the home group meetings, I told Jack I'd noticed Josh was absent from the service and asked if he was ill.

"No," said Jack, "but he's not himself. I'm worried about him. He's moody and incommunicative. He's gone surfing today and I fear he may be reverting to his pre-Zimmerman ways."

"I'll invite myself for a ride in the Mustang and see what comes of it," I said.

"Josh likes you, Ed, and I would appreciate your chatting with him."

"Speaking of cars," I said, "did you see the red Mazda Miata in the car-park?"

"Who could miss it?" Jack replied. "There aren't many of them on the road but I saw one just like it—same model, same color—on the Mooloolaba Esplanade last Monday. Carol and I were lunching there with former neighbors from our Buderim days."

As we drove home, Charlotte kept talking about home groups and I kept wondering if there were two identical Mazda Miatas on the Sunshine Coast.

32

At the Traffic Lights

Over lunch I told Charlotte of Jack's concern for Josh.

"I think Paul's new car is the cause of the problem," she said.

"You mean Josh's nose is out of joint because Paul's Mazda is better than Josh's Mustang?"

"No, no. Didn't you notice that Paul's new car is only a two-seater?"

"I did, but what has that got to do with it?"

"I think Josh has enjoyed driving Lauren, Anna, and Paul to church. Now the Mazda has broken up the foursome, he is left to shuttle his sister, but why bother when she can travel with Jack and Carol?"

"You think Josh's problem is the loss of his taxi service?"

Charlotte responded with a vehement "Of course not! Are you blind? It's obvious Josh is keen on Anna but the two-seater Mazda gives Paul a competitive advantage. Paul has room for only one passenger and, mark my words, it'll be Anna."

Charlotte's implied charge that my eyesight was defective when observing Cupid at work was well-deserved in light of my pretended ignorance of a deeper reason for Josh's moodiness. To avoid being regarded as a totally unromantic male, I began to tell Charlotte about my longstanding awareness of Josh's interest in Anna. Before I got past an account of my perceptive observations on the day of the Zimmermans' arrival from America, she said she needed to take a nap and left for the bedroom.

I would normally have followed but my mind was on Josh. He was in his mid-twenties, had never had a girlfriend, was clearly smitten by a beautiful American girl, but saw his chances of a relationship with her disappearing in a copper-red Mazda convertible driven by one of his few friends. Whatever Jack meant by Josh's reverting to his old ways, there was an additional factor not present in the pre-Zimmerman days—Anna. Knowing

Josh's shyness, I suspected Jack may not be aware of his son's romantic interest. Jack was expecting me to help so, with Charlotte asleep, I decided to go for a drive to think about the best approach to the problem.

A sunny spring day on the Sunshine Coast attracts a lot of day visitors so the traffic was thick as I drove south through Alexandra Headland. An unexpected parking spot near the Mooloolaba beach prompted me to abort my drive in favor of a walk. As I made my way along a path lined with pandanus palms and crowded with people walking dogs, riding bikes, pushing prams, or carrying surf boards, I thought I should relinquish my parking spot and drive somewhere quieter. I was about to turn back when I saw, fifty meters in front of me, a car painted avocado green. I didn't have to walk much further to discover it was a Mustang and I knew Josh must be in the area. With so many people about, I held little hope of meeting him but pressed on with my walk all the same.

Near the patrolled surfing beach, I sat on a deck to admire the view. The beach in front of me was crowded, particularly between the red and yellow flags designating the safe swimming area. If Josh was in the water, I expected he would most likely be beyond the blue flag where surfboards were permitted. I wandered along the beach in that direction, stood near the water and checked out each board rider. I couldn't see Josh and was about to return to my car when I heard his voice behind me: "What's an old guy dressed in church clothes doing on a surfing beach?"

That Josh would speak to an old guy in church clothes impressed me, eased my newly-aroused and uncomfortable self-awareness and helped me open up a conversation. "Charlotte's having a nap, I decided to go for a drive, ended up going for a walk, saw your car in the park and, forgetting I'd not changed since church, thought I might find you in the surfboard section of the beach. It looks like *you* found *me*."

"Not that I was looking for you," said Josh, "but suit trousers, a dress shirt and tie, and polished leather shoes are hardly beach wear and they do make you stand out. I surfed all morning and was resting under the trees up on the dunes when I saw this odd codger walking along the beach. I thought he might have been a dementia patient who'd escaped from a nursing home. When I realized it was you, I was tempted to greet you with, 'How did you get past matron?'"

I laughed, but inside I was apprehensive: my meeting with Josh seemed providential and I sensed I was meant to make the most of it, but how? If I initiated a counseling session on the beach, dressed as I was, his fellow lifesavers would think he'd been bailed up by a zealous member of a cult. Josh would think, "I'm absent from church for one Sunday and one of the heavies is after me before the day is out." Josh came to my relief when he said, "I'm heading for my car. Where are you parked?"

"A couple of hundred meters past you," I replied. "I'll walk with you if that's okay."

"Sure," he said. "You start off while I get my gear from under the trees. I'll meet you on the deck."

I passed close to the lifesavers' clubhouse where three young women dressed in bikinis were engaged in reciprocal flirtatious behavior with a couple of male lifesavers one of whom, his back turned to me, looked very like Paul Fitzgerald.

When I got to the deck, I looked back along the beach to see if Josh was coming but there was no sign of him. Had he done a bunk? If so, I'd be disappointed but would understand. A minute later he arrived from behind me carrying a towel, surf board and T-shirt. Instead of coming via the beach, he'd accessed the path along the foreshore from the top of the sand dune. Was he trying to avoid the clubhouse?

As we walked, I asked how his morning surf had gone but his response was surprisingly laconic given his normally passionate interest in the topic. When we reached his car, I made as if to keep going but Josh prevented me: "Ed, I'm not sure why you came looking for me. I imagined Stan Mullins might have sooled you onto me for skipping church this morning or Dad asked you to get to the bottom of my irritability at home. What I'm trying to say, Ed, is that I do need to talk with someone and I'm happy for it to be you."

"Josh, I actually didn't set out this afternoon to find you but you've been on my mind for some time, long before today. Let's get some chips and a drink at Fisheries on the Spit, my shout. There's a quiet spot among the trees by the river where we can chat."

As Josh drove along the narrow neck of land between the Pacific Ocean and the Mooloolah River, my mobile rang. Charlotte was awake and asking where I was. I told her I was in a Mustang taxi on the Mooloolaba Spit. She understood and said, "I'll see you when I see you."

With a Coke in one hand and a box of chips in the other, Josh and I walked through a clump of casuarinas to the river. Seated on a bench with a view of Point Cartwright and a fleet of fishing trawlers, we ate in silence for several minutes before Josh spoke: "You said I've been on your mind for some time. Why?"

"I'm not omniscient, but I think I have some idea of what you've been going through of late. If at any point I'm off the track, please stop me."

"Fire away."

"You've had your eye on Anna Zimmerman for a long time."

Josh blushed and said, "You're on track so far, but how did you know?'

"Blind Freddie would have seen it in your body language on numerous occasions: on the day she arrived from America, during the ride in your Mustang to Caloundra, while we chatted in the Coffee Club at Bulcock Beach, at the barbecue in your backyard, in church whenever the Zimmerman family sang." Josh's face was crimson. I tried to put him at ease. "If I was your age, I'd be vying with you for her attention. She's a sweet, beautiful, intelligent girl. How am I going?"

"Still on track."

"Then along comes your one-time friend, Paul Fitzgerald; Anna fancies him; you're bitterly disappointed; you're a pain to live with at home; and you can't face seeing them together at church."

"You're spot on," Ed, "but there's one point I'd like to make."

"Please do."

"I admit I'm jealous but doesn't the Bible say God gets jealous?"

"It does but I think we sometimes confuse legitimate jealousy with sinful jealousy. Sinful jealousy is related to a breach of the tenth commandment: 'You shall not covet.' It's akin to envy."

"When is jealousy legitimate?" asked Josh.

"When a legitimate relationship is threatened by a third party. God has a legitimate right to our love and submission and when something or someone comes between, he reacts in terms of jealousy. Any husband who really loves his wife will be, and should be, jealous—in the right sense—if another bloke makes eyes at her."

"I don't suppose I have a legitimate right to Anna but I am concerned for her."

"In what way?"

"I think Anna is rushing into a relationship with Paul before she really knows him."

"You could be right." I was tempted to share some of my misgivings about Paul but knew they might be groundless. "A lot of mistakes are made through hasty decisions. I used to tell my students to keep one road-width of objectivity between themselves and the object of their desire."

"What did you mean?" asked Josh.

"Decision making is like being at a crossroad. Should you cross over, turn right, left, or just stay put? Imagine you are standing before a set of traffic lights at a crossroad and you see a girl on the other side of the intersection. She's sweet, beautiful, and intelligent. You cross over and begin courting her. You're both Christians and want to know if the relationship is right for you. In effect, you want to know the answer to the question, 'What color was the traffic light on the other side of the intersection before

I crossed?' The problem is that it's difficult to see the color of the light after you've crossed."

A puzzled Josh asked, "Where are you going with this, Ed?"

"You said you thought Anna was rushing into her relationship with Paul. If you're right, it's as if she's crossed the intersection, got involved with Paul, her emotions are stirred, and it's difficult to distinguish those emotions from God's view of things. In other words, she doesn't know if she has God's green light on the relationship. To keep one road-width of objectivity between us and the object of our desire is to avoid getting too close too soon, to avoid a loss of common sense through clouded emotions, and to avoid severe pain if things don't work out."

"I get what you're saying," said Josh. "Your analogy applies to me as well as Anna. I've allowed my emotions to run away with themselves. In a sense I've got too close too soon; things haven't worked out, and I'm suffering for it. But where do I go from here?"

"You don't know for sure that Anna is God's choice for you, Josh? At the moment you see her on the other side of the intersection but in reality you've mentally and emotionally crossed the road. Pull your mind and emotions back into your body, remain before the traffic light and wait until you get a green light before you cross."

"That's a tough call," said Josh.

"Your emotions are controlled by your mind," I said. "I once heard a Christian psychiatrist say, 'The biggest sex organ in your body is your brain.' Fill your mind with matters other than Anna while you're waiting in front of the red light. Leave Anna with God. Don't even pray about her. That only reinforces her in your mind. Let others like me pray for her. You just wait for God's green light. We don't like waiting. Have you ever been in your Mustang at a stop light and it's stayed red for so long you're tempted to cross against the light thinking there's an electrical short in the system, and all of a sudden it changes to green?"

"Many times."

"Sometimes, Josh, you don't get a green light: you get a green arrow."

"What's your point?"

"Josh, if Anna is meant for you, God will deal with Paul as you wait patiently for a green light, hard as that may be. If Anna is not meant for you, keep waiting and you may get a green arrow, and when you follow it, you'll find round the corner someone better than Anna—if that's possible."

We sat silently, eating cold chips, sipping flat Coke, and shedding the odd tear—from both sets of eyes.

33

A Very Little While

With its roof folded down, Paul's convertible screeched to a halt as Charlotte and I stepped out of our car at SCIF the following Sunday. Charlotte gave me an I-told-you-so look as we saw Paul's passenger. Without bothering to open his car door, Paul vaulted out of his seat and raced around to open Anna's door. With a deep bow and an exaggerated flourish, he said, "At your service, ma'am." Anna gave him a smile, a bit forced I thought.

Turning to me, Paul asked, "What do you think of her?"

"I think she's sweet, beautiful, and intelligent," I replied.

"I meant the car," said Paul.

"No comparison," I said. I expected an "Edward" from Charlotte if I didn't say something about the car so I said I liked the color but declined an invitation to look under the bonnet. Anna seemed pleased and, taking Paul's arm, ushered him into church.

I made a point of not sitting behind Matthew Beecroft by sitting behind the Wilson family minus Josh. Paul and Anna were sitting alone several rows away. Just before the service began, Lauren asked Jack and Carol to move in towards the wall, then she stood up and beckoned to John and Elizabeth who had just arrived and were looking around for seats. I gave them a thumbs-up as they entered the row. It looked like their search for a new church was over.

After the opening hymn and invocatory prayer, Stan Mullins said, "I'm delighted to welcome to our fellowship John Delaney from Nambour and Elizabeth Wills from Caloundra. John and Elizabeth are students at USC and have expressed an interest in being part of our church. Please make them feel at home." As the congregation applauded, Lauren put an arm around Elizabeth and gave her a squeeze. Anna turned and gave a cheery wave.

Stan continued with his announcements: "We are encouraged by the interest in the proposed home groups. Please sign up at morning tea if you haven't already. Next Sunday we will post a list of home group leaders and venues."

I had no doubt the Wilsons' home would be an acceptable venue, since Jack was an elder, but I doubted I would be selected as a leader, given my eschatological leanings.

"Arrangements are already in place for our conference in December," said Stan. "We've appointed a planning committee and printed advertising leaflets for a mail-out to churches and organizations on the Sunshine Coast and beyond. At morning tea you will be asked by a member of the committee to help with promotion by distributing leaflets to friends who don't attend SCIF. To accommodate the expected numbers, we plan to hire a large marquee to be erected behind the church."

Before Andy gave his message, he reinforced Stan's announcement about the conference: "Dr. Harmon is a world-renowned author and conference speaker so it is a great privilege for our church to have him and his wife Susan with us in December. With only six weeks to go, I encourage everyone to support the committee and to work hard to make the conference a huge success."

Hebrews 10:21–25 was the focus of Andy's message. In my NIV, it read:

> Since we have a great priest over the house of God, [22]let us draw near to God with a sincere heart in full assurance of faith, having our hearts sprinkled to cleanse us from a guilty conscience and having our bodies washed with pure water. [23]Let us hold unswervingly to the hope we profess, for he who promised is faithful. [24]And let us consider how we may spur one another on toward love and good deeds. [25]Let us not give up meeting together, as some are in the habit of doing, but let us encourage one another —and all the more as you see the Day approaching.

As an opening sentence—I thought it was a bit corny, not to mention unoriginal—Andy began, "We're going to look at a row of lettuces in God's garden." He then proceeded to expound the exhortations in the passage beginning with "Let us." When he came to verse 25, he stressed the importance of church attendance, "Particularly," he said, "since many are lured away from a commitment to the local church through the attractions of the world. Paul said in 2 Timothy 3 that in the last days people would be 'lovers of pleasure rather than lovers of God.' In these last days we need to gather together regularly for mutual encouragement, especially, says the author, as we see the day of Christ's return approaching. The end is drawing near."

I had earlier questioned the application of "last days" in 2 Timothy 3 to *our* day so I didn't reflect further on it. I had no problem with Andy's urging regular church attendance; I had no problem with his understanding "the day" to refer to the day of Christ's return. I did have a problem, however, with his handling of the imminence expressed in the phrase, "all the more as you see the Day approaching."

The phrase contained a note of urgency but in Andy's view, the day was still approaching almost 2,000 years later, which seemed to minimize the urgency for the first century readers.

Andy kept saying "we" but the text said "you," which referred not to *us* but to *them*, the readers of the first century. They could see the day drawing near so the end was near for them. Andy said the end was near for us but that would mean it wasn't near for them. Apparently for Andy "approaching" meant one thing in the first century and another in the twenty-first century.

He seemed to be aware of the problem and tried to get around it by dragging in 2 Peter 3:8: "With the Lord a day is like a thousand years, and a thousand years are like a day." On the basis of this verse, he maintained that language suggesting an event was near could, from God's perspective, mean it was a long way off. I had often heard people use the verse in this way but it seemed like an exegetical dodge to make a text fit a presupposed paradigm.

Peter was quoting these poetical words from Psalm 90 to correct scoffers who thought the Lord had reneged on his promise. I imagined a conversation reflecting the thrust of the text:

> Scoffers: "You promised Christ would return. Year after year passes and still it hasn't happened. We don't think it's *going* to happen. You made an empty promise."
>
> The Lord: "What seems a long time to you is nothing to me because I live outside time. Forty years is like a snap of my fingers. My promise *will* be fulfilled—when I'm ready. Make no mistake about it."

We were not entitled to rip the quotation from its context in 2 Peter and apply it in other contexts as if it were some kind of mathematical formula at our disposal to make "last days" or even "last hour" mean "thousands of years"; "near" mean "far"; "soon" mean "not for a long time"; and "at the door" mean "miles away."

To drive home the nearness of Christ's return, Andy quoted from Hebrews 10:36–37 in the KJV:

> For ye have need of patience, that, after ye have done the will of God, ye might receive the promise. [37]For yet a little while, and he that shall come will come, and will not tarry.

In my NIV, it read:

> You need to persevere so that when you have done the will of God, you will receive what he has promised. [37]For in just a very little while, "He who is coming will come and will not delay."

"Few verses in the New Testament stress the nearness of Christ's return like these," I thought and wondered what Andy would do with them. He made the most of them. It wasn't difficult because he preached as if the "you" in the text referred to the congregation. But it didn't: the "you" referred to the readers of the original letter. They were urged to persevere because Christ's return was very, very close. I knew the KJV's "a little while" did not fully capture the nearness of the return and that the NIV was justified in adding the word "very" to represent the strength of the original language. Andy again resorted to the mathematical formula in 2 Peter 3 to get around the problem of how a coming promised in a very little while could still be coming after a very long while.

It was a naughty thought, but it seemed to me unethical to urge perseverance under difficult circumstances on the grounds that relief was just round the corner if it wasn't. I found it impossible to believe that the original readers would have understood "a very little while" to mean anything but a very little while.

If the King James Version of the first half of verse 37 was a bit weak, I rather enjoyed its rendering of the second half: "and will not tarry." Had Robyn Bradford never read these words? Just wait till the next time she said, "Should the Lord tarry."

I didn't have to wait long. I had no sooner caught up with John and Elizabeth to commend their decision to be part of SCIF than Robyn Bradford interrupted with, "Hi folks, I'm a member of the committee to arrange the end-times conference in December. I'm sure you're all excited about it." With that, she opened a large shoulder bag, handed each of us a bundle of fifty leaflets and urged us to "go into the highways and byways and compel them to come."

I accepted a bundle but the "outward and visible sign" on my face did not reflect "an inward and spiritual grace." John and Elizabeth were glad to help and offered to circulate leaflets to friends from their previous churches and to the members of Real Life. "As you hand out the leaflets," said Robyn, "stress that this is a not-to-be-missed event of critical importance in these last days. I look forward to seeing you at the conference with many of your friends, should the Lord tarry."

Had Robyn Bradford been asleep during the sermon? Didn't she listen when Andy read "and shall *not* tarry?" I was about to enlighten her but the presence of John and Elizabeth, coupled with a sudden surge of the recently deficient "inward and spiritual grace," restrained me. Robyn continued her promotional rounds and I pointed John and Elizabeth in the direction of the home-groups sign-up table.

As they moved away, Andy approached me and said, rather seriously, "Ed, if you've got some spare time this week, I'd like to catch up for a chat."

Since I had been feeling remiss in not having taken Andy bushwalking as I'd promised on his inauguration Sunday, I said, "Maybe we could chat and hike at the same time," I said. "If you can take a day off, I'll fit in and show you some of the local walking tracks."

"I'd like that," he said. "Wednesday's my day off. If you're free, let's do it."

I ran our plans past a compliant Charlotte and arranged to pick Andy up before breakfast on Wednesday. I looked forward to the hike but was curious to know what he had on his mind.

34

The Pastor's Concerns

Dressed in my Nike cap, T-shirt, board shorts and joggers, I arrived at Andy's house in Buderim at seven on Wednesday morning. In contrast to my city-slicker appearance, Andy looked the part of an Aussie bush walker, but not a seasoned one: from his broad-brimmed Akubra hat to his elastic-side riding boots, everything looked new. A safari shirt was tucked into khaki denim trousers supported by a wide leather belt with a long-horned steer on the silver buckle. I suspected the R.M. Williams store at Maroochydore had done quite well out of him. I smiled as I greeted him with, "You're supposed to have corks hanging all the way round your hat—to keep the flies away."

I had promised Andy months ago that I'd hike with him on the Blackall Range so we left Buderim via Mons Road, went north along the Bruce Highway to Nambour, and climbed the northern end of the range to Mapleton. Andy wanted to stop for breakfast but I told him better choices were available ten minutes away at Montville, if he could handle the roller-coaster ride along the range without getting car-sick."

"I'll be fine," he said, "but the breakfast had better be good." It was. Not only was Andy satisfied with the cheese and onion omelet, fresh croissants with marmalade jam, and the skinny caramel latte, but he sat on the cafe deck in awe of the view towards the coast. So far, Andy had given no indication of what he wanted to talk to me about. I didn't press him but fed his interest in the attractions of the trip by giving a tourist-guide commentary.

After breakfast Andy wanted to browse through Montville's art galleries and craft shops but when I suggested the family would enjoy doing that, he was persuaded that, as hikers, we needed to get out into the bush. A few kilometers out of town brought us to the Kondalilla Falls National Park.

"What a strange name," remarked Andy.

"'Kondalilla' is an aboriginal word meaning 'rushing waters.' You'll see why they called it that when we reach the falls," I said.

"How far are they?" asked Andy.

"The round trip is about 4.6 kilometers," I said. "It'll take us a couple of hours."

"Let's get going," said Andy.

After 400 meters we came to Picnic Creek where the track forked. We turned right and made our way through tall stands of eucalyptus trees to a lookout with spectacular views of the Obi Obi Valley. Sipping the cans of ginger beer Andy produced from his knapsack, we gazed in silence as a peregrine falcon soared high above the valley floor. When the silence became inordinately long, I wondered if it had more to do with the purpose of our hike than the Obi Obi Valley. It seemed appropriate to ask, "Andy, you said you wanted to have a chat with me this week. Now might be as good a time as any."

When Andy said, "I'll get straight to the point, Ed." I thought he was about to correct me for a theological aberration so was surprised when he continued, "It's about Anna. I couldn't ask for a better daughter but, at the moment, I'm concerned for her. I wanted to talk with you because you've seen your kids through adolescence and you've had more to do with the church young people than I have."

"If it'll help to share your concerns, Andy, the least I can do is be a good listener."

"You will have noticed that Anna has developed an interest in Paul Fitzgerald."

"I saw it coming months ago," I said.

"The relationship is one of my concerns: she's besotted with him; spends endless hours on the phone to him; meets with him daily at the university; goes on dates with him in his sports car; and comes home very late at night. At home she's irritable, sometimes rude to Linda and me, and is undisciplined with her studies. She's a bright girl, Ed, but her grades will suffer if she continues like this. Anna's only a teenager and I feel she's getting too involved for someone her age."

"Do you think Lauren might be able to help," I said. "They've been very close."

"She hardly ever sees Lauren now that she's so absorbed with Paul," said Andy. "And speaking of Paul, I have some misgivings about him: whenever he calls to pick up Anna, he never has time to chat so we can get to know him better; and on the few occasions when we have talked, the substance of the conversation has been Paul Fitzgerald. He's totally self-focused.

I'm convinced Anna is blinded to his character defects by his good looks. I know he's made a profession of faith but I'm not sure how genuine he is."

As Andy spoke, he massaged his forehead with one hand and drummed on the lookout guard rail with the fingers of the other. I felt for him but had no easy answer. He didn't need me to offer a platitudinous, "It's just a passing phase," or "I'll pray about it." I moved closer to him, gave the drumming fingers a gentle squeeze and remained silent for several minutes. Andy was the first to speak.

"What do *you* think of Paul?" he asked.

I didn't welcome the question. There was no doubt about Paul's egocentrism but should I tell Andy that I questioned Paul's veracity and was unsure of his fidelity to Anna? If I did, I felt I would add unnecessarily to Andy's misgivings by sharing my own, particularly since I could not affirm they were "beyond reasonable doubt." On the other hand, to speak positively about Paul also seemed inappropriate. I didn't want Andy to think I approved of the relationship. To be honest, I didn't. Faced with a dilemma, I prevaricated: "Like you, I've only seen Paul as he's presented himself. I can't say I've been close enough to know the real Paul—Paul as he is on the inside. I share your concern about the exclusiveness of the relationship. If only there were some way of getting them to mix within a group instead of hiving off on their own."

"Perhaps there is," said Andy. "I intended to talk with you later today about home groups but it may be relevant to talk about them now. Last night the elders met to consider who should lead them and in whose homes. Jack Wilson pushed successfully for you to lead the group at his house."

"I'd be happy to," I said, a little surprised that a relative newcomer, known to entertain strange ideas, should be given leadership responsibility, "but why do you say it might be relevant to our present conversation?" I asked.

"Why don't we make the home group at the Wilsons' a young people's home group?"

"The Sutherlands and Wilsons are hardly young," I said.

"The Wilson children are," said Andy, "and I know the new couple, John and Elizabeth, would be keen to be in your group. They told me how much they appreciated your lunch-time talks at the university."

"You're hoping Anna and Paul will join the group," I said.

"Exactly. I'll work—gently—on Anna and, if successful, she'll handle Paul."

"I've enjoyed being with young people for most of my professional life," I said, "so I hope all goes to plan." The smile on Andy's face showed signs of serenity instead of stress.

We had been standing at the lookout so long we needed to keep moving. The track wound beside rock pools to a view from the top of the falls. "I'd like to see them from the bottom," said an excited Andy. Knowing there were scores of steps on the return trip if we continued, I wasn't so keen but, since he'd already started, I followed reluctantly. The path crossed Skene Creek and the open forest gave way to cool rain forest packed with palms and tree ferns. When we reached the bottom, the sight of water cascading ninety meters down the escarpment improved my attitude and caused Andy to exclaim, "I can see why the aborigines called them the Kondalilla Falls."

As we made our way up the ridge past bunya pines and piccabeen palms, Andy was startled by a booming sound from above. "Whatever's that?" he shouted.

"A Wompoo Pigeon," I said, "a beautiful, purple-breasted bird that feeds on figs and other fruit. It's only one of more than a hundred bird species in the region." A rain forest was a new experience for Andy and, unfortunately, my tourist-guide commentary proved inadequate to answer all his questions.

With the ham and salad rolls Charlotte had packed in an Esky, supplemented by fruit, cheese and crackers from Andy's knapsack, we lunched well in the picnic area near the car park. After reflecting together on our morning's walk, Andy said in a serious tone, "Ed, there's another thing that's worrying me about Anna." I leaned forward and waited for him to go on. "You might remember my telling you months ago that as a child she suffered from nephritis."

"I do remember, Andy."

"Well, recently she complained of passing blood in her urine so we took her to Mark Mullins. He organized a test and the other day we got the results. Not good: the nephritis has recurred."

"How serious is it?" I asked.

"It could be just a passing urinary tract infection or it could be the beginning of longer term kidney disease. Mark has referred her to a nephrologist and together they will keep a close watch on her to minimize kidney damage should her condition turn chronic. Because she's young, there's a good chance that the problem will clear up but it's still a concern."

"I'm sure it is. Charlotte and I will support you in any way we can. Please keep us informed."

"We certainly will," said Andy, "but I would appreciate your keeping the matter confidential at this stage."

"Will do."

We arrived at the manse mid-afternoon to find Sam dribbling a soccer ball between garden beds and Linda pruning roses. With a warning to the footballer to keep clear of the rose bed, Linda greeted us warmly and inquired how the hikers had fared. I didn't need to say anything: Andy was ecstatic, almost to the point of speaking in tongues as he peppered his report with Kondalilla, Obi Obi, and Wompoo. I was pleased to see him so relaxed and was about to head home when Paul's Mazda convertible turned into the front yard and left an ugly skid mark on the lawn as he braked. Anna alighted and Paul drove off, exacerbating the skid mark.

"How was your day at USC, sweetheart?" asked Linda.

With a petulant "Much the same as usual," Anna went indoors with barely a nod towards Andy and me. Linda wiped a tear from moist eyes and Andy's ecstasy reverted to anxiety.

35

Escape or Endure?

Charlotte was saddened to hear about Anna's health and the stress within the Zimmerman family. "It's all Paul Fitzgerald's fault," she said. "I get bad vibes when he's around. His father's also behind it, I'm sure. Max blames you for influencing his son but I wouldn't be surprised if that's just a cover for an underhand humanistic stratagem to infiltrate the church and destroy our pastor's family. Don't underestimate the devil, Ed."

Not being sure what satanic machinations might be behind the Zimmermans' woes, I did not confirm Charlotte's analysis of the situation but I did share her concern so we planned to meet with Andy and Linda once a week to encourage them.

"Wednesday is Andy's regular day off," I said. "Why don't you and Linda make some arrangements for next week?"

"I'll give her a call in the morning. By the way, have you heard anything about home groups? I know nothing. I don't know if we're meeting in the Wilsons' home. I don't know if you're going to be a leader. The first meeting is supposed to be in two weeks' time and I'm still in the dark."

"I'm sorry, dear," I said, "I was so caught up with the Zimmermans' problems that I forgot to tell you that I've been asked to lead a home group next door and Andy would like us to involve the young people, particularly Anna and Paul. He thinks the social interaction with a wider circle than just Paul would be good for Anna."

"What night of the week will we meet on?" asked Charlotte.

"Nothing's been said about that. I imagine different groups will meet on different nights. We'll have to see what suits the Wilsons."

Within minutes, Charlotte was on the phone to Carol Wilson talking excitedly about implementing their preliminary plans for home group suppers and inviting her and Jack for breakfast next day to discuss further arrangements.

As we sat on the back veranda the following morning enjoying poached eggs, pancakes and percolated coffee, our guests and I were giving deserved praise for Charlotte's cuisine when we were interrupted by two small birds and a small dog. Aggressively evicting some sparrows from the bird table on the poinciana tree, two Mickey birds began to enforce their assumed territorial rights in keeping with their other name, Noisy Miners. Chuffey saw them as invading *his* territory and barked disproportionately to his size. When the noise finally subsided, we began to talk about home groups.

Carol felt the beginning of the week was too close to the weekend just passed; Jack thought the end of the week was too near the weekend coming; I exhibited outstanding conflict resolution by suggesting a mid-week meeting. We settled on Wednesday night with a seven o'clock start. Jack and Carol said they would encourage Josh and Lauren to attend; I agreed to invite John and Elizabeth; and it was left to the Zimmermans to work on Anna and Paul. I doubted Josh would come if he knew Anna and Paul would be there.

Jack said the elders wanted the home groups to reinforce the Sunday morning teaching through discussion of the text used in Andy's sermon. At the mention of the word "discussion," Charlotte nodded in my direction as if to remind me that discussion did not mean preaching. I returned the nod with a smile that justified her reminder, given my tendency to hog the floor.

The following Sunday, Stan Mullins announced that leaders, venues, and dates for home groups were confirmed and invited folk to choose a group that suited them and sign up for it in the church hall.

For his sermon, Andy took the first part of Hebrews 11. He admirably analyzed and illustrated faith from the accounts of Old Testament believers but, again, I was side-tracked when he read that Abraham lived in a tent. Why would Abraham do that if, as many taught, the land of Israel was such a long-term big thing? Robyn Bradford avidly followed news from the Middle East in expectation of fulfilled prophecy in relation to Israel—and kept me informed through her emails. Carol Wilson lent me copies of the *Last Days Bulletin* with the same emphasis. I wondered if Abraham was wincing at their misplaced optimism. He didn't place great store on the land. When he arrived, he lived in a tent. Surely if the land was so important in the long term, he would have built an enduring dwelling for his descendants. He didn't. He lived in a tent—for the whole of his life. Why? The answer was in front of me in the text: his hope was not pinned on the land but on "the city with foundations, whose architect and builder is God" (verses 9, 10). He was "longing for a better country—a heavenly one" (verse 16). Apparently, for Abraham, the land wasn't the big thing, just a shadow of the real thing, so he lived in a tent.

After the service, I waylaid John and Elizabeth as they headed to the church hall, fearing they might opt for a venue other than the Wilsons'.

"You wouldn't be going to check out the home group options by any chance?" I asked, with a smile.

John responded with a question: "Any suggestions?"

"A Wednesday night group at Maroochydore is highly recommended," I said. "It would suit people who live at Caloundra and Nambour."

"But who's leading it?" asked Elizabeth.

"I'm too humble to say," I replied.

"A humble leader is just what I want." Then, turning to John, she asked, "Do you want to be in Ed's group?"

John shrugged his shoulders, screwed up his face, and said, "Maroochydore is ideal and Wednesday night is fine but I'm not sure about . . . " After a pause long enough to put a frown on Elizabeth's face, he finally said, with a grin, "If it must be Ed's group, so be it."

Elizabeth relaxed, gave John a gentle flick and said, "He's such a tease, Ed."

Flushed with the initial success of my home group recruiting campaign, I was tempted to usurp the responsibility of the Wilsons and Zimmermans when I saw Lauren, Anna and Paul getting a drink—Josh wasn't at church. I thought better of it but couldn't resist a quick squiz at the list for our group before leaving for home: all seniors, except for John and Elizabeth.

"Is Andy's plan going to work?" I said to Charlotte as we drove home. "Only two young people have signed up for our group and neither of them is Anna or Paul."

"Give them time, Ed. There's a week and a half before our first meeting. I know you; you're over-excited."

"Am not," I said, with mock sullenness.

Sizzlers at Maroochydore was the venue for our first Wednesday get-together with the Zimmermans. Charlotte and I ordered the salad-bar smorgasbord deal but Andy and Linda settled for a cup of coffee. We soon discovered that their on-going concern about Anna's health had affected their appetites.

"You might have noticed Anna has developed some inflammation round her eyes," said Linda. "That's just one of the symptoms of her kidney disease. She gets frequent headaches and is more tired than usual. Andy and I are really worried about her."

Andy spoke up: "Mark Mullins has adjusted Anna's diet to reduce sodium and protein and has prescribed medication to reduce her blood pressure. Fortunately, she has completed her exams for the year but her studies next year will depend on changes to her health during the summer."

"Is Mark able to give an accurate prognosis at this stage?" Charlotte asked.

"He said that when acute nephritis recurs there's a one-in-three chance of its leading to what he called ESRD, End Stage Renal Disease," said Andy, "but it's too early to say whether Anna faces that depressing outcome."

"We're taking it one day at a time," Linda sighed. "Mark will monitor the performance of Anna's kidneys. If it improves, we'll be delighted; if it deteriorates to a 90 percent loss of function, then ESRD has set in and dialysis or a kidney transplant will be required."

Charlotte and I instinctively joined hands with Andy and Linda. The silence that followed was probably more comforting than verbal attempts at sympathy. Finally, I broke the silence with a brief prayer for the family and we resumed eating but there were no second visits to the salad bar.

Before the service on Sunday, I checked the sign-up sheet for my home group. I was disappointed: no change. My fears were not relieved when I noticed Paul and Anna, not to mention Josh, had not turned up for church. Andy's message was the basis for our discussion on Wednesday night. I needed to check my tendency to wander in the thickets of my own thoughts and concentrate in preparation for our first home group but I found it hard as I visualized the meeting as a monumental flop. I cheered myself up by recalling a story about the first meeting of the Social Apathy Group (SAG for short) at Oxford University. No one turned up and the meeting was regarded as an outstanding success. Andy began by reading Hebrews 11:32–38. I followed in my NIV:

> And what more shall I say? I do not have time to tell about Gideon, Barak, Samson, Jephthah, David, Samuel and the prophets, [33]who through faith conquered kingdoms administered justice, and gained what was promised; who shut the mouths of lions, [34]quenched the fury of the flames, and escaped the edge of the sword; whose weakness was turned to strength; and who became powerful in battle and routed foreign armies.[35]Women received back their dead, raised to life again. Others were tortured and refused to be released, so that they might gain a better resurrection. [36]Some faced jeers and flogging, while still others were chained and put in prison. [37]They were stoned; they were sawed in two;

they were put to death by the sword. They went about in sheepskins and goatskins, destitute, persecuted and mistreated—[38]the world was not worthy of them. They wandered in deserts and mountains, and in caves and holes in the ground.

"You could hardly call life a level playing field," said Andy. "For example, I know people who have been diagnosed with life-threatening illnesses, have prayed and astounded the doctors with their miraculously rapid recovery. On the other hand, I know people, similarly afflicted but equally godly, who have not recovered. For years they have suffered deteriorating health and chronic pain. It doesn't seem fair. The problem of pain, to use the title of one of C.S. Lewis's books, is an age-old one, and one that I've wrestled with for years. I don't have a slick answer for it but as I prepared during the week for this morning's message, I saw something in the text we just read that I'd never seen before and it offered help with the problem.

"I had read the passage many times but failed to notice that the people listed in the text—some named, some known by reputation, some unknown—were in two groups. Group 1 consisted of people who escaped their afflictions, people like Daniel who escaped the lions, people like his three friends who escaped the flames, women who escaped grief from the loss of loved ones. Group 2 began in the middle of verse 35 with the word 'Others.' None of the people in this group escaped. They endured—torture, abuse, imprisonment, homelessness, and horrifying deaths."

Andy was right and, like him, I'd not noticed the clear structure of the passage into two groups. Why had most translations of the Bible not paragraphed the passage to make these groups stand out? It was so obvious and, as Andy went on to show, so significant.

He asked the congregation, "Which group would you rather be in, group 1 or group 2?" We all opted for group 1. Then he said, "I've got some bad news for you. For every Daniel who escaped the lions, many have endured being killed and eaten by them rather than renounce their faith; for every Shadrach, Meshach, and Abednego who escaped the flames, hundreds endured being consumed by them as persecutors like the sixteenth-century English queen, Bloody Queen Mary—I'm not swearing—burnt scores of believers at the stake.

"While some of us may be blessed with the occasional group 1 experience, verse 1 of chapter 12 says we are to run the race before us with endurance. In that sense we are all group 2 people. We're not in the egg and spoon race; we're in the marathon."

Andy then asked another question: "Who had more faith, the people in group 1 or the people in group 2?" Perhaps thinking a miracle required more faith, some chose the group 1 people. The rest, probably suspecting it was a curly question, said nothing. Andy then read from verse 39: "These were *all* commended for their faith," and he stressed the word "all." He continued: "The people in both groups were men and women of faith. Never minimize the faith of those who do not experience the quick fix but who hang in for the long haul. Never assume that the sick who are not healed harbor sin or lack faith, as some would imply. They may actually be men and women of great faith, just group 2 people."

Andy had a third question: "Which group was Jesus in, group 1 or group 2?" and then he read from chapter 12, verses 2 and 3 (KJV) about Jesus, with emphasis on the word "endured":

> Looking unto Jesus the author and finisher of our faith; who for the joy that was set before him *endured* the cross, despising the shame, and is set down at the right hand of the throne of God. For consider him that *endured* such contradiction of sinners against himself, lest ye be wearied and faint in your minds.

"Jesus endured." said Andy. "He was in group 2. He could have been in group 1. In the garden of Gethsemane he told his disciples that twelve legions of angels were at his disposal, more than enough to put him in group 1, but he had prayed, "Not my will but yours be done." According to John 12:27–28, Jesus, deeply troubled as he faced the cross, chose to pray, "Father, glorify your name" rather than "Father, save me from this hour." In other words, rather than ask to be put into group 1, he submitted to doing what would bring greater glory to the Father. He left it to his Father to decide which group he would be in."

Andy spoke with great conviction making me think that he was conscious of the choice he faced in relation to Anna's health. Every father would want his daughter to escape kidney disease in preference to years of ill health. I felt for him. "Father, glorify your name" was not an easy prayer to pray.

After the service, I thanked Andy for the fresh thoughts he had brought through his message on Hebrews 11.

"Thanks, Ed," he said. "I didn't find it easy to speak this morning. It pained me to see Anna's usual seat empty." I was about to ask if her absence was due to her health but he anticipated my question with, "She's with Paul at a surf carnival he's competing in."

I didn't ask Andy if he'd succeeded in enlisting Anna for the home group. Was it because I didn't want to cause him more pain or because I didn't want to hear that Anna and Paul would not be attending? So far, the only people expected on Wednesday night were two Sutherlands, two Wilsons, and John and Elizabeth—who were sure to feel they'd gate-crashed a geriatric group.

36

Home Group

Early Monday morning, Jack and I went fishing at the Cod Hole. We arrived about 5:00 a.m. as the sun was rising. The fish must have been late risers: not even a nibble. We used the time to chat.

"Ed," said Jack, "I want to thank you for spending time with Josh the other Sunday afternoon. He told me about the over-dressed old man on Mooloolaba beach who chatted with him. He didn't go into detail about the conversation but it's made a difference, Ed. He's more relaxed in himself and much easier to live with, so thank you."

"That's encouraging," I said. "By the way, is he interested in the home group on Wednesday night?"

"He's very busy so I wouldn't count on him. Stan Mullins is opening up a second hardware store in Bundaberg in a week or two so Josh has extra accounting work to do."

"What about Lauren?"

"Every time I mention the home group she says she's snowed under with assignments."

The image of a monumental flop on Wednesday night returned but disappeared as I felt a strong jerk on my line and moments later hauled in a 35 cm bream. Jack soon caught another. By 7:30 we had more than enough for breakfast so headed home.

As we gutted the fish near the jetty, Jack said, "Home groups, as you know, are an innovation for SCIF. Carol and I are excited about using our place as a venue so we're really looking forward to Wednesday night and, I might add, very pleased that you'll be leading the group." I listened with mixed feelings: I was pleased the Wilsons were pleased but was unable to rise to the level of their excitement.

On Wednesday night, Charlotte served an early dinner after which I stayed to clean up the kitchen while she went next door to help Carol set up for supper. When I arrived about 6:45, the kitchen table displayed a set of Royal Doulton cups and saucers and enough sandwiches and cakes for half the church. A tray of sausage rolls sat on top of a bench waiting to be put in the oven. Jack ushered me into the living room where he had added kitchen chairs to the regular lounge furniture to form a rough circle for a dozen people. Charlotte and Carol joined us and for ten long minutes we sat silently in an empty circle. Charlotte looked at me and touched the sides of her mouth with her forefingers to induce a smile. I did my best but couldn't match Jack's beaming face.

He bounced to his feet at a knock on the door. As he showed John and Elizabeth into the room, Lauren emerged from her bedroom saying she needed a break from study and would keep John and Elizabeth company. Beaming even more brightly, Jack welcomed the small group as if it were a large group and included somewhat inflated phrases: "rare privilege . . . historic occasion . . . significant milestone . . . unique learning experience . . . outstanding Bible teacher"—he looked at me when he said that. He meant every word but I felt it was a bit over the top, especially when he introduced me as "our illustrious leader."

I added my welcome and said that Jack's overly generous remarks reminded me of a story I'd heard: "A wealthy American tourist was driving a large limousine through the mountains of northern Italy when he came to a high, narrow bridge across an alpine river. He was unable to cross because a stubborn donkey sat on its back legs in the middle of the bridge refusing to budge, in spite of the pushing, pulling and strident urging from a local peasant. The impatient tourist drove towards the donkey and sounded the limousine's very loud horn. The frightened donkey leapt to his feet and jumped to his death over the low parapet. The irate peasant threw up his hands, tore at his hair, and shouted, 'Too bigga da honk for too smalla da donk.'"

As if I had orchestrated sound effects for my story, a car horn sounded outside the house. Paul Fitzgerald had announced his arrival. A minute later, he entered the room followed by Anna. His expression seemed to say, "Here I am you lucky people." By the time folk milled around them and they got settled, two more arrivals further delayed the commencement of our first home group, Josh Wilson and Mark Mullins. Charlotte gave me an O-you-of-little-faith look.

Jack felt obliged to give another embroidered welcome but I did not repeat my donkey story, much as Paul's honking would have made an easy transition to it. After my own welcome to the recent arrivals, I said, "One of my first speaking engagements, decades ago, was to a group of high schoolers some of whom were very reluctantly present. As a novice, I began by asking, 'Why are we all here?' A smart-aleck student in the back row called out, 'Because we're not all there.' I was tempted to express my condolences for his intellectual limitations but thought better of it. I won't ask exactly the same question of you but a similar one: 'What do we hope to get from our home group?'" Anna was the first to speak.

"As long as I can remember, I've heard my father preach Sunday after Sunday. While I appreciate him, it's always good to hear different viewpoints on the Bible. I enjoyed Ed's sessions at Real Life recently and look forward to his input here."

I needn't have feared Paul would follow suit with a reference to my contribution to Real Life. With a smirk, he said, "I'm here to keep Anna on the straight and narrow." Anna made an effort to smile and seemed pleased when John spoke up and diverted attention away from her: "Elizabeth and I missed the intimacy of a home group in our previous churches so we're thrilled for the opportunity to meet informally to interact on biblical topics."

I was surprised Mark had joined the group. I thought he'd be leading one in his own home. He explained: "Cathy and I lead very busy lives and we both feel the need for spiritual refreshment. We want to be stretched in our thinking about theological issues and feel Ed will be a catalyst to that end. We plan to alternate in our attendance at the home group. Cathy will be here next week when I'll look after the children. Wednesday night is the one weeknight I'm never on call so this home group is just what we need."

With a pause in the responses, I was about to take over when Josh spoke up. "This will be my first and last home group for some time." He had everyone's attention. "Dad and Mum know that I've been mulling over an offer from work to help set up a branch hardware store in Bundaberg. Today I made up my mind. I'll be heading north next week. No offence to my parents or my sister, but it's time I learnt to fend for myself. I hope to be home some weekends but if I'm going to be part of the Bundaberg scene, I may as well get involved in a church up there." When Josh finished, he was surrounded by a circle of silent, serious faces.

"You'll leave a hole at the surf club, Josh," said Paul.

"I don't think anyone'll drown because I'm not there," he replied.

Lauren's "How will I manage without my big brother?" was followed by a "We'll miss you, Josh" from Anna. Josh said nothing but I detected a faint and telling smile.

The staggered start and the prolonged welcome prompted me to get the meeting under way. I handed out sheets containing Sunday morning's text from Hebrews 11 and 12 and we read part of it around the circle.

> And what more shall I say? I do not have time to tell about Gideon, Barak, Samson, Jephthah, David, Samuel and the prophets, [33]who through faith conquered kingdoms, administered justice, and gained what was promised; who shut the mouths of lions, [34]quenched the fury of the flames, and escaped the edge of the sword; whose weakness was turned to strength; and who became powerful in battle and routed foreign armies. [35]Women received back their dead, raised to life again. Others were tortured and refused to be released, so that they might gain a better resurrection. [36]Some faced jeers and flogging, while still others were chained and put in prison. [37]They were stoned; they were sawed in two; they were put to death by the sword. They went about in sheepskins and goatskins, destitute, persecuted and mistreated—[38]the world was not worthy of them. They wandered in deserts and mountains, and in caves and holes in the ground.
>
> [39]These were all commended for their faith, yet none of them received what had been promised. [40]God had planned something better for us so that only together with us would they be made perfect.

"Several of you missed Andy's sermon on Sunday so let's do a little revision." Paul interrupted: "I was competing in the Coolangatta Gold Ironman Race last weekend. I came third in a line-up of more than 500." He would have gone on but Anna interrupted: "I've heard all my father's sermons so there's no need to revise for me."

"Actually, Anna, no one had heard the sermon before last Sunday because your dad shared a discovery he made about the text only days before he preached. I thought it was very insightful. Let's see who remembers it. You all have a copy of the text in front of you. Take a pencil and draw a vertical line in the first paragraph to mark the end of what Andy called group 1 and the beginning of what he called group 2. It will help to remember that the people in group 1 had very different experiences from the people in group 2." Those who were present on Sunday promptly inserted the line in the right place; those not present took a little longer.

"Josh, would you mind telling us where you drew the line?" I asked.

"I put it before the word 'Others' in verse 35."

"What was the basis for your decision?"

"Everyone up to that point seemed to have a good news story and everyone after that a bad news story."

"A good observation. One way of representing the two groups might be 'good news/bad news.' Would 'success/failure' be a suitable description of the two groups?" I asked. Some nodded, one or two said "Yes" but Mark Mullins gave a strong "No." I asked him to explain his answer.

"I think the people in both groups were successful. In verse 38, the writer says of the people in group 2 that 'the world was not worthy of them.' They were treated as if they were not worthy to live in the world but God thought they were so special the world didn't deserve to have them."

"Excellent," I said. "So both groups were successful, Mark?"

"Absolutely."

"Another question for us all: 'What single word in verse 39 represents the secret of their success?'"

Almost in unison they said, "Faith."

"So you can be a man or woman of faith and miraculously escape death and be in group 1; or you can be a man or woman of faith and experience a horrifying death and be in group 2. If faith is common to both groups, it's not faith that determines the group we're in. What is it?"

Elizabeth spoke up. "I got some help with that question from Andy's reference to the prayer Jesus prayed when he was troubled: 'Father, glorify your name.' I think your question should be '*Who*, not *what*, determines the group we're in?' And the answer is 'a sovereign God who will do what brings him the greater glory.'"

"A very good answer, Elizabeth. By the way, what terms did Andy use to distinguish the two groups?"

"'Escaped' and 'endured,'" she said.

"What we've seen so far, then, is that God may respond to our faith with a miracle through which we escape from our troubles or he may respond to our faith with grace that enables us to endure our troubles. The bottom line, though, is that he decides."

I waited in case someone had a comment or question. No one spoke but the body language suggested that our revision of Andy's sermon had brought everyone up to speed on the matter of the two groups. I continued: "Is there anyone who would like to share an experience relevant to our topic."

"I would," said Charlotte. "I used to be a very active person, in good health and full of energy, but about three years ago, I experienced a severe case of chronic fatigue syndrome. Every day was a burden. I would get up in the morning with big plans for the day, few of which would be accomplished. I went to three specialists. They couldn't help. I prayed in faith that God would heal me quickly but it was a slow process and it's still ongoing. At first I was resentful and that only made my condition worse. I finally came to a point of acceptance and I prayed in the words of a song by Katie Wilkinson:

> May I run the race before me,
> Strong and bold to face the foe;
> Looking only unto Jesus
> As I onward go.

"I realize I'm anticipating the verses from chapter 12, but being in group 2 is really about running an endurance race with the eyes of faith on Jesus. I wanted to be in group 1 but God had other plans. As a group 2 person I get to see God at work in my life every day, giving me the strength and courage to achieve his goals in spite of my limitations."

I thanked Charlotte for her very relevant contribution and affirmed the truth of her experience from my own knowledge of her, but not before I noticed a quiet thoughtfulness had settled on the group and that Anna's eyes were moist. I said, "Let's reflect on what Charlotte has said as we read silently the first three verses of chapter 12 from our sheets.

> Therefore, since we are surrounded by such a great cloud of witnesses, let us throw off everything that hinders and the sin that so easily entangles, and let us run with perseverance the race marked out for us. ²Let us fix our eyes on Jesus, the author and perfecter of our faith, who for the joy set before him endured the cross, scorning its shame, and sat down at the right hand of the throne of God. ³Consider him who endured such opposition from sinful men, so that you will not grow weary and lose heart.

I asked, "Was Charlotte right in thinking this passage is particularly relevant to group 2?"

"Yes," said John, "because each verse talks about endurance. We are told to run with perseverance, which is endurance, and Jesus is twice said to have endured."

"That's right, John. Whether we like it or not, we are all in an endurance race and the writer says we must get rid of the things that hinder and the sin that entangles. Is there a distinction between things that hinder and sin?"

"I think so," said Jack. 'When I was a teenager, I was very keen on Rugby League. I practiced a couple of nights a week and at weekends I was playing in matches against other teams on the Sunshine Coast. Football was not sin; it was not wrong in itself, but I found it was a hindrance: my school work suffered; my competitive spirit made me aggressive, even off the field; I developed inappropriate speech and behavioral habits and, spiritually, I was going backwards. I knew fine Christian footballers for whom it was not a hindrance but for me it was. It had to go."

Jack's story created a reflective atmosphere. I waited in case others might like to share. Josh looked particularly thoughtful as though unsure about whether to speak. He did: "Recently, I've come to see that hindrances are not always out there but sometimes in here." He tapped his chest. "I've been hanging onto something in my heart that was a good thing but it was not helpful. It consumed my thinking and sapped my energy for things I should have been doing. My irritability at home made me a pain to the family. It's been a struggle to let go but now that I have, I'm more at peace and I feel I'm going forwards instead of backwards."

The reflective atmosphere intensified. Jack gave Carol's hand a squeeze, both of them quite moved by their son's honesty. I had no doubt that the something Josh had been hanging onto was a someone. A lesser person might have tried to score a point by using the word "someone" and looking at her—or his rival—as he spoke, but there was not the slightest whiff of sour grapes.

Before we went to supper, I suggested we close the session by having Charlotte pray the verse of the song she had quoted earlier:

> May I run the race before me,
> Strong and bold to face the foe;
> Looking only unto Jesus
> As I onward go.

When she finished, half a dozen indicated they had made the prayer their own by voicing a sincere "Amen."

At supper the sausage rolls and sandwiches were a big hit. I was pleased that the group did justice to Charlotte and Carol's preparation and I was also pleased to see healthy cross-generational communication as John and Elizabeth conversed with Jack and Carol, and Josh thanked Charlotte for the words she'd shared. Paul was jingling the keys of his Mazda convertible but Anna took no notice: she was enjoying renewed friendship with Lauren.

Mark approached me holding a Royal Doulton cup of tea and curling a little finger in jocular imitation of high society. He invited me into the lounge and we sat next to a low table from which he picked up his Bible and said, "I've got a question about tonight's text," he said, and proceeded to read Hebrews 11:39–40:

> These were all commended for their faith, yet none of them received what had been promised. [40]God had planned something better for us so that only together with us would they be made perfect.

"My question is this: What were the Old Testament believers promised that they didn't have?"

"Mark," I said, "they were promised an 'eternal inheritance' (Hebrews 9:15) which explains why Abraham 'was looking forward to the city with foundations, whose architect and builder is God' (Hebrews 11:10), and why the Old Testament believers were 'longing for a better country—a heavenly one' (Hebrews 11:16). However, Hebrews 11:13 says, 'they did not receive the things promised; they only saw them and welcomed them from a distance.'"

"Is Abraham still waiting to go to heaven?" pursued Mark. "If so, it would seem that no one has yet gone to heaven. Not a pleasant thought if the Christian funerals I've been to are anything to go on."

"I believe Abraham is in heaven," I said, in an effort to cool Mark's growing concern. Then, without waiting for him to respond, I added, "Next week's study may help us with your question so I suggest we wait until then to explore the matter further." The word "may" was intended, on the one hand, to give Mark hope that he would soon get an answer and, on the other hand, to cover my uncertainty about whether I could answer his question from next week's study? Did I even want to raise the topic at next week's meeting? My postponement of the issue reflected a fear that Mark could see the implications of my belief that Abraham was in heaven. He was opening a can of very big worms and I needed time to think about how to deal with them.

"Have you forgotten that it's Cathy's turn to come next week," he said with a smile.

I *had* forgotten, but having been reminded, I didn't think it fair to tell him that Cathy could help him with his question following next week's meeting. I arranged to meet with him on Sunday afternoon, rather reluctantly. The elders had entrusted me with the leadership of a home group and here I was about to get involved in a discussion that could put me at odds with clause 24, not to mention Mark's father, the chairman of elders.

37

Is Abraham in Heaven?

Charlotte and Carol spent so much time in each other's company, they commissioned Jack and me to hinge a panel in the side fence to form a gate between our backyards. The result was tangible evidence of the bond that had developed between the two families.

Early on the Saturday morning after our first home group meeting, Charlotte and I were drinking coffee on the back veranda when we heard a click from the gate latch and excited barking from Chuffey. I stood to see Jack at the foot of the stairs. He beckoned as he said, "Come on over. Josh is about to leave for Bundaberg." Carrying our cups of coffee, we went through the gate to find Josh closing a very full boot and attaching his surfboard to the roof rack with bungee cords.

He then stood by the open front door of the car surrounded by a teary mother and sister and a stoic father, lost for words as he hugged his son. Charlotte's eyes were sympathetically moist; my feelings were ambivalent, a mixture of optimism about a new life for Josh and apprehension that his present loneliness might be exacerbated in a strange city. As I shook his hand, he said, "Thank you," but did not elaborate. I said I'd keep in touch. We all followed the car as he backed it onto the street; then, revving the engine, he gave a cheery wave, a noisy demonstration of the Mustang's powers of acceleration, and headed north. He seemed to be the happiest member of the group.

Prior to the service at SCIF the following day, I noticed a greater level of interaction between age groups and even between traditionalist and more contemporary members. Gates were opening in fences other than in our backyard. "There must have been a good attendance at home groups," I thought. Andy confirmed my thinking before his sermon: "The elders are delighted that 80 percent of the church met in home groups during the week and reports indicate that 'a good time was had by all.' Your discussion this week will be on the text of this morning's message taken from Hebrews 12:18–29." In my NIV it read:

> You have not come to a mountain that can be touched and that is burning with fire; to darkness, gloom and storm; [19]to a trumpet blast or to such a voice speaking words that those who heard it begged that no further word be spoken to them, [20]because they could not bear what was commanded: "If even an animal touches the mountain, it must be stoned." [21]The sight was so terrifying that Moses said, "I am trembling with fear."
>
> [22]But you have come to Mount Zion, to the heavenly Jerusalem, the city of the living God. You have come to thousands upon thousands of angels in joyful assembly, [23]to the church of the firstborn, whose names are written in heaven. You have come to God, the judge of all men, to the spirits of righteous men made perfect, [24]to Jesus the mediator of a new covenant, and to the sprinkled blood that speaks a better word than the blood of Abel.
>
> [25]See to it that you do not refuse him who speaks. If they did not escape when they refused him who warned them on earth, how much less will we, if we turn away from him who warns us from heaven? [26]At that time his voice shook the earth, but now he has promised, "Once more I will shake not only the earth but also the heavens." [27]The words "once more" indicate the removing of what can be shaken—that is, created things—so that what cannot be shaken may remain.
>
> [28]Therefore, since we are receiving a kingdom that cannot be shaken, let us be thankful, and so worship God acceptably with reverence and awe, [29]for our "God is a consuming fire."

Andy shaped his sermon around the differences between the first paragraph, beginning with "You have not come" and the second paragraph, beginning with "But you have come." He contrasted the gloom of Mount Sinai with the glory of Mount Zion; he spoke of Moses the mediator of the old covenant and of Jesus the mediator of a new covenant. He finished by urging us to heed the warning in the third paragraph and to respond with worship as in the fourth paragraph.

As I listened, I evaluated his message according to Campbell Morgan's three characteristics of a good sermon: truth, clarity, and passion. Initially, I gave him five stars for each one: what he said was orthodox; I had no difficulty in following his line of thought; and throughout he was "burning with fire" like Mount Sinai. On reflection, however, I reduced his rating for truth to four stars, not because of what he said but because of what was unsaid. I sensed there was a missing note and because that missing note was what I felt the readers of Hebrews would have been passionate about, I cut Andy back to four stars for passion as well. The missing note related to the clauses, "You have come to Mount Zion" and "We are receiving a kingdom." Knowing that my concern was based more on feeling than fact, I determined to give it more thought, particularly before I met with Mark Mullins mid-afternoon.

Charlotte went to the bedroom after lunch for her Sunday afternoon nap; I went to the study. In an hour's time, Mark would be pursuing the question of Abraham's current position in the after-life and I knew related questions would surface that might affect my status in *this* life. I did some reading on the Hebrews passage that had sparked his question, made some notes, and then drove to Gloria Jean's coffee shop in Buderim.

I found Mark sitting at a table for two with his large, black, leather-covered Bible in front of him. I humbly placed my small, red, pocket New Testament on the table and took our coffee orders to the counter. I returned to find Mark had opened his Bible to Hebrews 11 so, not bothering with small talk, I waited for him to revisit the question he had raised at the home group. I didn't have long to wait.

"Ed, I've read Hebrews right through since Wednesday to make sure the question I raised is relevant to the context of the book. I believe it is. When I asked if Abraham was in heaven, you said you believed he was but you didn't tell me why. I'm keen to hear your reasons."

I felt put on the spot, as if Mark were forcing me to take the worms out of the tin one at a time. My pocket New Testament beside his big Bible looked as insignificant as I felt. I began my response cautiously: "Mark, I've been on a theological or, more specifically, eschatological journey for a couple of years and I don't profess to have everything worked out. When I said that I believed Abraham was in heaven, I used the word 'believe' less as used in the Apostles' Creed and more as in 'I believe we're in for a wet summer.' My rather loose conviction that Abraham is in heaven is based on the assumption that my journey has been heading in the right direction. To be honest, I'm reluctant to enlarge on my wanderings because they've been taking me away from views that are held strongly at SCIF."

"Ed, my medical studies and experience have taught me to diagnose in order to determine whether a patient's physical or mental condition is consistent with good health or indicative of some disease. I often sit in church diagnosing the preacher, asking myself, as it were, whether the symptoms presented in his sermon match the good health presented in the Bible. I don't listen with a negative mindset but with a desire to be sure of the truth.

If your journey *is* heading in the right direction, I want to go there so please feel at ease in sharing with me. As a doctor, I take the issue of patient confidentiality seriously. I extend to you the same degree of confidentiality with respect to anything you share with me this afternoon. Furthermore, I am the one who has taken the initiative to ask about matters that put pressure on you so you need not fear that you are disloyal to SCIF if you answer the questions honestly."

"I appreciate your encouraging comments, Mark. If we start with the question you asked about whether Abraham is in heaven, I'm sure it will open up the issues I have been wrestling with of late. Please read Hebrews 11:39–40." As Mark read the verses, I determined to involve him as much as possible in discussing them to avoid any impression that I was urging him to adopt my point of view.

> These were all commended for their faith, yet none of them received what had been promised. [40]God had planned something better for us so that only together with us would they be made perfect.

"It's very easy when reading a passage like this to think that the word 'us' refers to us who live in the twenty-first century, but does it, Mark?"

"I must admit that I've tended to include myself when pronouns like 'us' occur in the Bible," he said, "but in this case, 'us' refers to the writer and the original readers of the letter to the Hebrews."

"Correct," I said. "And who is represented by 'them?'"

"Abraham and the men and women of faith in the Old Testament, many of whom are mentioned in this chapter."

"Right. So we have two groups both of which are to be made perfect at the same time. When we compare the two verses, it would appear that the words 'what had been promised' and the words 'made perfect' refer to the same thing. Would you agree?"

Mark re-read the verses, thought for a moment and replied, "Seems reasonable. At least the former would seem to include the latter."

"What had Abraham been promised that he hadn't received?" I asked.

"His eternal inheritance, entrance into the heavenly city," said Mark.

"Yes," I said. "The connection between the promise and the city is clear from Hebrews 11:9–10." I read the verses:

> By faith he made his home in the promised land like a stranger in a foreign country; he lived in tents, as did Isaac and Jacob, who were heirs with him of the same promise. [10]For he was looking forward to the city with foundations, whose architect and builder is God.

Mark sought clarification: "Let me see if I'm on the right track. You seem to be saying that to be made perfect is to experience the promise of entering into the heavenly city and that this is to happen at the same time for both the Old Testament believers and the readers of the book of Hebrews."

"That's a good summary," I said. "And what word in the text supports your statement that it will happen for both groups at the same time?"

"The word 'together,'" he said.

"That's how the NIV has translated the Greek which says, 'Not without us.'"

"Sounds like 'together' to me." He reflected for several minutes then exclaimed: "The word 'together' occurs in 1 Thessalonians 4:17. It may be a parallel reference."

I waited as he turned to the passage and read:

> After that, we who are still alive and are left will be caught up together with them in the clouds to meet the Lord in the air. And so we will be with the Lord forever.

Mark was so excited at the perceived relevance of what he'd just read that he continued: "Here are the same two groups experiencing together, on one occasion, entry into the presence of the Lord. The occasion is the return of Christ and the experience is the resurrection of the dead and the rapture of the living."

I knew Mark was well-grounded in end-times teaching about the rapture so I assumed his excitement meant that his futuristic understanding of the rapture answered his questions about Hebrews 11:39–40. The worms might remain in the can after all. I was wrong. He continued: "So Abraham is not in the heavenly city yet because the rapture has not yet occurred. He's still waiting. And if Abraham is not in the heavenly city, no one is. And what about all those words of comfort given at Christian funerals where the bereaved are told their deceased loved ones have entered the pearly gates and are walking on streets of gold?"

I assumed Mark's question was rhetorical and remained silent. His conclusion was valid if the rapture was still future. I was not about to suggest otherwise. I hoped he would just go away and devise an alternative funeral service for departed Christians. Our coffees were cold but we sipped them in silence nevertheless. As I looked at Mark's reflective face, I could almost hear the cogs whirring inside. It was asking too much to think he would let the matter rest. He broke the silence: "Ed, you said you believed Abraham *was* in heaven. I asked earlier for your reasons and so far I haven't heard one of them." He said no more but the look on his face said he would not tolerate any attempt to dodge the issue.

Mark went to order fresh coffees while I hoped my mobile would ring with an urgent message from Charlotte to come home immediately because important visitors had unexpectedly arrived. As I looked wistfully at the silent phone in my hand, I struggled to know where to begin my response to Mark.

The expectant look on Mark's face was still there when he returned with the drinks. I fortified myself with a long sip and said, "Mark, your link between Hebrews 11:39–40 and the rapture in 1 Thessalonians 4 seems reasonable. Both passages refer to the fulfilment of eschatological hope for the dead and the living at a particular occasion in the future. If that occasion is still future then, as you logically pointed out, Abraham is not in the heavenly city. I think you can see why I haven't rushed into explaining why I believe Abraham *is* in heaven."

Mark spread his lips and hissed as he breathed in through his clenched teeth. "I certainly can," he said. For some moments he was silent and I wondered if his commitment to confidentiality was caving in to compromise, under a higher obligation to blow the whistle on me. When he said, "You're a brave man, Ed," I didn't know if he was calling me a hero or a heretic. His prolonged, intense look made me feel like a patient about to receive a terminal diagnosis. Instead, Mark asked, "Am I correct in thinking that my request for reasons for your believing Abraham is in heaven boils down to a request for why you believe the second coming of Christ has already occurred?"

"You've forced me out of the closet," Mark.

"It's a legal maxim that 'No man should be condemned unheard' so please feel free to share the grounds for your position but, given that I'm reeling from shock, don't be surprised if I side with the prosecution rather than the defense."

If only my phone would ring. It didn't, but Mark's did. I only heard his side of the short conversation: "What happened? . . . I'm on my way." Pocketing his mobile phone, he said, "Ed, I have to go. Ryan has come off his bike and grazed his leg. Nothing serious by the sound of it but Cathy's worked up and wants me to check him out. I'm sorry, but we'll have to adjourn this discussion till another time."

Before I could say anything, he was gone. *He* might have been sorry; *I* wasn't. Not that I was totally relieved: Mark's reference to adjourning the session left me feeling like a criminal on remand pending an appearance before the prosecutor on a date to be determined.

38

Just Around the Corner

Charlotte and I continued to meet with Andy and Linda at Sizzlers. The anticipation of reunion with the Harmons and the growing interest in the conference restored their appetites so all four of us made the most of our smorgasbord meals. At our third meeting, after an update on Anna's deteriorating health, Andy said, "Enough about *our* situation, what's happening with the Sutherlands?"

Charlotte gave an enthusiastic account of our first home group and I mentioned how we had farewelled Josh Wilson as he left for Bundaberg.

"Anna came home beaming last Wednesday night," said Linda, "and was more conversational than she's been in weeks. She can't wait for tonight's meeting. She also made reference to Josh's departure. I sensed she was sorry he would no longer be part of the group."

I felt Linda may have been hoping Anna's affections were shifting from Paul to Josh but, not knowing how to pursue the matter, I changed the topic by asking Andy about the conference.

"Chuck and Susan Harmon are excited about their visit and so are we. Because he's so well-known from his books, we're expecting a good turnout. Later this week the conference committee will be sending out another round of promotional material with the added detail that Dr. Harmon's topic will be, 'The last book in the Bible: an urgent message for these last days.' On Sunday morning, we'll be enlisting volunteers to help with fitting out the tent before the conference, and with car parking, catering, and ushering during the conference."

Outwardly I tried to empathize with Andy's excitement but inwardly I wondered if Dr. Harmon's views would only confirm G.K. Chesterton's comment in *Orthodoxy* about the book of Revelation: "Though St. John the

Evangelist saw many strange monsters in his vision, he saw no creature so wild as one of his own commentators!"

Attendance that evening at the home group was the same as the previous Wednesday night except for the absence of Josh and the presence of Cathy Mullins in place of Mark. Cathy's effervescent personality enabled her to converse with ease and encouraged me to believe that Mark had maintained his commitment to confidentiality. I was reminded of my own need to respect patient confidentiality when, the report at Sizzlers of Anna's health still fresh in my mind, I noticed her pallid face and puffy eyes. I hoped her obvious pleasure at being part of the home group hid her symptoms from others. When I gave opportunity for people to share personal matters with the group, Anna said nothing about her health and nor did I. After several prayed for group members and the forthcoming conference, we began our discussion of last Sunday's sermon.

"Time for a quiz on Andy's sermon last Sunday," I said. Several opened their Bibles to Hebrews 12 causing me to quip, "At least some of you know what chapter he preached on—and where to find answers to the questions I'm about to ask." One or two sheepishly closed their Bibles and I smiled to allay their embarrassment.

"Andy's sermon was largely a series of contrasts," I said. "What two mountains were contrasted?"

"Mount Sinai and Mount Zion," answered Lauren.

"What else did Andy contrast?" I asked. Rapid answers followed:

"The old covenant and the new covenant," said Elizabeth.

"The gloom of the one and the glory of the other," added Charlotte.

"Moses the mediator of the one and Jesus the mediator of the other," said Anna.

"Well done," I said. "Sounds like you were all awake during the sermon. Let's read the text Andy preached on and look for other contrasts that may be in it." We read Hebrews 12:18–29. I read verse 18 and invited the others to each read a verse clockwise round the room:

> You have not come to a mountain that can be touched and that is burning with fire; to darkness, gloom and storm; [19]to a trumpet blast or to such a voice speaking words that those who heard it begged that no further word be spoken to them, [20]because they could not bear what was commanded: "If even an animal touches the mountain, it must be stoned." [21]The sight was so terrifying that Moses said, "I am trembling with fear."
>
> [22]But you have come to Mount Zion, to the heavenly Jerusalem, the city of the living God. You have come to thousands upon thousands of angels in joyful assembly, [23]to the church

of the firstborn, whose names are written in heaven. You have come to God, the judge of all men, to the spirits of righteous men made perfect, ²⁴to Jesus the mediator of a new covenant, and to the sprinkled blood that speaks a better word than the blood of Abel.

²⁵See to it that you do not refuse him who speaks. If they did not escape when they refused him who warned them on earth, how much less will we, if we turn away from him who warns us from heaven? ²⁶At that time his voice shook the earth, but now he has promised, "Once more I will shake not only the earth but also the heavens." ²⁷The words "once more" indicate the removing of what can be shaken—that is, created things—so that what cannot be shaken may remain.

²⁸Therefore, since we are receiving a kingdom that cannot be shaken, let us be thankful, and so worship God acceptably with reverence and awe, ²⁹for our "God is a consuming fire."

"Did anyone observe any other contrasts in the passage?" I asked.

John said, "There's a contrast in verses 26–28 between a heaven and earth that can be shaken and a coming kingdom that cannot be shaken."

"A perceptive observation," I said. I was about to ask if others had noticed additional contrasts but John continued, "Ed, I see a problem here: at Real Life you quoted a passage at the end of Matthew 16 where Jesus said some of his disciples would not die before he returned to usher in his kingdom. The problem is that the passage we are considering here in Hebrews 12 says that heaven and earth will not only be shaken but removed before the kingdom comes. Heaven and earth are still with us, so did the kingdom really come when Jesus said it would?"

"A very good question, John," I said. "The solution to the problem is not to disregard the clear time frame Jesus gave for the coming of the kingdom. He said it was at hand when he was on earth and, as you point out, he said it would come before some of his disciples died. That much is plain. The solution rests with our understanding of the shaking and removal of heaven and earth. You will notice that verse 26 is a quotation. It comes from Haggai 2:6 where the prophet, like other Old Testament prophets, used descriptions of astronomical upheavals to represent the commotions on earth described in the very next verse (Haggai 2:7) as a shaking of the nations. Later in the same chapter (verses 21–22), he uses similar language."

"What then is the meaning of the quotation in Hebrews 12," asked John, "if the words are not to be taken literally?"

"In preparation for tonight's home group, I made some notes from Adam Clarke's commentary on this passage. He says the shaking of the earth and the heavens probably refers to 'the approaching destruction of Jerusalem, and the total abolition of the political and ecclesiastical constitution of the Jews; the one being signified by the *earth*, the other by *heaven*; for the Jewish state and worship are frequently thus termed in the prophetic writings.'

"John, earlier this evening, you insightfully noted the contrast in Hebrews 12:26–28 between a heaven and earth that can be shaken and a coming kingdom that cannot be shaken. If Adam Clarke is correct in identifying the shaking of heaven and earth with the destruction of Jerusalem, then it is reasonable to think that the kingdom the Hebrews were receiving is the very same kingdom that Jesus predicted would come with power before some of the disciples died. The destruction of Jerusalem occurred in AD 70, about forty years after Jesus' prediction, so its fulfilment was quite feasible."

Thankfully John let the matter rest. How satisfied he was with my answer I didn't know. The puzzled looks on some faces in the circle made me wonder if they were totally confused or, worse, knew what I was saying but disapproved because it was seriously at variance with what they believed.

I suddenly realized what I had done. I had brought into an authorized meeting of SCIF members, views that had previously only been touched on with individuals or at the Real Life meetings. I decided to retreat to safer ground by discussing the warning in verse 25 and the call to worship in verse 28. Before I could start, Jack said he had a question. I was pleased he did not pursue the issue John had raised but my relief was short-lived.

"Ed," he said, "in verse 22, the writer says the Hebrew Christians 'have come to Mount Zion, to the heavenly Jerusalem, the city of the living God.' Does that mean they would soon die and go to heaven?"

"Jack, to answer your question we need to see that the writer is making a significant contrast between his readers and the Old Testament believers. Take, for example, the Old Testament believer, Abraham, as recorded in Hebrews 11:9–10:

> By faith he [Abraham] made his home in the promised land like a stranger in a foreign country; he lived in tents, as did Isaac and Jacob, who were heirs with him of the same promise. For he was looking forward to the city with foundations, whose architect and builder is God.

"Abraham was looking forward to 'the heavenly Jerusalem, the city of the living God,' to use the words you quoted." Cathy interrupted my line of reasoning:

"Ed, I've been reading ahead in Hebrews to prepare for Andy's sermon next Sunday on chapter 13. In verse 14 of that chapter it says, 'For here we do not have an enduring city, but we are looking for the city that is to come.' This seems to be saying much the same about the first century Christians as you just read about Abraham in chapter 11. Both groups were looking forward to entering the heavenly city so why do you speak of a *significant* contrast?"

"You're right, Cathy, that there is a similarity between the Old Testament believers and the New Testament believers, with both groups anticipating heaven, but there is this difference: if you look at Hebrews 11:13 you'll see that the Old Testament believers only saw the city from a distance but, according to the verse Jack quoted, Hebrews 12:22, the readers '*have come* to the heavenly Jerusalem, the city of the living God.' For one group, the heavenly city was a long way off; for the other group, it was just around the corner. That is a significant contrast."

Aware that his question had not really been answered, Jack revisited it: "I'm still unclear about the meaning of their having come to the heavenly Jerusalem. Were they about to die or not?"

"Sorry, Jack," I apologized, and then paused to consider how I could satisfy him without provoking further, more controversial, questions. With some prevarication, I said, "Jack, the Old Testament believers did not go to heaven when they died but they believed that they would enter the heavenly city in the distant future. The New Testament believers were told that they were closer (I should have said 'close') to entering the city, namely, at the second coming of Christ. On that occasion they would be joined by believers who had died, including those of the Old Testament like Abraham."

Jack seemed to be happy with my answer but I suspected that his understanding of the word "closer" meant closer for the Hebrews than for Abraham. I did not tell him that the words, "*have come* to Mount Zion, to the heavenly Jerusalem," seemed to imply that the Hebrews were on the verge of entering in, that what Abraham had seen afar off was for them very close because the coming of Christ was very close. Verse 28 says these same Hebrew Christians were "receiving a kingdom." The coming of Christ and the coming of the kingdom were promised to occur before some of the disciples died (Matthew 16:27–28). At the time of the writing of Hebrews, both events were therefore very close so the verb "have come" was not inappropriate.

I hurriedly steered the focus of the group to the safe topic of worship in verse 28 of the passage we'd read at the beginning of our discussion. I'd had enough eschatological controversy of late without inviting more. My relationship with Cathy's husband Mark was under serious threat over whether Abraham had gone to heaven at a rapture that was already passed and now Cathy had elicited from me a comment that was dangerously akin to the same topic. Was it merely ironic or had Mark already spoken with his wife about my shocking views? What would they talk about later that evening when Mark asked about the home group? How long would it be before Mark reported me to his father, Stan Mullins, chairman of the church elders, or before Cathy's crusading mother, Robyn Bradford, used her recently acquired computing skills to circulate my heretical views?

39

Conference Preparations

The very next day, Robyn sent me an email. My name was one of many in the address field. I was surprised at the extent of her contact list but relieved that the content of the email was about the fast-approaching conference and not my heretical views. Robyn, as chair of the promotions sub-committee, was on the job. With a passion I admired, but did not share, she wrote:

> Dear Brothers and Sisters,
>
> How privileged we are to live in the final days of this present age with the exciting prospect of being caught up to meet the Lord in the air at the soon-to-occur rapture of the saints.
>
> Should the Lord tarry, we will also have the privilege of participating in SCIF's first-ever prophetic conference. Noted end-times speaker, Dr. Chuck Harmon, will unveil from the book of Revelation the horrors that await the unbeliever and the glories that await the believer.
>
> The conference is therefore of relevance to all so let us labor diligently to promote this strategic event. Colorful leaflets are available in the church foyer for distribution in your neighborhood and attached to this email is a copy for you to forward to friends.
>
> Having read all of Dr. Harmon's books, I can assure you that his messages will interest, inform, and influence those you invite.
>
> Yours, as we see the day approaching,
> Robyn Bradford.

Robyn's email was followed by daily conference updates and passionate promotional pleas laced with five-minutes-to-midnight comments.

My resolve not to letter-box my neighborhood and my skepticism about the value of the conference provoked serious self-analysis. Was I so sure of the error of Chuck Harmon's position that my pessimistic attitude was justified? Was I afraid to expose myself to his teaching lest he make a stronger case for *his* position than I could make for *mine*? Would all my months of eschatological wrestling prove to be in vain? Given that I held a view at variance with the church, not to mention many better scholars than myself, should I not acknowledge my pride and adopt a more teachable spirit? I used to tell my students that tertiary study involved consideration of alternative views to our own and here I was hypocritically prejudging Dr. Harmon before hearing him.

To assuage a mild attack of guilt, I decided to forward the conference brochure to Luke Rodman and David Barnes with a brief and innocuous note: "You may be interested in the attached." David would be pleased that I appeared to be siding with the truth and was trying to rescue Luke from error. If the two of them came to the conference, I was sure their motivations would differ.

On the Wednesday before the conference, we had no sooner arrived at Sizzlers than the Zimmermans pulled up beside our car with two passengers in the back seat. The Harmons had arrived two days earlier than expected. Andy and Linda were overjoyed, a noticeable contrast to the sadness of previous Wednesdays when they had delivered progressively disappointing health reports on Anna's loss of kidney function.

After brief introductions in the car park, we ordered six salad-bar meals and requested a round table to facilitate conversation. Since their arrival in Australia, Andy and Linda had begun to blend into the local population but Chuck and Susan Harmon were so conspicuously American that Aussie heads among the lunch clientele turned as if a couple of burka-clad women had entered a Jewish synagogue. Chuck appeared to be a young sixty-year old. Andy was tall but Chuck was a head taller. For a lunch meal at Sizzlers at the start of a Sunshine Coast summer, he was over-dressed with his red-checked sports jacket, cream silk shirt, and dark, silver-speckled bow tie. His unwrinkled, smoothly shaved face contrasted with the more weathered look of sun-drenched Queenslanders. Susan Harmon, dressed in various shades of pink from her scarf to her high-heeled shoes, looked equally out of place. She appeared to be considerably younger than Chuck and quite handsome though the heavy layers of makeup, including pink lipstick, left me wondering what the real Susan Harmon looked like under the camouflage.

If external differences initially put distance between us, the warmth and genuineness of the Harmons' Southern charm soon drew us together. Within minutes, Charlotte and I were chatting with them like old friends. By the time we had sampled the salad and dessert bars to our gastronomical satisfaction, we had ranged in our conversation topics from the joys of grandparenting to the similarities and differences between the American Democrats and the Australian Labor Party.

When I returned to the table with a cup of coffee, I found Susan had changed places with her husband so I was now seated beside Chuck. With his wife chatting with Linda, he turned to me and said, "Andy tells me you're a retired New Testament professor."

Overlooking his misuse of the word "professor" in an Australian context, I made a brief reference to my teaching career at AIMS and asked, "Have you always been interested in the book of Revelation?"

"Before I went to theological seminary, I steered clear of the book, regarding it as too confusing and controversial, but through my studies I saw how the book fits into God's plan for the consummation of the ages and I've loved it, studied it, and preached it ever since."

I had no doubt about the direction Chuck would take in his exposition but I tried not to betray indifference: "I commend you for tackling such a difficult New Testament book as the focus for the conference."

"It's true that many find the book difficult and for that reason they neglect it," he said. "I hope to generate a renewed interest in Revelation during the conference by showing the big picture of the book and, in particular, its relevance at this crisis point in human history."

"Do you feel the book of Revelation is more relevant to our generation than to previous generations?"

"Indeed I do. The whole of Revelation from chapter 4 onwards refers to the future and since chapter 3 concludes with a reference to our generation in its description of the Laodicean age, the age we are living in, that future is soon to become the present. We are on the verge of what has been called 'the climax of the ages.'"

Two questions came to my mind: *Was* most of the book of Revelation yet to be fulfilled and *was* the letter to the Laodiceans prophetic of our generation? I was tempted to raise the questions but felt it would be in poor taste to begin arguing with a friend of the pastor and the newly-arrived guest speaker at a conference much anticipated by the church. However, Chuck noticed my hesitation in replying to his comment and asked, "Is that how you see the book of Revelation?"

He was putting me in the hot seat. I tried to wriggle out of it. "Chuck, a few minutes ago, I commended you for tackling the difficult book of Revelation. I confess that I am among those who find it difficult so I envy your assurance about how it should be interpreted." Chuck smiled and I felt my stratagem was working but when with a penetrating gaze he prolonged the smile but said nothing, I tried again: "I'm looking forward to your conference talks which, I'm sure, will help me towards the kind of assurance you have." He smiled again. Meanwhile, I tried to justify to myself the use of the words "looking forward" on the grounds that his talks would indeed give me greater assurance about the book of Revelation, assurance not that his views were correct but that they were wrong and could therefore be eliminated from my search for the correct interpretation. But I was prejudging the man again so committed myself to attending the conference with an open mind.

I was pleased when Andy rescued me from the hot seat by interrupting the buzz of conversation around the table: "We need to get these good folks home for a rest. They haven't fully recovered from jet lag and they face a busy few days. There'll be plenty of time to get to know them better during the exciting weekend before us. Don't forget tomorrow morning." I recalled that with such a busy week, home groups had been cancelled and members were urged to meet at the church on Thursday morning for a working bee.

On the way home, Charlotte exuded some of Andy's excitement. "What a lovely couple! I'm really looking forward to getting to know Susan better and to listening to Chuck's talks. We're in for a wonderful weekend, Ed, and I hope you're not planning to sabotage it by intruding with your weird ideas."

Somewhat abashed by her comment, I struggled to relieve her concerns by saying, "I don't have all the answers, Charlotte, and you'll be pleased to know I intend to keep an open mind as I listen to the talks on Revelation. An open mind doesn't mean an unthinking mind but if, perchance, I disagree with something Chuck says, I promise I won't cause a scene by interrupting his message." She seemed happy with my response.

When Charlotte went for an afternoon nap, I checked my emails. Two caught my attention. The first was from David Barnes:

> Ed, many thanks for your invitation to the prophetic conference this coming weekend. I'm planning to attend. Chuck Harmon's books have considerably helped my understanding of eschatology and his views are certainly in line with the doctrinal position of AIMS. I look forward to catching up with you.

The second email was from Luke Rodman. My expectation that his interest in the conference would differ from David's was confirmed when he began his email without reference to the invitation I'd sent. He told me he was working as a defense lawyer in a prestigious law firm and was studying part-time at AIMS on his MDiv, enjoying it but not always agreeing with everything taught. To my surprise, he added a PS to the email: "By the way, thanks for the invite to the end-times conference. I'm trying to adjust my schedule to fit it in."

The news that David and Luke were planning to attend the conference added to Charlotte's excitement. "That *is* good news," she gushed. "Should we save their having to travel several times to the coast by inviting them to stay with us?"

She was thinking my thoughts after me but instead of responding with a simple, "Yes," I asked, "You're sure it's not too much for you?"

My use of domestic psychology to cement her suggestion in place seemed to work. With her body language showing umbrage that I seemed to doubt her hospitality skills, she said, "We *do* have a couple of spare bedrooms, Edward, and what's a couple of extra mouths to feed. Get on your computer and tell them they'll be welcome."

I was pleased at her enthusiasm and doubly pleased when both David and Luke wrote accepting our invitation. Having two friends from the past for the weekend might offset my expected dissatisfaction with the content of the convention sessions.

When Charlotte and I arrived at the church shortly after 6:00 a.m. next morning, I was surprised to see a score of adults chatting in the car park. I expected all the volunteers to be retirees but was pleased to see John and Elizabeth, Anna and Lauren, and working people like Mark Mullins who had taken the morning off to lend a hand. The good turn-out reflected the enthusiasm for SCIF's first eschatology conference.

Stan Mullins gathered the group together and outlined the tasks for the day: assisting the professionals in the erection of the marquee and the platform, placing seating for the crowds expected to attend the conference, setting up a bookstall at the entrance to the marquee, and preparing the church hall for the conference meals.

A huge semi-trailer arrived on schedule and within minutes the driver and his offsider took control in directing the volunteers. It was hot work carrying canvas sections, spreading them out, and hammering in dozens of steel tent pegs. When all was ready for raising the three huge center poles, we lined up with a long rope and formed what looked like a tug-of-war team. In short time the marquee rose and we felt we deserved a break.

As we made our way to the hall for a drink, I noticed passing cars slow down or stop, the occupants no doubt wondering at first if a circus had come to town, but driving on when they saw the long banner Robyn Bradford had attached to the fence. It read: "Friday night to Sunday morning. Come and hear why the end is near. Details at the door of the tent."

In the hall a dozen large trestle tables had been set up and covered with butcher paper, smaller tables were nested in every available corner, crockery was stacked on the servery, salad vegetables were spread out on kitchen benches, and large saucepans of pasta and potatoes were boiling on the stove. Morning tea had not been forgotten: tea, coffee, cold drinks and an assortment of sandwiches and cakes awaited the workers.

With a coffee in one hand and a paper plate in the other, loaded with egg and lettuce sandwiches and a custard slice, I made my way to some empty seats in a corner. I was soon joined by Mark Mullins, similarly loaded with refreshments.

"It's good to see so many enthusiastic volunteers," he said.

"At the rate we're going, the tent should be fitted out by lunch time," I replied.

"Are you looking forward to the teaching this weekend, Ed?"

"It should be thought-provoking, Mark. I'm sure Dr. Harmon will be a stimulating speaker. I met him yesterday and we had a bit of a chat. He's quite passionate about his topic."

"Speaking of yesterday, Ed, I was sorry there was no home group last night. It was my turn to attend and I was really looking forward to it, hoping to get some answers to my questions, and Cathy's. She came home from last Wednesday's meeting full of questions but thrilled that she'd been able to contribute to the discussion."

Fearing that in chatting about their questions my views had surfaced, I tried, unsuccessfully, to change the subject by asking, "How is Ryan after his bike accident?"

"He's fine. Just a graze. A dab of Dettol, a couple of Band-Aids and some sympathy and he was happily back on his bike. Which reminds me, Ed: Ryan's accident interrupted our recent conversation at Gloria Jean's coffee shop. You were responding to my question about whether Abraham was in heaven when Cathy phoned. I rushed home but as I drove there, I confess I was flabbergasted, thinking less about Ryan and more about your suggestion that Christ has already returned."

"I'm sorry to have caused you concern, Mark. The journey to my present—and to be honest, tentative—position has not been easy but one controlling factor has been a commitment to hearing the text of Scripture even though it puts me offside with the position of others. I have no plans to be a disruptive influence in your family, in our home group, or in the church."

"Ed, I appreciate your candor. Permit me to be candid too." I braced myself as Mark continued. "Ed, I've given a lot of thought to our discussion at Gloria Jean's last Sunday week and I've come to the conclusion that your position, albeit tentative, is so left of center as to be inadmissible. I can't believe that so many could be so wrong for so long. I only hope that the conference this weekend will help you to reject your tentative position and affirm the position of the church."

"What does Cathy think about the issue?" I asked.

"I've avoided it for two reasons: one, I promised I would respect your confidence, and I have; and, two, I want to protect Cathy from having to answer embarrassing questions about you that her mother might ask. Robyn is suspicious—and justifiably so—of your end-times view."

Stan Mullins interrupted our conversation by recalling us to work. I thanked Mark for his frankness and returned, somewhat subdued, to help with setting up the stage and placing 300 chairs in position, sure there were too many and not sure if I wanted to sit on any one of them.

40

A Panoramic View of Revelation

I woke on Friday morning with unexpected enthusiasm for the weekend ahead. If I wasn't free to publicly discuss eschatology with the guest speaker, I anticipated vigorous debate on our back veranda with my friends from AIMS. Charlotte was excited too: she looked forward to being the perfect hostess to David and Luke at home, and at church she looked forward to Chuck Harmon's talks and her role as part of the catering team. I only hoped her joy would sustain her should she extend herself beyond her normal endurance limits.

The opening session of the conference was scheduled for 7:30 p.m. Charlotte and I arrived at the tent site at 6:30. She had further work to do in the kitchen in preparation for Saturday's meals and I was rostered as a door steward before the meeting and a salesman at the book table after it. We were by no means the first to arrive: Arthur Bradford was up a step-ladder adjusting the angle of the flood lights over the entrance; Jack Wilson was on stage testing the microphone by counting into it; John and Elizabeth, torches in hand and dressed in orange iridescent jackets, were stationed at the gate as parking attendants. They did not have to wait long for the first carload of visitors to arrive, my signal to position myself opposite Cathy Mullins in the foyer of the tent. Together we handed out song sheets and conference programs along with a warm welcome. We were kept so busy that, to my surprise, the tent was more than half full by 7:15 and people were still pouring in.

I hardly recognized Luke Rodman. The former wispy-bearded student I had known was clean-shaven and dressed like a successful partner in a large law firm. I asked him to keep two seats for Charlotte and me. David Barnes arrived just before starting time. He was not alone. With him was a short bald-headed man wearing half-frame glasses, none other than Alex

Symons. I did my best to avoid discrimination in welcoming them in spite of vivid recollections of the circumstances of my dismissal from AIMS. Alex was pleasant enough but the smile he gave from one side of his mouth seemed to say, "Dr. Harmon's going to set you straight, mate."

People were still coming in as the opening song was being sung to the accompaniment of an electronic keyboard hired for the occasion and played by Linda Zimmerman. I felt sure that technical unfamiliarity with the instrument rather than a generous spirit had induced Mrs. Beecroft to relinquish the organ stool. The sound of almost 300 people singing "How Great Thou Art" stirred even my stoic emotions.

When the last of the latecomers had arrived, I joined Luke. Charlotte was still in the kitchen but arrived as Stan Mullins was welcoming everyone. He was not his confident self, perhaps because he was not used to large crowds or because he was overawed at the success of the conference planning. If the latter, I shared his sentiment. Robyn Bradford's emails had paid off. Stan invited people to stand when he asked, "Who's from the Sunshine Coast?" More than half the audience stood. It took him nearly ten minutes to cover the remainder as he extended the geographical range of his questions that included, "Is there anyone here from further north than Maryborough?" Josh Wilson called out "Bundaberg" and stood with a dozen others. At least fifty people stood when Brisbane was mentioned. Toowoomba in the west was not far behind and even Lismore in northern New South Wales was represented. Charlotte turned to me, not with an O-you-of-little-faith look but with open mouth and hands held against her cheeks in wonderment. I nodded with an affirming smile. Two rows in front of me I saw a bald head turn to David Barnes. Alex Symons was also impressed.

Stan was about to give some announcements when a group of five young people stood and shouted, "You forgot Tasmania." By this time Stan had gained more confidence and responded with "A very warm welcome to half the population of Tasmania." A number of people laughed at Stan's uncharacteristic attempt at humor. He then held up the conference program and urged everyone to take note of session times and to complete the tear-off booking slip if meals were required.

After a Southern Gospel song from the Zimmerman family, Andy came to the microphone and said, "Who's from Tennessee in the United States?" Chuck and Susan Harmon, who were seated on the platform behind Andy, stood with the rest of the Zimmerman family.

"Our family is from Tennessee," said Andy, "and we *did* know the Harmons when we lived in the States, very well indeed. Chuck was the senior pastor of the church where I served before coming to Australia. I can assure you from personal experience that the Harmons are the finest of people and that our guest speaker is a gifted pastor, author, and radio and conference speaker, particularly on the topic before us this weekend. After you hear him tonight, you will want to return for the other sessions listed in your program. You will also want to purchase his best-known book, *Hurtling to Armageddon*, and others he has written, all available from the bookstall in the foyer."

Andy had the audience sing the conference theme song, "He's Coming Soon," and then said, "Please welcome our guest speaker, Dr. Chuck Harmon, all the way from the United States of America. Prolonged applause and the odd whistle—not, of course, from SCIF members—allowed Chuck time to adjust the microphone to his height and to arrange his notes on the lectern.

"Susan and I are delighted to be visiting our dear friends the Zimmermans and to have this opportunity to spend the weekend with y'all. By the way, if you should have trouble understanding my accent, I'll call on Andy to translate for you. Thank you for your applause. It's nice to have it *before* I speak because I don't always get it *after* I speak. I'm reminded of an occasion back home when the emcee at our son's twenty-first birthday celebration began to behave strangely. He pulled a large table into the center of the room on which he placed a smaller table and then added a chair to the smaller table. The stack was about seven feet high. He turned to us all and said, 'Would you like to see me do a double somersault over this pile of furniture?' We all expressed our eagerness for such a daring spectacle so he limbered up with a few stretch exercises, went to the side of the room and, like an athlete at the starting block, prepared for a run-up. We waited expectantly. To our surprise, he rose slowly, walked seriously to the center of the room and said, 'This could be dangerous: I could knock the chair on the way over, fall and break my neck. Just in case I don't come out this alive, I'd appreciate y'all giving me my applause before I perform.' We all clapped. He started for the starting block but before he reached it, he paused, turned, and returned to the center of the room. With his hands on his hips, he shook his head and said, "If y'all think I'm gonna risk my life for such a lousy applause as that, you've got another think coming.' We never did get to see him do that double somersault."

Chuck then put his hands on his hips, looked sternly around the tent and said, "If, after the applause you gave me, you think I'm gonna speak . . . " He paused, relaxed his hands and said with a smile, "I mean, because of your enthusiastic applause, you *will* get to hear the message tonight." An even louder applause followed.

As the basis for his message, Chuck read the whole of the first chapter of Revelation and then said, "The book of Revelation divides Christians into at least three categories: there are those who understand it and love it; those who read it but don't understand it; and those who avoid it as too difficult and controversial. I hope that all of you will come to love it because it is such an important book for our generation, undoubtedly the last generation before the return of Christ." Robyn Bradford gave a loud "Amen, brother."

As I listened to Chuck, I mentally assigned myself to one of the three categories, conscious that I could move up a notch or two but not sure if I wanted to arrive at his understanding of the book. With a degree of effort, I recommitted to an open mind.

Chuck continued: "Look again at verse 19: 'Write, therefore, what you have seen, what is now and what will take place later.' This verse gives us the framework for an understanding of the whole book. Note the three time references in the verse: 'have seen' refers to the past, to the vision John saw in chapter 1 of Christ among the seven golden lampstands; 'what is now' refers to the seven churches in Asia whose then-present condition is recorded in the letters of chapters 2 and 3; and 'what will take place later' refers to the future. After a peek into heaven (chapters 4 and 5), John covers future events such as the tribulation (chapters 6 to 18), the second coming and millennium (chapters 19 and 20), and the eternal state in the new Jerusalem (chapters 21 and 22)."

"Easy-peasy," I thought. "That should solve the problems of people in categories two and three. Let's hope there are no hidden nasties in the fine print."

"The book of Revelation," Chuck summarized, "is thus a panoramic view of history from the first century to the end of time and beyond. Some of you may be wondering if the book of Revelation gives us any clues as to what stage of human history we are at and how soon the prophecies will begin to be fulfilled. I believe it does.

"The seven churches of chapters 2 and 3 represent successive stages in history beginning with Ephesus, which depicts the apostolic age, and ending with Laodicea, which represents the condition of the church immediately before the rapture."

Chuck proceeded to link the suffering church at Smyrna with the persecuted church of the second and third centuries, Pergamum with the state church founded by Constantine in the fourth century, Thyatira with the Roman church of the Middle Ages, Sardis with the reformation church of the sixteenth century, and Philadelphia with the era of missions from the eighteenth century. "The last of the seven," said Chuck, "predicts our day. On every hand we see lukewarmness, the very conditions Paul said in 2 Timothy 3 would characterize the last days: love of self, love of money, and love of pleasure. Never have we seen the world in the church as in our day: rock music in place of the rich heritage of our hymnody; quasi-religious floor shows in place of gospel proclamation; and the veneration of megachurch celebrities in place of the worship of God."

Chuck, cranking up for the climax of his message and overdressed for a sub-tropical summer, was wiping the sweat from his face like Pavarotti at the highpoint of an operatic aria. The audience was getting worked up too with outbursts of "Sock it to 'em, Chuck," and "Preach it, brother." Charlotte was clenching her fists as she nodded her head. I kept cool and dignified, as usual, as Chuck maintained his fervor: "We are in the last days of the last days, brothers and sisters. The Laodicean age has been with us for 200 years and in decline throughout that time. Christianity is at its lowest point ever and only the divine intervention of the rapture can rescue the believing remnant from the encircling morass. As our theme song says, 'He's coming soon!' But listen to our text, friends. The very first verse of the book says it is a revelation of 'what must soon take place' and verse 3 says, 'Blessed are those who hear it and take to heart what is written in it, because the time is near.' How blessed we are to be part of the rapture generation. 'Lift up your heads for your redemption draws near.'"

Chuck sat down accompanied by widespread amens and hallelujahs as Stan came forward to lead the theme song and to advertise the bookstall and Saturday's sessions. As they sang, I asked Charlotte to keep an eye on Luke and David and took up my position at the book table.

Business was brisk, some of Chuck's titles selling out within the first ten minutes. Alex Symons caught my eye as he pushed past the crowd in front of the table. Looking over his half-frames, he called chirpily, "Good to see you spreading the truth, Edward." Inwardly I winced and forced a smile for the next customer.

Well after 9:30, Charlotte brought our guests to the foyer and we went home for a late supper and a robust post-mortem on the first session of SCIF's inaugural prophetic conference.

41

Questioning the Panoramic View

Seated in the lounge sipping hot coffee and snacking on Charlotte's cheese muffins and lamingtons, we relished the company of friends from a previous life. Charlotte looked worn out so I marveled as for forty minutes she participated in the conversation. She then excused herself with, "Some of us have had a long day and, with another busy day tomorrow, I'll say 'Good night.'" I was pleased David and Luke showed no signs of following her lead because, late as it was, I wanted to hear their impressions of Chuck's message.

David seemed to read my thoughts as he asked, "What did you think of Dr. Harmon's talk, Ed?"

I replied guardedly: "He was easy to listen to, he has a good sense of humor, and he's certainly very passionate."

David didn't need much discernment to know my comments were evasive so he pressed a little harder: "What did you think of his use of Revelation 1:19 as the key to the whole book?"

"The three tenses in the text certainly reflect the content of the whole book. From John's perspective, there was a past: he'd just seen a vision of Christ; there was a present: he was living in the time of the seven churches—he's even said to have been a member of the church at Ephesus; and there was a future: a number of issues awaited fulfilment."

Luke broke in: "Ed, surely you don't mean you agree with everything he said."

Luke was tempting me away from my effort to keep the peace. I refused to be drawn. "Luke, your use of the word 'surely' suggests *you* don't agree with everything he said."

"You're right there."

"For example?"

"Do you want to get to bed tonight?"

"Give us one example," I said, "and we'll call it a day." I hoped the inclusive 'us' would prevent David from feeling we were about to gang up on him.

Luke sat forward on the edge of his armchair and, with a legal forefinger piercing the air, said, "Take Dr. Harmon's use of the clause, 'Write... what will take place later.' He believes 'later' refers to what will take place after the rapture. In his scheme of things, the rapture is yet to occur so most of Revelation has not been fulfilled in 2,000 years. That's a very long time yet Revelation 1:1 says the events of the book are 'soon to take place' and Revelation 1:3 says 'the time is near.' The words 'soon' and 'near' hardly square with 2,000 years but they are not inconsistent with 'later.' I put it to you that Dr. Harmon is reading his futurism into the text rather than getting it out of the text."

I felt Luke had a point but I was reluctant to affirm it so was pleased when David spoke up. "Luke, to pick up on your last sentence, I don't think Dr. Harmon professes to get his futurism out of the text you quoted. He merely sees the text as applying to a view of the future that he believes on other grounds."

"You're right, David. I stand corrected," Luke admitted, "but how do futurists like Dr. Harmon handle the imminence expressed in Revelation 1:1, 3?"

David continued: "Take the word 'soon.' The Greek behind it can also mean 'quickly' so it can refer, not to a time in the immediate future, but to speedy action when the time comes."

"I agree that the Greek can mean 'quickly' but that does not of itself justify postponing an event," Luke replied. "The use of 'quickly' frequently implies 'soon.' For example, in Acts 22:18 when Paul is told to get out of Jerusalem quickly, there is no suggestion that he delay his departure but that it be executed both soon and quickly. Again, when Jesus told Judas in John 13:27 to carry out the betrayal quickly, he meant 'without delay.' Besides, Revelation 1:3 says 'the time is near.' The phrase was given as a reason that the first century recipients of the prophecy would be blessed if they heard and obeyed its message—'because the time is near.' If the time were not near but 2,000 years away, the reason for the blessing is nullified. What do futurists do with 'the time is near'?"

"One way futurists handle the phrase is to note that the word 'time' refers not to a point in time but to a season. This season began in the days of the apostles and will be consummated at the return of Christ. 'The time is near' would mean that the beginning of the season is at hand."

I excused myself to get a book from the office that might help our discussion. When I returned, Luke was mounting a renewed attack on David's position so I placed the book on the coffee table and listened.

QUESTIONING THE PANORAMIC VIEW 197

"David, I've listened carefully to your attempts to prop up the yet-to-be-fulfilled view of most of Revelation as held by Dr. Harmon and I am not convinced. The soon-cum-quickly reference in Revelation 1:1 is repeated in verse 6 of the last chapter after all the events held to be yet future have been described. It is reasonable to think that the repetition at the end indicates that what is soon to occur is not the beginning of the season but the whole."

David was now thoughtful, or was he just tired? It was close to midnight and we had spent enough time on Luke's one example of doubt about Chuck's preaching so I said, "The time is near for us to go to bed so we ought to go soon." As Luke chuckled and David smiled graciously, I continued: "I'd like to wrap up our stimulating discussion by reading two sentences that are relevant to the words 'soon' and 'the time is near'. Milton Terry, in his book, *Biblical Hermeneutics* writes:

> If the seer, writing a few years before the terrible catastrophe, had the destruction of Jerusalem and its attendant woes before him, all these expressions have a force and definiteness which every interpreter must recognize. But if the things contemplated were in the distant future, these simple words of time must be subjected to the most violent and unnatural treatment in order to make the statements of the writer compatible with the exposition.

I didn't comment. There was no need: Luke's smirk and David's frown told me they had both seen Terry's point. I had contributed very little to the discussion during the evening and now, perhaps, I had said too much. However, we parted amicably for a much needed rest and arranged to meet for breakfast at 8:00 a.m.

An hour before breakfast, the noise of chinking crockery sounded louder than Charlotte's efforts at quietness intended. I should have gone to bed earlier. I got up to find her in good spirits with no criticism of the late-night discussion on eschatology and pleased to have my help in preparing breakfast. When David and Luke emerged, Charlotte asked us to begin with the first course while she prepared the second. She cooked as we drank apple juice and ate muesli topped with stewed apricots and yoghurt.

Charlotte, joining us for fried tomatoes, bacon and omelet, began the conversation: "What time did you guys turn in?" We looked at each other without saying a word. "I gather from your silence that it was quite a while after I retired," she said. "Well, if you won't answer that question, try this one: What topic of conversation absorbed you so far into the night?"

David spoke up: "It's all my fault we were late to bed: I asked your husband what he thought of Dr. Harmon's message last night and away we went."

"And Ed gave you an earful of his own views of the end times."

"Not at all," said David. "He was uncharacteristically quiet on the subject. Luke and I had most to say."

Charlotte gave me an endearing rub on the back as she said, "I'm pleased to hear it but, speaking of last night, it was the first time I'd heard the view that the seven churches in Asia represent seven periods of church history. Is that a commonly held view?"

The affectionate rub on the back kept me from responding but Luke had no such reservations, not that he answered the question: "It's not a view I espouse."

David was more to the point: "The view is probably less common than it used to be. Some interpreters, the historicists, treat the whole book of Revelation as Dr. Harmon treated chapters 2 and 3 but not all futurists follow that line. You still hear people talk about our being in the Laodicean age but many of them probably don't know what the other six churches are supposed to represent."

Charlotte turned to Luke and asked, "And why don't you espouse that view, Luke?"

I could see a repetition of the dynamics in last night's discussion but was powerless to prevent it. While Charlotte's tone of voice reflected a note of discontent that the youthful Luke should disagree with our American expert, I sensed at the same time she was interested to know what he thought. He wasted no time in telling her.

"For a start, there is nothing in the text to suggest the seven churches are intended to represent the Roman church, the reformation church, or any other church or historical period. The scheme is wholly the work of imaginative interpreters who have made connections, some of them scant indeed, between what is said in the letters and what they know of history. If you asked a group of church historians to read the letter to Sardis and make a case for seeing the reformation church in it, they would throw it out of court for lack of evidence."

Charlotte was not to be silenced: "Luke, the seven successive periods of church history mentioned by Dr. Harmon remain whether or not a connection with the seven churches of Asia was intended or not. Your strong objection to the connection seems unjustified given that no harm seems to have been done."

"I don't agree," said Luke. "Our job as interpreters is to discern what *was* intended by the biblical authors. We cannot treat this reckless handling of the text with indifference because, in doing so, we convey the impression that reading into the Scriptures what is not there is acceptable and it isn't. Furthermore, the view that the seven churches are prophetic of stages in church history raises questions for futurism."

"Such as?" asked David.

"The book of Revelation was written to the churches of Asia and was meant to be a blessing to them which implies they would understand what was being written. There's no way they could have seen hidden references to popes and reformers centuries in the future. The biggest problem for the futurists, however, is that when Revelation was written, the recipients were in the apostolic age with, according to Dr. Harmon, six more historical periods to come before the rapture. Had they known the cryptic significance of the seven churches they'd have had no reason to expect an any-moment rapture as understood by futurists."

"You're assuming that readers of the first century were expected to understand the historical significance of the seven letters," said David. "Only in hindsight can the historical connection be discerned."

"And when did hindsight kick in? Stage 2, stage 3? Did the reformers of the sixteenth century in stage 5 have hindsight about the significance of the preceding four periods? If so, the any-time rapture theory wouldn't apply to them with two more historical periods to go. If they didn't see the significance, was it because they lacked discernment or because no historical significance existed? Or is it only futurists of the present day who are gifted with the hindsight to make the right connections?"

The awkward silence that followed Luke's prosecution of futurism was thankfully broken by excited barking from Chuffey. Within minutes, Josh Wilson appeared at the kitchen door looking as though life in Bundaberg suited him well, or was he just glad to be home? Either way, it was good to see him so happy. I introduced him to our guests and commented on the sizable contingent from Bundaberg at the conference.

"Robyn Bradford's daily promotional bulletins induced me to advertise the conference in the church I attend in Bundaberg," said Josh. "Chuck Harmon is well-known among the members through his writings so several were keen to hear him in person. I've got three guys staying next door and Mum organized for the rest to be billeted elsewhere. What a great turnout last night. What did you think of it, Ed?"

Before I could answer, even in neutral terms, Charlotte interrupted with, "Ed, it's after nine and round two at the tent starts at 10:30. We need to get moving."

Charlotte's words, "round two at the tent," triggered a flashback to my youth: I was a teenager in Sideshow Alley at the Brisbane agricultural show, standing in front of Jimmy Sharman's tent. The bass drum was banging, a troupe of boxers posed muscularly on a platform above the crowd, and Jimmy's gravel voice cried out to the crowd, "Who'll take a glove?" in anticipation of the first fight of the day.

42

The Rapture and the Tribulation

Robyn Bradford was like a ten-year-old on Christmas morning for whom Santa had delivered every item on her wish list. Whenever I looked up she was audibly expressing her excitement somewhere else: exclaiming on the success of the first session to the Tasmanians; marveling to the Bundaberg contingent how rapidly the tent was filling half an hour before starting time; recommending a Harmon book to a passer-by at the bookstall; or applauding the last-minute erection of a three-meter banner above the platform. I too was pleased to see the banner but for a different reason. Charlotte had produced it in her studio over several weeks. After painting a magnificent cloud formation with beams of light dispersing from a radiant central point, she artistically printed "He's Coming Soon."

Sam Zimmerman and Ryan Mullins were equally excited as they crawled in and out of tent flaps in a game of hide and seek. They were less excited when the ubiquitous Bradford forced the sublimation of their energies by conscripting them to pick up programs left behind the previous evening.

Up on the platform, hidden talents were being revealed: the aged Matthew Beecroft was removing a violin from a weathered case and John and Elizabeth were adjusting their lips to a trumpet and clarinet respectively. With Mrs. Beecroft (surprise, surprise) on the Roland keyboard and Andy on the guitar, the group added to the pre-session atmosphere with an admirable performance.

As ushers went down the aisles asking people to pack together where there were empty seats, Mark Mullins, the session chairman, announced at the conclusion of one of the band's numbers, "You've been listening to the Sunshine Coast Independent Fellowship Second-Coming Conference Band." The unsolicited gold-medal applause elicited a standing ovation from Robyn Bradford (as if she'd just opened the best present on her Christmas list) and a (for me) first-ever smile on Matthew Beecroft's face. Mark invited the audience to sing with the band while the few remaining seats were filling. As they sang 'When the trumpet of the Lord shall sound and time shall be no more,' John accompanied them with a virtuosic improvisation on his trumpet.

More hidden talent emerged before Chuck rose to speak as Cathy Mullins, with a rich contralto voice, sang a SCIF favorite from Sankey's *Sacred Songs and Solos*:

> It may be at morn, when the day is awaking,
> When sunlight through darkness and shadow is breaking
> That Jesus will come in the fullness of glory
> To receive from the world His own.

Unexpectedly, Chuck stood next to Cathy for a duet on the last verse, harmonizing impressively:

> Oh, joy! oh, delight! should we go without dying,
> No sickness, no sadness, no dread and no crying.
> Caught up through the clouds with our Lord into glory,
> When Jesus receives His own.

The audience was so moved, they joined spontaneously in singing the final chorus:

> O Lord Jesus, how long, how long
> Ere we shout the glad song,
> Christ returneth! Hallelujah!
> Hallelujah! Amen. Hallelujah! Amen.

The stirring of my emotions throughout the singing caused me to reflect. Was I simply caught up in the atmosphere created by the music or was the indwelling Spirit, contrary to my current eschatological thinking, resonating with the theology of the song? My expectation that Chuck's topic for the morning would be in keeping with the theme of the song was confirmed within minutes.

"If you've been blessed as much as I have so far this morning, we could all go home now and feel it was worth coming," Chuck began, followed by a chorus of amens. "I particularly enjoyed your enthusiastic singing of the opening song and the stirring trumpet playing that accompanied it." With an outstretched open palm, he pointed to John. The audience applauded, John blushed, and Elizabeth gave him an affectionate smile. "But, good as that trumpet playing was," Chuck continued, "there's a trumpet call I'm going to enjoy even more. It's mentioned in 1 Thessalonians 4.' I followed in my Bible as he read:

> According to the Lord's own word, we tell you that we who are still alive, who are left till the coming of the Lord, will certainly not precede those who have fallen asleep. [16]For the Lord himself will come down from heaven, with a loud command, with the voice of the archangel and with the trumpet call of God, and the dead in Christ will rise first. [17]After that, we who are still alive and are left will be caught up together with them in the clouds to meet the Lord in the air. And so we will be with the Lord forever.

"What a trumpet blast that will be!" exclaimed Chuck. "Paul calls it 'the last trumpet' in 1 Corinthians 15:52, at the sound of which 'we will all be changed—in a flash, in the twinkling of an eye,' transported to heaven without dying, in company with those who have died in Christ before us."

I feared Chuck had forgotten that the conference was about the book of Revelation but my fears were unfounded as he continued: "The trumpet call we've just read about relates to the rapture of the church prior to the great tribulation and you may wonder where it fits into the book of Revelation. Some see a reference to it in Revelation 4:1:

> After this I looked, and there before me was a door standing open in heaven. And the voice I had first heard speaking to me like a trumpet said, "Come up here, and I will show you what must take place after this."

I knew some futurists used the verse in support of the rapture on the basis of the words "trumpet" and "Come up here" and I was appalled to think Chuck might be among them. How could it refer to the rapture? The context shows that John was simply ushered into a visionary state for the purpose of seeing what lay in the future. At best he heard a trumpet-like voice, not a trumpet, and no one else is said to have gone with him.

Chuck eased my concern by rejecting the rapture-interpretation of the verse, but when he stressed that the rapture occurs before the tribulation and that the tribulation is the subject of most of the remaining chapters of Revelation, I expected he would offer alternative texts from the early chapters of Revelation that *did* speak of the rapture. Surprisingly, he didn't.

Most of Chuck's message was about the tribulation. He nominated candidates for the antichrist, "an unspeakably cruel dictator," and speculated on the application of the mark of the beast and its associated economic restrictions. He then gave a literal and lurid account of the catastrophes to occur during the tribulation. His emaciated famine victims made starving children on charity fund-raising posters seem well-fed; his description of the incineration of a third of earth's trees ignited by falling fire balls, made the average Australian bushfire look like a backyard barbecue; and his gory depiction of lacerated and dismembered bodies as wild beasts emerged from jungles to rip and devour, unsettled squeamish listeners and left everyone subdued—but not for long. Determined to speak about "the next climactic event on the prophetic calendar," Chuck revisited the rapture in spite of its absence from Revelation.

"Brothers and sisters," he said, "I am convinced that the horrific events I have described are soon to be inflicted on this wicked world." Chuck paused as his listeners remained enshrouded with a palpable hush. He continued: "But—and it's a big 'but'—we won't be here! As we sang earlier, prior to the devastation of the tribulation we'll be "caught up through the clouds with our Lord into glory." The shroud lifted and the audience erupted with multiple hallelujahs.

Chuck finished with a plug for his hot-off-the-press *How to Avoid the Tribulation* prompting Robyn Bradford to lead a pack of eager buyers in the direction of the bookstall. They arrived before the sales assistants and stood looking like a crowd outside a Myer department store waiting for the doors to open on a Boxing Day sale.

I ambled into the hall hoping to get a drink before the first lunch sitting. One other person had the same idea: Josh Wilson was sitting alone at a round table with a hot drink in his hand and a preoccupied look on his face. Noticing a cloud of steam rising from an urn on the lunch counter, I made a coffee and began chatting to the workers preparing the meal, thinking Josh would be best left to his thoughts. He didn't think so and signaled me over.

Rather bluntly I asked, "Has the tribulation disturbed you?"

After an unexpectedly long pause during which I realized his preoccupation was more personal than eschatological, he whispered, "I'm worried about Anna. She hasn't been to either of the meetings. I thought she might have been away with Paul but her brother Sam told me as I came out of the tent that she's at home in bed with a kidney illness."

While I was realizing the reason for Linda's replacement at the keyboard by Mrs. Beecroft, Josh continued: "That's pretty serious isn't it, Ed?"

"It can be, but modern medicine will be more than a match for whatever ails her so I'm sure she'll be fine." My attempt at calming Josh did not seem to work. His visible concern showed that his months in Bundaberg away from Anna had not lessened his interest in her. I felt for him but did not want to pursue the kidney conversation. Andy and Linda were not advertising Anna's condition and I knew Sam was out of step with family policy in exposing it. I changed the subject but not before asking Josh to keep Anna's condition to himself.

"Chuck was in fine rhetorical form this morning," I remarked.

"He did get a bit worked up," Josh replied rather flatly, "but, for your encouragement, Ed, I think your Caloundra-Coffee-Club take on the antichrist was better than Chuck's. It makes much more sense to think Revelation is describing a person of relevance to the first century readers than someone who would emerge twenty centuries later. What did *you* think of Chuck's talk?"

"I was very puzzled about one aspect of it."

"O yeah," said Josh, brightening up a little, "and what would that be?"

I wasn't keen to involve a son of one of the elders in matters at variance with the church's Statement of Faith so I hesitated. Josh placed both elbows on the table, cupped his chin in his hands and gazed at me intently as if to say, "I'm waiting." I was about to yield to his unspoken entreaty when David Barnes arrived, coffee and lunch plate in hand. I introduced him to Josh and anticipated with relief a change in the direction of the conversation. Josh was not so easily diverted. He resumed his earlier posture and said, "Ed was about to comment on Chuck's talk this morning."

"Excellent! I was about to ask what he thought of it. We're all ears, Ed," said David, as he adopted Josh's pose. I was cornered.

Determined to start on a positive note, I said, "Chuck commendably distanced himself from the view that sees the rapture in Revelation 4:1 where John receives the invitation, 'Come up here, and I will show you what must take place after this.' I have no doubt it has nothing to do with the rapture. However,"—I paused and the elbow-supported chins leaned forward as if their owners were urging me to continue, in anticipation of a controversial note—"I would have thought, given Chuck's assertion that the rapture occurs before the tribulation, that he would have shown us passage after passage where John refers to the rapture, to assure his suffering readers they would not have to endure the horrors of the tribulation, the alleged subject of much of the book. Why would John spend so much time describing events that his readers were not to experience and so little, if any, on an event of great significance for them?" The chin supports were folded as Josh and David leaned back reflectively. David broke the silence.

"Ed, you suggest the rapture may get little, if any, mention in the early chapters of Revelation but I think it is clearly referred to in the letter to the church at Philadelphia. Let me read Revelation 3:10:

> Since you have kept my command to endure patiently, I will also keep you from the hour of trial that is going to come upon the whole world to test those who live on the earth.

"That surely is about escaping the tribulation via the rapture."

"Those who wear pretribulation spectacles when making such a point, David, are begging the question. When we look a little deeper, the text is less clearly about the rapture. For a start, reputable commentators differ over whether the words, 'I will keep you from,' promise *escape from* the tribulation or *protection during* the tribulation. The letter to Philadelphia was written to people living many centuries before the supposed great tribulation, which still hasn't come. They have certainly escaped that event but not via rapture but via death. In this case there is no clear reference in the text to the rapture."

"So you believe the church goes through the tribulation?" interrupted David.

"David, I'm not convinced that 'the hour of trial' refers to the so-called future 'great tribulation.' If that tribulation is as far removed from the Philadelphians as many think, it's irrelevant for Jesus to be promising them either escape or protection. It makes much more sense to understand the text as referring to something around the corner to them than a million miles away, something threatening them for which the promise in the text would be not only relevant but encouraging. And I think there is a suggestion that the threatened trial *was* close at hand. The phrase, 'the hour of trial that is going to come,' contains the Greek word *mellō* which is translated 'about to' in verse 16 of this chapter. Verse 10 could well be translated 'the hour of trial that is about to come.' Such a translation represents a text far more applicable to the first century readers. It is unfortunate that the eschatological presuppositions of many readers hinder their openness to such a translation."

Josh's puzzled look gave birth to a question: "Ed, if as you say the hour of trial was just 'around the corner,' when did it happen?"

"Jesus may have answered your question when he said in Matthew 24:34, 'I tell you the truth, this generation will certainly not pass away until all these things have happened.' As for the 'all things' he spoke of, consider Matthew 24:7: 'Nation will rise against nation, and kingdom against kingdom. There will be famines and earthquakes in various places.' And in verse 9 he told his disciples they would be 'hated by all nations.' All of this sounds very much like a widespread 'hour of trial' that could well have occurred in Philadelphia before the end of the generation Jesus addressed and, given that the discourse in Matthew 24 was spoken years before Revelation was written, it is not unreasonable to think that for the church at Philadelphia it was just around the corner."

Josh was silent and David merely stroked his chin and said, "Mm."

The reflective silence that followed David's "Mm" was interrupted by the arrival of Alex Symons carrying a generously loaded lunch plate. I felt he greeted David more affably than me but, even so, he was friendlier than he'd been prior to my leaving AIMS. In fact, he was uncharacteristically buoyant and lost no time in accounting for it.

"You'd need a heart of granite not to be moved by the message this morning," he began. "I had to wipe tears away as we sang 'When the trumpet of the Lord shall sound' knowing that very soon we shall hear that glorious summons. Don't you agree, David?"

As David nodded and said, "Certainly," I was afraid Alex was about to ask me the same question. Instead, he turned to me, somewhat less buoyantly, and asked, "How are *you* handling Chuck's teaching, Edward?" He always called me "Edward," never "Ed." His body language and a meaningful emphasis on the word "you" implied that Chuck had me on the back foot. I was determined not to give too much away or to engage in acrimonious debate so I said, "I had lunch with Chuck and his wife the other day and we got on well together."

Never one to be put off, Alex hit me with the question I thought I'd escaped: "And are you as certain as David that the last trump and the associated rapture of the saints are soon to occur?"

As I considered my response, I was consoled by the thought that, unlike David, I had no career to protect but was free to speak openly even if it meant relaxing my earlier determination to avoid conflict. If Alex was determined to press my buttons, let him. He might regret it.

43

Jesus' Teaching Raises Doubts

The smug look on Alex's face said he knew how I would answer the question about an imminent rapture and that it would put me offside with the theme of the conference. I was certainly not going to give him the satisfaction of answering his yes-no question with a monosyllable. I decided to unpack the question: "Alex, if I understand your question correctly, you are asking if I believe that very soon we are going to hear a trumpet blast following which we will all be translated to heaven and escape the tribulation."

"Spot on," he said.

"In that case, your question picks up nicely on three emphases in Chuck's address: the last trump, the rapture, and the tribulation."

Leaning back in his chair with arms folded, Alex said, "Right again," even more smugly, and fully aware that I was avoiding a direct answer.

"Let's begin with the last trump, Alex. As Chuck noted, it is mentioned in 1 Corinthians 15 and 1 Thessalonians 4 in the context of the rapture. I certainly think the two passages are referring to the same event." Alex pursed his lips and nodded with an audible "mm-mm." I continued: "But there is a third passage about a last trumpet in the book that we are studying so it's appropriate that we consider it." I opened to Revelation 10:7 and read:

> But in the days when the seventh angel is about to sound his trumpet, the mystery of God will be accomplished, just as he announced to his servants the prophets.

"And what point do you want to make from the passage?" asked Alex, in a more conciliatory tone as if I were coming around to his point of view.

"This trumpet is the last of seven and is not unreasonably to be considered with the last trumpet of Corinthians and Thessalonians. Furthermore, the wording of the text links it rather comprehensively with prophetic fulfilment."

"It does indeed," said Alex. "It sounds like the eschatological prodigal is finally returning to the futurist fold."

"Before you kill the fatted calf, Alex, let's look at a more detailed description of events associated with the sounding of the seventh trumpet. I opened to Revelation 11:15–19 and read:

> The seventh angel sounded his trumpet, and there were loud voices in heaven, which said:
>
> "The kingdom of the world has become the kingdom of our Lord and of his Christ, and he will reign for ever and ever."
> [16]And the twenty-four elders, who were seated on their thrones before God, fell on their faces and worshiped God, [17]saying: "We give thanks to you, Lord God Almighty, the One who is and who was, because you have taken your great power and have begun to reign. [18]The nations were angry; and your wrath has come. The time has come for judging the dead, and for rewarding your servants the prophets and your saints and those who reverence your name, both small and great—and for destroying those who destroy the earth."
> [19]Then God's temple in heaven was opened, and within his temple was seen the ark of his covenant. And there came flashes of lightning, rumblings, peals of thunder, an earthquake and a great hailstorm.

"You associate the last trump with the rapture. I won't argue about that but the passage we just read associates it with much more, with things, for example, that Jesus said would occur before some of his disciples died."

His conciliatory tone fully evaporated. Alex exploded: "Don't tell me you were sucked in by that bearded idiot who in one of your evening classes implied Christ returned in the first century."

"You'll be interested to know that Luke Rodman is at this conference," I said. "He's not wearing a beard but he is an intelligent defense lawyer."

"Thanks for the warning. I hope I manage to avoid him. I don't want him defending his heresy. Better still, I hope Chuck prosecutes an unassailable case against him."

"Alex," I said, "let's not be diverted from your question. You asked me if I was as certain as David that the last trump was soon to sound. To be blunt, I'm not. You think it will sound in the near future; I am open, on biblical grounds, to believe it may have sounded in the distant past, before some of the disciples died."

"I can't believe what I'm hearing. What a blessing the college got rid of you when it did," Alex fumed.

I didn't expose the real reason he'd sacked me, not in the presence of David and Josh, the former looking disconcerted and the latter straightening up with folded arms in anticipation of a good fight. I expected Alex to chicken out of the fight and storm off leaving his loaded lunch plate untouched.

I was therefore quite surprised when, with half a sausage roll in his mouth, he mumbled, "I think I'm going to enjoy this." I thought he spoke of the sausage roll but he continued: "I can't wait to hear you make a fool of yourself." At the risk of confirming his opinion of my intellectual limitations, I began, hoping he would keep stuffing himself so he couldn't interrupt me and that his mind might be as open as his mouth which was gaping in readiness for the other half of the sausage roll.

"Alex, note the issues associated with the last trumpet according to the passage we just read from Revelation 11: the inauguration of the kingdom of God, judgment and reward, the opening of God's temple in heaven." I continued in spite of a sarcastic "So what?" from Alex. "Keeping these issues in mind, listen as I read from Matthew 16:27-28:

> For the Son of Man is going to come in his Father's glory with his angels, and then he will reward each person according to what he has done. I tell you the truth, some who are standing here will not taste death before they see the Son of Man coming in his kingdom.

"Here we have similar issues, rewards according to works and the arrival of the kingdom of God, 'with power' according to the parallel passage in Mark 9:1. All of this is associated with the coming of Christ and is to take place before some of his disciples died."

Alex interrupted: "Don't you read the context when you study the Bible? What you read from Matthew 16, not to mention the parallels in Mark and Luke, is followed by, and fulfilled in, the transfiguration of Christ—about a week after Jesus' prediction. Surely that was before some of them died."

"I'm glad you mentioned that, Alex. It's not an uncommon view but it doesn't add up. At the transfiguration, there was certainly a display of glory but did Jesus *come* on that occasion? Did he come with his angels? Did the kingdom of God come with power? Were rewards distributed at the transfiguration? That some would not die before the kingdom came suggests that others would, hardly a reference to an event to occur within a week, but not inappropriate for an event before the present generation passed."

Josh unfolded his arms and asked, "Ed, I noticed that Revelation mentions the opening of God's temple in heaven in association with the last trump. Where does that fit in?" A mute and rather disgruntled Alex perked up at the question, perhaps thinking he had an ally in Josh.

"An astute observation, Josh, and a relevant question. With the opening of the temple, the ark of the covenant is seen. Under the old covenant, such a sight was hidden from all but the high priest and he only saw it once a year when he entered the Most Holy Place on the Day of Atonement. Here in Revelation 11, at the sounding of the last trumpet, it is openly disclosed in keeping with the words of Hebrews 9:8: 'the way into the Most Holy Place had not yet been disclosed as long as the first tabernacle was still standing.' It was still standing right up until AD 70 when the Romans destroyed the city of Jerusalem and its temple. That catastrophic event marked the ultimate end of the old covenant. The temple, the priesthood, the sacrificial system were no more. When Hebrews was written, the old covenant was still being observed but it was soon to disappear. As Hebrews 8:13 says, 'By calling this covenant "new," he has made the first one obsolete; and what is obsolete and aging will soon disappear.' Josh, your question raises the very real possibility that the last trump we've been hearing about is not future but past, that it does not consummate human history but inaugurates the kingdom of God and the age of the new covenant where access into the presence of God is available not just to a high priest but to all. The thought of inauguration is implied in the use of the word 'begun' in the translation of Revelation 11:17 that we read earlier: 'We give thanks to you, Lord God Almighty, the One who is and who was, because you have taken your great power and have *begun* to reign.'"

Alex was so appalled at what he had just heard that he put down his half-eaten second sausage roll and simply shook his head many times while staring at me in utter disbelief, as if I were a lost cause. He relaxed a little when David commented, "Ed, what you've just said cuts across the church's widely held eschatological position. You've relied heavily on Matthew 16:27-28 which, as you know, is given a range of interpretations including Alex's link with the transfiguration."

At this point, Alex broke in with, "Rub it in, David."

David continued: "Is what you claim supported elsewhere in the teaching of Jesus or are you tenuously relying on a single and much-disputed passage to bolster your narrowly-held eschatological position?"

"Yes and no," I replied.

"So you're unsure of your position," Alex interjected.

"On the contrary, Alex, I say 'Yes' to support from Jesus elsewhere and 'No' to sole reliance on Matthew 16:27-28." Almost in unison David and Alex asked where Jesus said anything like what I'd been claiming.

"Let me read the opening verses of a parable in Luke 19. I read verses 11 to 15:

> While they were listening to this, he went on to tell them a parable, because he was near Jerusalem and the people thought that the kingdom of God was going to appear at once. [12]He said: "A man of noble birth went to a distant country to have himself appointed king and then to return. [13]So he called ten of his servants and gave them ten minas. 'Put this money to work,' he said, 'until I come back.' [14]But his subjects hated him and sent a delegation after him to say, 'We don't want this man to be our king.' [15]He was made king, however, and returned home. Then he sent for the servants to whom he had given the money, in order to find out what they had gained with it."

I knew the parable was well-known to David and Alex and I knew that they regarded the return of the king as unfulfilled. Paradoxically, their body language betrayed both skepticism and intense interest to know what I would say. I was sure my comments would only confirm their doubts about my orthodoxy, not to mention my intelligence, but I began all the same.

"The parable was spoken shortly before Jesus rode into Jerusalem on a donkey. On that occasion the crowd cried, 'Blessed is the king who comes in the name of the Lord.' Jesus anticipated their expectation and stressed that the kingdom of God was not to be inaugurated immediately."

"Take note!" said Alex. "It didn't come when *they* expected, nor when *you* expected."

Ignoring the interruption, I continued: "We have tended to interpret the parable with a focus on the departing nobleman and his return to judge his servants. Because much of the parable deals with the allocation of rewards, we lose sight of the citizens mentioned as the nobleman departs for the far country. Their cry, 'We don't want this man to be our king,' parallels the cry of the Jews at the crucifixion of Jesus, 'We have no king but Caesar,' and reflects the Jewish leaders' objection to the inscription Pilate put above the cross, 'The King of the Jews.'

"The citizens reappear at the end of the parable when the nobleman, now installed as king, says, 'But those enemies of mine who did not want me to be king over them—bring them here and kill them in front of me.' You're right, Alex, the nobleman did not return as king immediately but he did return during the lifetime of those who rejected him."

"But Ed," interposed David, "aren't you building too strong a case on too weak a foundation? We've always regarded the distribution of rewards to the servants as occurring at the final judgment so why shouldn't the rebellious citizens be punished at the same time?"

With Alex inserting "Exactly!" and "Good question, David!" between approving nods, I felt outnumbered but forged ahead. "Yes, David, that has been the traditional view of the parable but allow me to suggest grounds for rethinking that view. First, the teaching of Jesus shortly before his crucifixion is replete with references to the judgment that was to come upon the Jews at the destruction of Jerusalem in about forty years." Flipping through the chapters towards the end of Matthew's gospel, I proceeded to support my assertion. I began by reading Matthew 21:38–41, part of the parable of the tenants:

> But when the tenants saw the son, they said to each other, "This is the heir. Come, let's kill him and take his inheritance." [39]So they took him and threw him out of the vineyard and killed him. [40]Therefore, when the owner of the vineyard comes, what will he do to those tenants?
>
> [41]"He will bring those wretches to a wretched end," they replied, "and he will rent the vineyard to other tenants, who will give him his share of the crop at harvest time."

Again David broke in: "But, Ed, the parable says the tenants would experience their wretched end 'when the owner of the vineyard comes.' Are you not begging the question in assuming that the coming and the accompanying judgment mentioned in the parable supports your notion of inauguration rather than consummation?"

"Good question, David, but more important than my interpretation or yours is that given by Jesus. Listen to what he said in verse 43:

> Therefore I tell you that the kingdom of God will be taken away from you and given to a people who will produce its fruit.

Note the sequence of events here: a coming is followed by judgment, and the kingdom of God is taken from the Jews and offered to others. We saw in Matthew 16:27–28, the same conjunction of coming, judgement, and kingdom, all before some of the disciples died."

"Wait on," yelled Alex, "what right have you to think this parable speaks of events to occur within that generation?"

"You're an intelligent man, Alex," I said. "Please tell me: Does Jesus' prediction that the kingdom of God would be taken from the Jews and given to others, including the Gentiles, belong in the first century or at a time still future to us following the second coming of Christ, as you understand that event?"

Alex paused and then mumbled, "I'll have to think about that."

Leaving him to his thoughts, I continued, "The reaction of the Jewish leaders to Jesus' parables is significant: 'they knew he was talking about them.' They were the ones who would kill the son; they were the ones from whom the kingdom of God would be taken; and they were the ones who would meet with a wretched end which Jesus declared in Matthew 23:35 would come on their generation. So, to return to your question, Alex, it is not unreasonable to think the parable *does* speak of events to occur within that generation."

Shrugging his shoulders to the accompaniment of disapproving grunts, Alex rose from the table and, turning to David, said, "It's time we were going. The afternoon session will be starting soon." David gave a not unfriendly wave as he meekly followed the AIMS chairman to the tent where "soon" would mean a wait of forty minutes before Matthew Beecroft tucked his violin under his chin and with the rest of the SCIF Second-Coming Conference Band played the introduction to "He's Coming Soon."

Left alone with Josh, I refrained from speaking for two reasons: one, I had been talking too much already; and, two, I recalled Josh's concern for Anna and felt he deserved to be left in peace. I was about to go when he said, "Ed, thanks for the honest sharing of your thoughts. You held my interest and made more sense than some of the views I've heard over the years. Besides, you've helped me take my mind off Anna. Worrying about her isn't going to make her well. Do you think anyone would miss me if I skipped the next session and paid her a visit? I won't dob Sam in for revealing Anna's problem."

"A visit from you might be just the medicine she needs," I replied.

Josh brightened visibly and left me alone, rather hurriedly given he'd had no lunch. I was tempted to skip the Saturday afternoon session myself as I recalled the soporific effect of afternoon sermons on warm summer days. However, I resisted the temptation to absent myself from Chuck's predictable interpretations because he promised a question time after the message during which I hoped the odd Luke Rodman—or even Edward Sutherland—might ask a question that would stir the eschatological pot.

44

The Harlot and the Bride

Josh was not the only one missing from the afternoon session of the conference. Numbers were down. I presumed some SCIF members had gone home for a siesta and that some of our country and interstate visitors were surfing at Mooloolaba or touring the Blackall Range for views of the Glasshouse Mountains, Kondalilla Falls, or works of art at Montville galleries. However, there were a few new faces. Martin Forbes, the physics lecturer from USC, was there with several students I recognized from my speaking visits to the Real Life group.

The congregational singing lacked energy due to the smaller numbers and the hot weather. Mark Mullins, the meeting chairman, aware of the pervasive lethargy in the incubator-like tent, tried to lighten the atmosphere with a joke: "In spite of the heat, I'm sure none of you will drop off this afternoon. I did hear of a long-winded and boring speaker who, unlike Dr. Harmon, was so good at inducing sleep that on one occasion the chairman, who was sitting directly behind the podium, thought he should silence the ponderous preacher. Ignoring the intended usage of the gavel he held in his hand, he aimed carefully, then threw it forcefully at the back of the speaker's head, hoping to put him out of action. Unfortunately, the speaker gestured at the wrong moment, the gavel missed its target and continued on its trajectory until it hit an old man in the front row. As he lapsed into a state of unconsciousness, his final words were, 'Hit me again; I can still hear him.'"

The eruption of widespread laughter followed by enthusiastic singing of "He's Coming Soon" showed Mark's story had fulfilled its purpose. Before introducing Chuck, Mark mentioned the scheduled question time: "Dr. Harmon has kindly offered to answer questions arising from his message this afternoon and from his previous talks. His message will be followed by a half-hour break for tea and coffee and an opportunity to place your questions in the designated box at the book table." The prospect of having Chuck address personal eschatological issues seemed to further rouse the audience, some already beginning to write their questions.

"Some of you," said Chuck, "may be attending your first session of the conference so I will give a quick overview of our previous sessions to help you place this afternoon's topic in context. The first three chapters of the book of Revelation concern the church in this present age. After that there is no mention of the church because it has been raptured to heaven thus escaping the horrors of the seven-year tribulation. This afternoon we will consider further events during the tribulation period which precedes the glorious return of our Lord Jesus Christ to usher in his earthly millennial reign, followed by the judgment of unbelievers, and the new heaven and new earth."

Alex Symons, who was sitting two rows in front and to my right, turned in my direction. Bending his head to see over his half-frame spectacles, he looked at me with a smirk that seemed to say, "That's it in a nutshell, Edward, so abandon your heretical notions and get with it." Robyn Bradford was sitting near the aisle in my row beaming with approval towards the platform as if to say, "Chuck, it's wonderful to hear end-times truth so faithfully expounded." A glimpse of Martin Forbes and Luke Rodman showed the former looking nonplussed and the latter skeptical. My deadpan expression betrayed a just-as-I-expected reaction to Chuck's dispensational eschatology and I wondered, as he continued, if the rest of the message would be equally predictable. His brief introduction had already made me apprehensive about the exegetical standard to be expected. He certainly had no right to think the absence of the word "church" after Revelation 3 in any way confirmed that subsequent chapters were post-rapture; any more than the absence of the word "disciple" from the New Testament after Acts 21 meant the authors of the epistles had no interest in discipleship. His argument had as little validity as that of the Irishman who, when charged with murder, said to the prosecutor, "You say you have two witnesses who saw me commit the murder; I have a hundred witnesses who will testify on the Bible that they *didn't* see me commit the murder." I emerged from my reflective mood as Chuck launched into his topic.

"This afternoon I will speak about two women mentioned in the book of Revelation." Chuck seemed to have everyone's attention as the notebooks and pencils were brought out. I knew which women he had in mind but was keen to hear what he would say about them. He continued: "Our description of the great tribulation this morning focused on the natural and human catastrophes that will occur at that time; now I want to focus on the religious conditions that will prevail. And that's where the first woman comes in. Let's read about her in Revelation 17:3–6:

> Then the angel carried me away in the Spirit into a wilderness. There I saw a woman sitting on a scarlet beast that was covered with blasphemous names and had seven heads and ten horns. ⁴The woman was dressed in purple and scarlet, and was glittering with gold, precious stones and pearls. She held a golden cup in her hand, filled with abominable things and the filth of her adulteries. ⁵This title was written on her forehead:
>
> MYSTERY
>
> BABYLON THE GREAT
>
> THE MOTHER OF PROSTITUTES
>
> AND OF THE ABOMINATIONS OF THE EARTH.
>
> ⁶I saw that the woman was drunk with the blood of the saints, the blood of those who bore testimony to Jesus.

"How are we to understand the prostitute of Revelation?" asked Chuck, and proceeded to answer his rhetorical question. "I agree with Dr. Dwight Pentecost, who equates her with 'the apostate religious system that exists in the tribulation.'" For most of his message, Chuck denounced trends in the present age that would culminate during the tribulation in what Dr. Pentecost described as "all professing Christendom united in a single system under one head." Targeted by Chuck's withering denunciation were the papacy, Pentecostalism, the World Council of Churches, an assortment of false cults, the ordination of women, so-called Christian rock music, and a number of American mega-churches. I imagined the audible scratching of pencils on notebooks reflected a smug separation from every trend under fire and a self-satisfied assurance that the rapture would guarantee escape from the Babylonian whore's apostasy.

Quoting Revelation 18, Chuck sounded a note of victory as he announced the fall of Babylon accompanied by a string of woes that threatened her fiery and rapid ruin. He elicited a chorus of hallelujahs when he offset the gory description of Babylon's demise with, "But, brothers and sisters, we will not be there. Well before Babylon falls, we will have been raptured to heaven away from the filth and the abominations of the Babylonian whore."

I felt like shouting "Hallelujah" because Chuck was nearing the end of the depressing account of the tribulation, an account that had consumed most of the Saturday morning and afternoon sessions of the convention. I couldn't help wondering why the apostle John would devote almost two-thirds of his book of Revelation to a seven-year period 2,000 or more years away that neither the seven churches of Asia he addressed in his book nor those Chuck addressed in the tent, would experience. As I reflected, Chuck launched into the second part of his address.

"Both of the women we are considering are mentioned in Revelation 19, a chapter in which there is great rejoicing, for two reasons: one, because the first woman has been condemned (Revelation 19:1–3); two, because the second woman is about to be married." Chuck read about her in Revelation 19 and 21.

> Revelation 19:6–9: Then I heard what sounded like a great multitude, like the roar of rushing waters and like loud peals of thunder, shouting: "Hallelujah! For the Lord God Almighty reigns. [7]Let us rejoice and be glad and give him glory! For the wedding of the Lamb has come, and his bride has made herself ready. [8]Fine linen, bright and clean, was given her to wear." (Fine linen stands for the righteous acts of the saints). [9]Then the angel said to me, "Write: 'Blessed are those who are invited to the wedding supper of the Lamb!'"

> Revelation 21:2, 9–10: I saw the Holy City, the new Jerusalem, coming down out of heaven from God, prepared as a bride beautifully dressed for her husband.
> [9]One of the seven angels who had the seven bowls full of the seven last plagues came and said to me, "Come, I will show you the bride, the wife of the Lamb." [10]And he carried me away in the Spirit to a mountain great and high, and showed me the Holy City, Jerusalem, coming down out of heaven from God.

Chuck spent time contrasting the filthy abominations of the scarlet woman with the righteous deeds of the beautifully-adorned bride. He noted that both women were represented as cities, Babylon on the one hand and the new Jerusalem on the other. Of the bride, Chuck said, "At the rapture Christ will come *for* his bride and take her to heaven where the marriage of the Lamb will be celebrated. At his second coming, he will return to earth *with* his bride prior to the millennium."

As Chuck spoke, I thought of Jesus' parable of the wedding feast in Matthew 22:1–14. There he likened the kingdom of God to a wedding feast. Was to be at the wedding feast to be part of the kingdom of God? Is that what John meant when he wrote, "Blessed are those who are invited to the wedding supper of the Lamb!" (Revelation 19:9), blessed because they are in the kingdom of God?

The marriage supper was beginning to look less like a mere function, a wedding-reception party, and more like a celebration inaugurated with the coming of the kingdom, before some of the disciples died, an ongoing, never-ending celebration of our eternal union with Christ as his bride. And since the bride and the city were equated (Revelation 21:2, 9–10), to be at the feast was not only to be in the kingdom but also in the new Jerusalem, the old Jerusalem having been destroyed, as indicated in the parable where the king "sent his army and destroyed those murderers and burned their city"—a very suggestive reference to AD 70. After that the invitation was widened and "the wedding hall was filled with guests," perhaps a reference to the offer of the kingdom to the Gentiles.

I emerged from my ruminations as Chuck wound up his talk. He challenged his listeners to ensure they were destined to attend the wedding of the Lamb then Mark closed the meeting with a benediction, announced that afternoon tea was available, and reminded folk to submit their questions before the next session.

I felt I should contribute a question but before I finished writing, I sensed someone had sat next to me. I turned to see a serious-faced Josh Wilson.

"Got a minute, Ed?"

"Sure, Josh. Just give me thirty seconds." I finished scribbling the question, folded the paper, put it in my shirt pocket and asked, "How did you get on at Anna's place?"

"Linda graciously invited me into the living room where Anna was sitting in an armchair, a pillow behind her back and a pouf beneath her feet. She looked so different: her face was swollen and her eyes puffy yet she smiled sweetly and said she was glad to have a visitor. You can imagine my mixed emotions. She asked how the conference was going so I tried to paint a glowing picture that might take her mind off her illness. Before long I sensed she was getting drowsy, at which point Linda asked that I not prolong my visit. As Linda made her way to the front door, somewhat rashly, I took one of Anna's hands in both of mine and said, 'I'm really sorry to see you like this, Anna.' She didn't withdraw her hand, which helped to assuage my fear that I was overly forward in taking it in the first place. My final words were, 'I'll be thinking of you. I hope you'll soon be well and that I might come and visit you again.' I can't tell you how pleased I was to hear her say, 'I'd like that.' I gave her hand a squeeze and you won't believe it but she squeezed me back. I won't be able to wash my hands for a week."

"Did Linda give you any details about Anna's condition?" I asked.

"When I got to the front door, I found Linda on the veranda looking down the stairs with her back to me. I thought it meant I had overstayed my welcome so I started down the stairs but turned after a few steps to thank her for permitting my visit. Words did not come when I saw her eyes filled with tears. Mine quickly moistened.

"Linda broke the silence: 'Josh, your visit will have meant a lot to Anna. Whenever Lauren visits, Anna asks how you're getting on in Bundaberg. I only cut short your visit because she gets very weary and the doctor has ordered rest. Be assured you're very welcome.'

"'Linda,' I said, 'I hope you don't mind my asking, but how serious is Anna's condition?'

"'Very serious,' she replied. 'We've known for some time that Anna has a kidney disease called nephritis. She is now experiencing nausea, headaches, swelling in the face and legs, and blood in her urine. These symptoms indicate serious deterioration in her condition so she could well be facing a kidney transplant. Unfortunately, neither Andy nor I have a blood group compatible with Anna's so if we can't get a donor soon she may have to undergo dialysis which involves hooking her up to an artificial kidney machine to cleanse her blood.'

"By this time Linda was very emotional and I was too choked up to speak. I simply placed my palms and fingers together, pointed them to heaven hoping Linda would understand that I would be praying, and continued down the stairs. End of story, Ed."

I gave Josh a hug and said, "Let's get a coffee." On the way to the hall I dropped my question in the box at the book table. People were already returning to the tent so we had no trouble finding a quiet corner in the hall for a quick drink. I encouraged Josh to attend the next session on the grounds that some of the questions might be interesting but mainly to divert his mind from his concern for Anna.

When the conference band struck up the introduction to "He's Coming Soon," Josh followed me into the tent, rather reluctantly. Up on the platform Stan Mullins was emptying the contents of the question box into a large bowl. He then welcomed everyone and advised that he would draw questions from the bowl at random and read them out before handing them to Chuck for his response.

Many of the questions were trivial, ranging from "Will my pet dog be in heaven?" to "If the number 144,000 is to be taken literally, is their virginity also to be understood literally?" To Chuck's credit, he dealt with them expeditiously and when my question was selected I thought (humbly) that he would be pleased to consider a more serious matter. Stan read the question: "In your talk earlier, you referred to the fall of Babylon in Revelation 18. Its fall is also recorded in Revelation 14:8 after which we read in verse 13, 'Blessed are the dead who die in the Lord *from now on*.'" Stan pleased me by stressing the words I had emphasized then continued with my question: "The words, 'from now on' suggest that a turning point has been reached; that believers who die *after* the fall of Babylon have an advantage over those who died *before* the fall of Babylon. The fall of Babylon is supposed to occur after the rapture, that is, after dead believers are resurrected. How can those who die in the Lord *after* the fall of Babylon be better off than those who were resurrected *at* the rapture?"

Stan shook his head and winced as he handed the question to Chuck who received it with a wry smile and said. "Christians who die *subsequent* to the rapture are certainly not more blessed than those who experience the resurrection *at* the rapture so we must conclude that the questioner is making too much of the words "from now on" or is splitting chronological hairs between the rapture and the fall of Babylon. They are certainly separate but not by many years."

It was time for *me* to wince. If I was making too much of the words "from now on," Chuck was not making anything of them. As for lightly dismissing the chronological gap, his eschatological paradigm majored on slotting events in their right place, with its range of judgments, resurrections, even comings, and insistence on events occurring pre-this or post-that. If taken seriously, my question raised a number of issues but either Chuck didn't see them or, if he did, he didn't want to go there. He was wearing his dispensational pre-millennial spectacles and if that view were threatened, he must wriggle around the text at all costs. I didn't have a clear answer to my own question but Chuck's answer had not helped me. Perhaps there might be another question in the bowl that would point in the right direction.

More trivial questions followed. I was bored until Stan started to read a question that I suspected came from Luke Rodman for, after the first few words, he seemed to know what followed. He rose up from *his* bored position and sat back with arms folded, eager to hear Chuck's response. The question read, "The prostitute is called 'Babylon the Great'; Babylon is commonly associated with Rome; the beast on which the prostitute sits is also thought to be Rome with its seven hills symbolized by the beast's seven heads. However, in Revelation 17:16, the beast destroys the prostitute. Did Rome destroy Rome or does Babylon *not* signify Rome after all?"

Stan passed the question to Chuck who paused as he re-read it. "Mm!" he murmured. "An insightful question. Fortunately, I have the answer in a comment by C.I. Scofield written in the margin of my Bible." He paused as he found the note and read: "Two 'Babylons' are to be distinguished in the Revelation: ecclesiastical Babylon, which is apostate Christendom, headed up under the Papacy; and political Babylon, which is the Beast's confederated empire, the last form of Gentile world-dominion. Ecclesiastical Babylon is 'the great whore' (Rev. 17:1), and is destroyed by political Babylon (Rev. 17:15–18).''

Luke's arms were still folded and the look on his face said that he was not satisfied. If *he* was unhappy with Chuck's answer to *his* question, and *I* was unhappy with Chuck's answer to *my* question, perhaps we could help each other by sharing our concerns. I resolved to catch up with him during the meal break.

Josh had sat beside me throughout the question time but I saw no noticeable lifting of his spirits. He seemed to be enduring rather than enjoying it and to be relieved when the last question was answered and the meeting closed. With a languid look, he turned and said, "Ed, I think I'll go home and have an early night. Thanks for being a friend." I gave his arm a gentle squeeze and he was gone, leaving me to seek an answer to my question.

45

Babylon is Not Rome

I didn't have to look for Luke Rodman. As Josh took off in one direction, Luke appeared from another. Dispensing with formalities, he said, "I'll bet my bottom dollar that you submitted the question about the advantage of dying after the fall of Babylon."

"Your bottom dollar's safe. I did submit the question and I'm sure I'd be right in ascribing to you the question that raised doubts about the Roman connection with Babylon."

"Spot on!" he said. "And I'm cornering you before someone less friendly does. I'm convinced that our two questions are related."

"I hope you're right," I said. "Let's grab a coffee and find an isolated table in the hall where we can chat without interruption."

Never one to curb plain speaking, Luke said, "Good idea: we don't want an eavesdropper spreading the word that paramours of the Babylonian prostitute have infiltrated the camp."

Once settled with our coffees, I asked, "How are our questions related, Luke?"

"My question concerned the identification of Babylon. I believe the correct answer to that question will help answer your question."

"You have my attention. Please continue."

"With the help of two witnesses, Milton Terry's *Biblical Hermeneutics*, and J.S. Russell's *The Parousia*, I will present the case that Babylon does not represent Rome. Dr. Harmon believes Babylon *does* represent Rome. I will argue that there is a better alternative." As Luke Rodman the lawyer prepared to give evidence, I took an imaginary seat in the "gallery" to weigh it.

"Babylon is described as 'the great city' in Revelation 16:19 and 17:18. The same phrase exactly is used in Revelation 11:8 of the city where Christ was crucified, undoubtedly Jerusalem. Unless it can be shown that

Revelation speaks of two great cities, we must at least be open to the possibility that Babylon represents Jerusalem."

At the risk of being ejected from the court, I interrupted from the "gallery": "You'll have to do better than that, Counselor."

"Hold your horses; I'm just getting started and my plea for an open mind appears to be met with a closed mind. Consider this:

"The book of Revelation, which likens Babylon to a prostitute, has more allusions to the Old Testament than any other book in the New Testament. In the Old Testament, the imagery of prostitution is a common description of unfaithful Jerusalem, certainly not Rome. Note Isaiah 1:21: 'See how the faithful city has become a harlot.' Jeremiah 2:20 calls Jerusalem a prostitute and Ezekiel 16 graphically enlarges on Jerusalem's prostitution. The analogy emphasizes Jerusalem's unfaithfulness to the God with whom she was in covenant relationship. The city of Rome never had such a relationship."

"You could have something there, Luke. Is that it?"

"No way! I'm just warming up. Listen to the description of Babylon in Revelation 16:19:

> The great city split into three parts, and the cities of the nations collapsed. God remembered Babylon the Great and gave her the cup filled with the wine of the fury of his wrath.

"Again, John appears to be drawing on two Old Testament descriptions of Jerusalem and applying them to Babylon in the book of Revelation. First, Ezekiel 5:1–5, 12 speaks of a three-way split of Jerusalem involving God's judgment through plague, famine, and sword, all of which, in Luke 21:11, 24, Jesus predicted in the context of the fall of Jerusalem. Second, in Isaiah 51:17, Jerusalem drinks the cup of God's wrath, similar language to that used in Revelation with respect to the fall of Babylon."

As Luke continued to build his case, the crack in my mind that had begun to open widened but, so ingrained was the traditional Roman connection, I was not convinced "beyond reasonable doubt"—but Luke was not finished.

"Babylon the prostitute was also Babylon the persecutor of apostles, prophets, and saints in general. She is said to be drunk with their blood (Revelation 17:6) and at her downfall, they are told in Revelation 18:20: 'Rejoice over her' because 'God has judged her for the way she treated you.'"

"Hang on, Luke, if I'm right about where you're going with this, you're forgetting that history shows Rome drunk with the blood of martyrs. Don't you know what went on in the Colosseum, not to mention the provinces of the Roman Empire? It's invalid to argue your case on selective evidence that supports it while neglecting clear evidence that doesn't. You just quoted

Revelation 18:20 but you didn't mention verse 24 which would seem to fit better with Rome than Jerusalem. Listen as I read: 'In her was found the blood of prophets and of the saints, of all who have been killed on the earth.' Surely 'on the earth' indicates widespread persecution more applicable to Rome than Jerusalem."

Luke paid me an unexpected compliment by saying, "You'd make a good lawyer, Ed. You're right. The phrase 'on the earth' does seem to have universal application but, if pressed, the phrase is also a problem for the Rome advocates." Consider: Chuck sees the fall of Babylon as still future and if he looks back over the centuries where persecution of Christians occurred, he will see clearly that Rome was not always involved. Moslems, Hindus, and communists have often been persecutors of the church in places far beyond the realm of Rome."

"But isn't the universal language at least *more* applicable to Rome than Jerusalem," I said.

"Not necessarily," replied Luke. "The Greek word translated 'earth' can also be translated 'land,' in which case the reference would be to the land of Israel not to all parts of the world. Ed, I'm well aware of the atrocities perpetrated by Rome against Christians but hear me out before you continue to play defense lawyer for the Babylon-is-Rome proponents. I call as my star witness none other than Jesus himself."

"This better be good," I said, as I imagined Jesus facing interrogation by Luke. He began to apostrophize Jesus as if he were on the stand, even turning his head in the direction of his invisible star witness when he addressed him and turning it the opposite way when the witness replied.

> Luke: How would you rate Jerusalem as a persecutor?
>
> Star Witness: As recorded in Luke 13:33, I once said to the Pharisees, "Surely no prophet can die outside Jerusalem!"
>
> Luke: But Jerusalem has not been responsible for the death of every martyr.
>
> Star Witness: True, but her record of persecution was so abominable that I foretold her coming judgment on that account in a long tirade against the Jews of Jerusalem, as recorded in Matthew 23:33–36: "You snakes! You brood of vipers! How will you escape being condemned to hell? Therefore I am sending you prophets and wise men and teachers. Some of them you will kill and crucify; others you will flog in your synagogues and pursue from town to town. And so upon you will come all the righteous blood that has been shed on earth, from the blood of righteous

Abel to the blood of Zechariah son of Berekiah, whom you murdered between the temple and the altar. I tell you the truth, all this will come on this generation."

Luke: When you said "this generation," did you mean Jews then living would experience judgment within their lifetime?

Star Witness: I certainly did! Within forty years the city of Jerusalem was destroyed by the Romans in horrifying circumstances.

Luke was enjoying his role play but I interrupted him all the same. "I don't doubt that the destruction of Jerusalem was punishment for its persecution of God's servants, but why should one believe that the fall of Babylon is the fall of Jerusalem and not the punishment of Rome for *its* role as persecutor?"

"A reasonable and not unexpected question from someone with a closed mind, Ed, but don't forget that Babylon is a prostitute, a biblical symbol of spiritual unfaithfulness. Instead of heeding the prophets, the Jews killed them; instead of living righteously, they shed righteous blood; instead of their synagogues being centers of worship, they were scenes of flogging. Furthermore, if we take Revelation 1:1, 3 seriously, the events of the book were to take place 'soon'; they were 'near.' Which city fits better with these words, Rome, which did not fall for 400 years (much later if you listen to Chuck), or Jerusalem, which fell in 40 years?"

I didn't answer Luke's question but my thoughtful silence no doubt suggested to him that my mind had become more open than he credited. I could see that if the whore of Babylon represented Jerusalem and not Rome then Luke's question to Chuck, "Did Rome destroy Rome?" was not a problem because Rome certainly destroyed Jerusalem. When I finally broke the silence, it was to ask Luke to elaborate on how the identification of Babylon with Jerusalem would help with the question I had asked Chuck.

"I'm famished," said Luke. "People are lining up to collect meals at the servery so let's join them. A good feed will fortify us for grappling with your question towards a better answer than Chuck offered. Feeling hungry myself, I followed Luke as he headed for the end of the long queue. On the way, Martin Forbes caught up with me and after a "Good to see you, Ed," he asked, "Were you happy with the answer to your question about your dog's eternal destiny?"

Failing naively to interpret the smile on Martin's face, I replied, "That wasn't my question."

"No," said Martin, "but there were a couple of questions asked that could have come from you."

"One of them did and I know the author of the other one." At that moment Luke turned and said, "Guilty, your honor."

After the introductions, Martin said, "If you felt as I did after hearing the answers to your questions, I suspect you're still in the dark."

"I think Ed is," said Luke, with a sly grin in my direction, "but I'm working on him."

Ignoring Luke's dig, I told Martin that we were on a meal break from a serious consideration of an alternative to the traditional identification of Babylon in the book of Revelation, an alternative that Luke claimed was the magic key to answering my question."

"I'm not into magic," said Martin, "but I did feel the depth of your questions called for an answer out of the ordinary. Would I be intruding if I joined as a spectator when you continue your discussion?"

I was delighted at the thought of having someone with me in the "gallery" but I deferred to Luke as the legal expert and he, not averse to performing before an audience in the court, assented. With plates loaded with chicken schnitzel, mashed potato, cherry tomatoes, and hot French bread laced with garlic butter, we headed for our still-vacant table in the corner.

46

A Better Hope

In between mouthfuls of chicken schnitzel and French bread, we indulged in small talk. I asked Martin if he had caught up with his former student, Cathy Mullins, and Luke quizzed him on life as a Christian lecturer in science at a secular university. However, our conversation didn't last long. Martin wanted the focus to shift from him to Luke's "magic key"; Luke seemed keen to resume his role as chief advocate for the Babylon-is-Jerusalem position; and I was eager to see how his view would help with the answer to my question so summarily dismissed by Chuck.

"Martin," said Luke, "you will recall that I asked Chuck, "Did Rome destroy Rome?" I felt the question was valid because in Revelation 17 the beast destroys the prostitute riding on its back, both, according to Chuck, representing Rome. I agree that the beast with seven heads, said to be seven hills in Revelation 17:9, is Rome. But is the Babylonian prostitute Rome? Earlier I presented a case to Ed that it represents Jerusalem not Rome."

"Luke," I said, "it would be helpful to Martin if you briefly reviewed the points you made before dinner."

With consummate skill, Luke summarized his case for Jerusalem, Martin nodding at intervals as if convinced by the arguments. Even I was more convinced by the repetition of the case than before but I still had a question: "Luke, Revelation 17:3 depicts the prostitute riding on the back of the beast suggesting a relationship that was hardly true of Jerusalem and Rome. How do you square that with your case?"

"Good question, Ed, but note that for a hundred years Rome undergirded Jerusalem and Judea politically with a succession of Roman governors and the Herodian dynasty of kings whose authority to reign over the Kingdom of Judea came from Rome. Certainly not every Jew liked the

Roman connection but recall the words of the Jews to Pontius Pilate prior to the crucifixion of Jesus, 'We have no king but Caesar.'"

"Fair enough," I said, "but to move on, you were going to explain how Babylon's being Jerusalem could help answer the question I put to Chuck."

"Ed, you rightly indicated in your question that the announcement in Revelation 14:8 of Babylon's fall, is followed in verse 13 by the words, 'Blessed are the dead who die in the Lord from now on.' If Babylon is Jerusalem, the words 'from now on' would refer to the fall of Jerusalem in AD 70. The question then becomes, 'What is so significant about the fall of Jerusalem that believers who die *after* that event are better off than those who died *before* it?'"

"You have the floor, Luke, so please answer the question," I said, as Martin and I sat back, keen interest lining our faces.

"Fasten your seat belts," urged Luke, "because we are going to cover a range of texts in quick time, some of which, at first, may seem isolated but in my summation I will show their relevance to the matter before us. Jesus said some of his disciples would not die before three things happened: his return, the inauguration of the kingdom of God, and divine judgment. You can check them out in Matthew 16:27 and 28 and the parallel in Mark 8:38 and 9:1."

"But where does Babylon come into it?" I interrupted.

"All in good time, Ed." I mentally kicked myself for my impatience.

Luke continued. "In Luke 21, Jesus predicts the destruction of Jerusalem, his second coming, the redemption of the disciples, and the coming of the kingdom of God."

Martin interrupted: "But Luke, could there not be many years, even centuries, between those events?"

"That's the common view, Martin, but when the time phrases in the text, all of them in the context of the destruction of Jerusalem, are taken seriously, long periods of time are excluded. As I read the time phrases with emphasis, please note that the pronouns 'you' and 'your' refer not to us but to the four disciples mentioned in Mark 13:3–4 with whom Jesus was speaking." Luke then read the following excerpts from Luke 21:

> "At that time they will see the Son of Man coming" (verse 27).
>
> "When these things begin to take place, stand up and lift up your heads, because your redemption is drawing near" (verse 28).
>
> "When you see these things happening, you know that the kingdom of God is near" (verse 31).
>
> "I tell you the truth, this generation will certainly not pass away until all these things have happened" (verse 32).

"I'm well aware that interpreters try to make 'this generation' mean something other than 'the people living at that time' but the time phrases just quoted are against them, not to mention the use by Jesus of 'this generation' elsewhere, for example, Luke 17:25, and the fact that some of the disciples would not die before Jesus and the kingdom came. By the way, I think Jesus knew there would be a lot of exegetical squabbles over verse 32 so he prefaced it with 'I tell you the truth,' as if to say, 'Some of you are not going to believe me but what follows is the truth.' Furthermore, the insertion of 'certainly' in the NIV translation reflects the very strong future construction used in the Greek."

Turning to me, Luke said, "Ed, since you've waited patiently for the Babylon connection, let's go there. I've already given you evidence that Jerusalem is represented in the book of Revelation as Babylon, so when Luke 21 predicts the fall of Jerusalem, it is reasonable to regard it as the fall of Babylon recorded in Revelation 14:8. In addition, the issues associated with the destruction of Jerusalem are to be associated with the fall of Babylon, namely, the coming of Christ, the coming of the kingdom of God, judgment, and the redemption of the disciples."

"Luke," I said, "pardon my interrupting, but I see where you're going with this and, if I may, I'd like to share part of a conversation I had over lunch with Alex Symons and David Barnes from AIMS. I think it's relevant and I'd like your take on it."

"Fire away, Ed."

"Thanks, Luke. I'll be brief. Much of what you have said entered into our conversation."

"You talked about these matters with Alex Symons?" Luke asked with an astounded tone.

"I did and at one stage I feared he was going to choke on a sausage roll he was eating. I certainly didn't sense any inclination to alter his firmly held views."

"I'm not surprised," said Luke. "Now which part of your conversation did you want to share?"

"We were talking about the rapture which is believed to occur at the last trumpet. I threw in a possible connection with the seventh trumpet of Revelation 11 which is associated with matters not unlike those you have been addressing: the inauguration of the kingdom of God, the judgment of the dead, and the rewarding of the righteous."

"Ed, we're on the same page. I believe Revelation 11 is very relevant to what I've been saying and warrants my summing up the case for a strong connection between the two questions we asked Chuck. You asked, with reference to Revelation 14:8, 13, how the fall of Babylon can be a point beyond which Christians who die are better off. A good question when one recalls that the popular view is that the fall of Babylon occurs after the rapture. Let me sum up the reasons that believers who die *after* the fall of Babylon are better off than those who die *before* it.

1. The fall of Babylon is the fall of Jerusalem, which occurred in AD 70.
2. AD 70 is about 40 years after the death of Christ, that is, about one generation.
3. Within one generation, before some disciples died, Jesus said he would return.
4. His return would mean the resurrection of believers who had died.
5. Believers who had died were, before his return, in a disembodied state.
6. A disembodied state, following his return, would not be the lot of departed saints.
7. Departed saints from then on would immediately receive their resurrected bodies.
8. To receive a resurrected body at death is to be better off than to be disembodied.

"I rest my case," said Luke.

Martin had a question: "Luke, your case rests on point 1, the identification of Babylon with Jerusalem. Not all agree with that point so what happens to your case if Babylon is not Jerusalem?"

"A good question, Martin, but not a problem. You are thinking that point 1, because it is the first point, is foundational to the argument and that a faulty foundation means the collapse of the argument. Babylon is only in focus because both Ed and I asked questions about it and I am trying to show Ed that the answer to *my* question about Babylon helps with the answer to *his* question about Babylon. However, points 2 to 8 hold good without point 1. Christ promised he would return within a generation, before some of the disciples died. If you don't like Babylon as the critical point of demarcation in Revelation 14:13, think of the phrase, 'from now on,' as a reference to the return of Christ."

Martin had another question: "Luke, your claim that the return of Christ occurred in the first century flies in the face of long-established creeds and confessions of the Christian church. The *Apostles' Creed*, for example, says, 'From there [heaven] he will come to judge the living and the dead.' Aren't you going out on a dangerously thin limb?"

"Another excellent question, Martin, and one that I will respond to very cautiously. The creeds, such as the one you mentioned—not composed by the apostles by the way—are attempts to interpret and summarize important truths of the Christian church in keeping with the Scriptures. The high regard in which they have been held for centuries cannot be lightly disregarded. However, as human constructions their interpretations are not infallible and they certainly must never be placed on a level with Scripture. I am bound to respect the authority of Scripture and will happily change my views if I am shown to be in breach of it, but Scripture, not the creeds, will always be the touchstone by which my orthodoxy is judged."

Although I agreed with Luke's response, it left me unsettled. Who was I to question centuries of universal adherence to the Apostles' Creed and others such as the fourth century Nicene Creed? If we start tampering with the latter, we will end up denying the deity of Christ and agreeing with Arius, forerunner of the Jehovah's Witnesses, whose heresies the Council of Nicaea was addressing. Martin's "dangerously thin limb" was beginning to look thinner by the minute and I was not sure I had the guts to go there. Would it not be safer to cling to the trunk?

Either to assuage my doubts or to beat Martin in the competition to outsmart Luke, I threw in a hypothetical: "Luke, I can imagine many at this conference, if made aware of your position, would not only call you a heretic who had embraced the error of Hymenaeus and Philetus, who in Paul's day claimed the resurrection had already occurred (2 Timothy 2:17–18), but would also accuse you of robbing them of the 'blessed hope' of Christ's return (Titus 2:13)."

"You're not wrong there, Ed. I would not only be accused but found guilty and severely sentenced without a fair trial. But since this is all in our imagination, Ed, bear with me as I imagine what I would say to my accusers should they allow me the right of defense." Luke proceeded to address his accusers as if they were present and we were absent:

> In case you've forgotten what it means to beg the question, let me remind you. It means to assume the truth of what you are trying to prove. You are begging the question big time. Since the resurrection had not occurred when Hymenaeus and Philetus made their claim, it was certainly false but leaves open the question as to when the resurrection would occur. Their error does not prove your position is true—nor mine either, for that matter. However, you are assuming your position is true when you accuse me of their error. Instead of begging the question, address the arguments I have used in support of a first-century resurrection.

Luke was getting worked up as he apostrophized his opponents and I feared that he would expatiate on the evidence from Jesus and the apostles for a second advent that for them was near, not far, and that he would forget the second part of the imaginary accusation by conference attendees. He continued his case but not as I had feared.

> Not only did you beg the question, you accused me of robbing Christians of the "blessed hope" of Christ's return as described in Titus 2:13. One could argue that *your* view robs the early Christians of the "blessed hope." They were waiting expectantly for the return of Christ only to be disappointed, if your view is correct. Biblical hope is not wishful thinking but assurance, conviction, with respect to a future event. Did they really have such hope if it was not realized? Does someone who claims to have hope of going to heaven but who ends up in hell really have hope?
>
> Suppose, for the purpose of argument, that there are 2,000 years between AD 70 and the return of Christ, as you understand it. In your view, Christians who die during that long period have to wait till the end of the 2,000 years to receive their resurrection bodies. In my view they are resurrected at the moment of death. I don't rob people of hope; I offer them a better hope.

At that point, the Luke who was so absorbed in addressing his imaginary accusers, came back to us and interrupted our silent reflection with, "Has anyone noticed that we are the only people in the dining room? We're going to be late for the evening session."

47

The Millennium and the New Jerusalem

We *were* late for the evening session, very late. Chuck had not only begun his message, he was 500 years into the millennium. Fortunately, the back row of seats was empty so we were able to sneak in unnoticed. Chuck had everyone's attention as he described a world where lambs frolicked happily with lions and where snakes were safely kept as pets; a world where those who returned with Christ lived next door to survivors of the tribulation, the former sexless, sinless, and immortal, the latter bearing children and subject to sin, sickness, and death; a world without war and political unrest with Christ reigning visibly as King of kings from his headquarters in Jerusalem.

The skeptic in me felt that Chuck's millennium was an unreal world, perhaps fabricated to accommodate a questionable eschatological paradigm. Chuck's talk purported to be an exposition of Revelation 20, the only chapter in the Bible that specifically refers to a millennium, but much of what he said, from the lambs and lions to Jerusalem and even earth itself, came not from the chapter but from the major and minor prophets. I was not convinced that any of the texts quoted referred to the millennium. Chuck's treatment of them lacked serious exegesis based on their historical and literary contexts and came across as proof texts to prop up an entrenched millennial view. My concerns seemed not to be shared by people sitting in the rows in front of me: they were vigorously jotting down the references in their notebooks, with full approval I feared.

When Chuck claimed that during the millennium there would be a rebuilt temple on top of a mountain, an elaborate system of animal sacrifices, Sabbath observance, and celebration of the Passover and Feast of Tabernacles, I was appalled. I felt history was going backwards. It didn't help when Chuck stressed that the sacrifices would only be memorials of

Christ's death, not means of atonement. "So much for the Lord's supper," I thought. Chuck drew heavily from the later chapters in Ezekiel but when I checked Ezekiel 43:25–27, I found references to daily *sin* offerings and to God's accepting people when they perform the prescribed rituals. "So much for the finished work of Christ and salvation by faith alone," I thought. Luke's supposed breach of long-established creeds was beginning to look like a peccadillo.

Throughout his presentation, Chuck spoke with an air of authority suggesting his view of the millennium was unquestionably correct. I envied his confidence without sharing his convictions. I had a number of unanswered questions about Revelation 20 that robbed me of the ability to expound the chapter clearly. If Chuck learnt of my difficulties with the passage, I imagined his saying to me, "I like the view I hold better than the one you don't." I mentally replied, "One can know that a strange creature is not an elephant without knowing what it is."

I wondered later if Chuck might not be more empathetic to my uncertainties and less sure of his millennial position—probably inherited—if he pondered the following four considerations:

1. Revelation 20 is undoubtedly one of the most controversial chapters in the Bible. Reputable scholars are divided not only over the meaning of the finer points, but even of major elements in the big picture. One only has to google "views of the millennium" to see the great diversity that exists among Christians on the topic. One website offers an article entitled, "Why I Changed My Mind about the Millennium"; another offers "The Three Prevailing Millennium Views"; and amazon.com advertises a book entitled, *The Meaning of the Millennium: Four Views*.

2. Another consideration worthy of Chuck's attention comes out of the very first verse in Revelation 20. John sees an angel carrying a large chain with which to bind Satan. Even Chuck should be open to understanding the chain as symbolic, given that Satan is a spiritual being incapable of being bound by a literal chain. If the first verse contains symbolic language, Chuck should consider that such language might be found in other verses also.

3. Related to the previous consideration is the nature of apocalyptic language. Symbolism is a prominent feature of such language. Few people doubt that a prostitute riding on the back of a beast with seven heads is symbolic. Many, however, are less willing to acknowledge that "a thousand years" might also be symbolic. Such a consideration is not a problem for those who understand the nature of apocalyptic language.

For them, the numbers in phrases such as "ten days" (Revelation 2:10), "seven horns and seven eyes, which are the seven spirits of God" (Revelation 5:6), and "144,000 from all the tribes of Israel" (Revelation 7:4), can reasonably be understood as symbolic. The thousand years of Revelation 20 is also worthy of such treatment. Many see the 1,000 years as representing a very long time just as "ten days" may represent a rather short time. One should also be open to the possibility that the Greek scholar, William Milligan, in his Baird Lecture for 1885 was correct when he said: "The fundamental principle to be kept clearly and resolutely in view is this, that the thousand years express no period of time. Like so many other expressions of the Apocalypse, their real is different from their apparent meaning. They are not to be taken literally. They embody an idea; and that idea, whether applied to the subjugation of Satan or to the triumph of the saints, is the idea of completeness. Satan is bound for a thousand years—i.e. he is completely bound. The saints reign for a thousand years—i.e. they are introduced into a state of perfect and glorious victory."

4. Chuck might be less dogmatic in his interpretation of Revelation 20 if he were willing to reconsider his approach to the book as a whole. His adoption of a sequential approach to Revelation means that he regards each section of the book as following the previous one chronologically: current age, rapture, tribulation, second coming, millennium, judgment, new Jerusalem, all in order from left to right on a long timeline. However, an alternative approach regards the components of Revelation as involving repetition so that, just as the seven bowls (Revelation 16) concern issues covered by the seven trumpets (Revelation 8, 9, 11), so Revelation 20, rather than describing a fixed block of time in the future, may be dealing with truths that are taught elsewhere. The major elements of Revelation 20, the binding and defeat of Satan, the resurrection of the dead, the reign of saints with Christ, and divine judgment, are not unique to Revelation 20. The repetition approach is contrasted with the sequential approach in a graphic description of J. S. Russell: "If we may venture to use such an illustration we should say that the visions are not *telescopic*, looking at the distant; but *kaleidoscopic*,—every turn of the instrument producing a new combination of images, exquisitely beautiful and gorgeous, while the elements that compose the picture remain substantially the same."

The Sunshine Coast Independent Fellowship Second-Coming Conference was coming to an end. Apart from tomorrow's regular Sunday morning service, this was the last meeting and Chuck was determined to make the most of it so he begged permission to move on from the millennium to the new Jerusalem. The turning of pages in the notebooks anticipated a new topic and suggested that permission was happily granted.

Chuck's literalism continued into Revelation 21 and 22 as he described a new Jerusalem in the shape of a cube whose three dimensions were each well over 2,000 kilometers. I could conceive of a city with such a length and breadth but such a height challenged my imagination. The golden streets, the pearly gates, and the twelve precious stones in the foundations were all treated as literal. In support of his view, Chuck quoted with approval a writer who said that that if "gold" and "pearls" didn't mean "gold" and "pearls" then the accuracy of the Bible was in question. Chuck's reasoning was as convincing as if he'd said that Jesus had leaves instead of hair because he said, "I am the vine." I cringed inwardly and looked left at Luke who was cringing outwardly and then right at Martin who was either dozing or praying, his eyes closed and his chin on his chest.

Chuck seemed disinclined to wrestle with whether the author *intended* the text to be taken literally or symbolically, preferring the easier but unreliable approach: if you *can* take a passage literally, you *should*. Surely he knew that apocalyptic literature is by nature full of figurative language. It made more sense to regard the precious materials as metaphorical support for Revelation 21:11 where the city is said to shine with the glory of God. While I didn't agree with Chuck's hermeneutics at this point, I didn't want to lose my perspective. Whatever the true state of the new Jerusalem, I was sure the experience of glory would outshine the images used to depict it, whatever it might *actually* look like.

In an attempt to keep myself awake and to stimulate the attention of my two friends, I took from my pocket an unused dinner serviette and wrote, "Turn your phones on and I'll send you a text message." I showed it to Luke. The wrinkles from his face disappeared, he gave me a thumbs-up, and proceeded to adjust his phone. I then nudged Martin. His "Where-am-I?" reaction revealed he'd been sleeping not praying. When he saw the note, he quickly overcame his embarrassment and took out his phone. I felt a bit like a high-school student influencing a couple of mates to misbehave in the back row at a school assembly. I started the digital conversation with a question to both of them:

Me: Is the new Jerusalem up there or down here?

Martin: Not sure but always thought the pearly gates were up there.

Me: Fair enough. After all, it's called the "heavenly Jerusalem" in Hebrews 12:22.

Luke: True, but what do you make of Revelation 21:2–3 where the city comes down from heaven and God lives with people, declaring them *his* people and himself *their* God?

Martin: Those words remind me of the terms of the new covenant in Jeremiah 31:33 and Ezekiel 37:27.

Me: Does that suggest because we are in the new covenant now, we are in the new Jerusalem now?

Luke: Perhaps in a "now-not-yet" sense. Hebrews 12:22 suggests the "now" possibility. When Hebrews 13:14 was written, the city was *about* to come, according to the Greek behind the text.

Me: How do you reconcile that with the new Jerusalem's coming down *after* the appearance of the new heaven and earth (Revelation 21:1–2)? That hasn't happened yet, has it?

Luke: The passing of the old heaven and earth (Revelation 21:1) would seem to be the removal of "the old order of things" (Revelation 21:4), to be replaced with a new order, not new planets and mountain ranges.

Me: That might square with Hebrews 12:26–28 where the removal of heaven and earth (apocalyptically speaking) leads to the coming of the kingdom which Jesus said would happen before some of his disciples died (Matthew 16:28).

Martin: Would someone please pull all the pieces together: I'm getting confused.

Luke: Here's my tentative take. With the old order/covenant/creation passing away when the old Jerusalem fell, the new Jerusalem came which we enjoy down here as a foretaste of much better things to come when we go up there. As Milton Terry puts it: "heaven begun on earth."

I was glad Luke used the word "tentative" because I was not prepared to lightly embrace the thoughts of three "high school boys" texting at the back of the "assembly" when they should have been paying attention to what the "principal" was saying at the front. After Luke summed up, we switched our phones off and gave our attention to Chuck who was continuing his description of the new Jerusalem.

Verses from Revelation 21 and 22 that he read served only to confirm my earlier doubts about his literalism and even made our digital conversation somewhat attractive. When he read about the bride's being the city (21:9–10), I failed to see how he could maintain its literal dimensions and building materials. When he read about the leaves on the tree of life being for "the healing of the nations" (22:2), I thought, "Who needs healing after the millennium, after the wicked have been consigned to the lake of fire? A lot of nations could do with some healing now." And when he read the invitation from the Spirit and the bride to those who are thirsty to come and drink of the water of life which flows down the main street of the city (22:1, 17), I felt it challenged today's church to engage in the task of evangelism. I used to think those outside the city—which I took to be heaven—"the dogs, those who practice magic arts, the sexually immoral, the murderers, the idolaters and everyone who loves and practices falsehood" (Revelation 22:15), were in hell, but I was wrong for they were invited to come and drink of water that was available within the city—hardly possible for people in hell.

My reflections about the new Jerusalem, even if short of the mark, had certainly challenged me: I had drunk of the water of life; I was a participant in the new covenant; I was part of the bride of Christ; my citizenship was in heaven. Nations and neighbors around me were outside (22:15). I had a responsibility to tell them how to get inside (22:14). Eschatology needed to be more than a discussion about the future: it needed to impact the present, to motivate me to help those with an eternally bleak future to exchange it for the glory of the new Jerusalem.

Chuck was finishing off his message. It had been full of good news for Christians: with Christ for a thousand years in the millennium, with Christ forever in the new Jerusalem. To heighten the anticipation of these future blessings, he stressed that they must soon take place, by quoting the words of the angel to John: "These words are trustworthy and true. The Lord, the God of the spirits of the prophets, sent his angel to show his servants the things that must soon take place" (22:6). As he said, "We will soon be with Christ in that heavenly city, the new Jerusalem," the Roland keyboard, played by Chuck's wife Susan, sounded the introduction to Frederic Weatherly's song, "The Holy City." Susan timed it so that Chuck could transition seamlessly from sermon to song. The emotional ambience was palpable. As Chuck sang, I continued to grapple with two issues: how events that must soon take place 2,000 years ago still had not taken place; and how "soon" meant "soon" now but didn't mean "soon" then.

When Chuck got to the last verse of the song, I stopped my mental grappling and began to share the emotions of those around me:

> And once again the scene was chang'd,
> New earth there seem'd to be,
> I saw the Holy City
> Beside the tideless sea;

> The light of God was on its streets,
> The gates were open wide,
> And all who would might enter,
> And no one was denied.
> No need of moon or stars by night,
> Or sun to shine by day,
> It was the new Jerusalem,
> That would not pass away.

After the hallelujahs subsided, Chuck urged his audience not to miss the Sunday morning service and to invite friends and neighbors to come, particularly unbelievers, as he planned to wrap up the series with a message entitled, "The Urgency of the Hour."

As folk moved to the hall for the final supper, Charlotte saw me sitting in the back row and said, "Ed, it's been a long day; I need to go home. I'll go with Carol Wilson and leave you to bring Luke and David when you're ready." I stood for a goodnight peck and she was gone. Martin stood alongside.

"Sorry, Martin," I said, "I don't give my kisses to everyone."

With a mock grimace, he said, "I'm pleased to hear it. I wondered if you've time for a chat. It's not personal so Luke and David are welcome." Alex Symons's shiny bald head led me to David who was pleased to join us for supper. I was unable to draw him away, however, without a caustic comment from Alex: "Still holding to your offbeat notions, Edward?" Without waiting for a reply, not that I wished to respond, he continued: "If Chuck hasn't managed to straighten you out, I'd say you're a lost cause." Exceptional grace kicked in as I said, "Have a pleasant evening, Alex," and taking David in tow, the four of us headed for coffee and SCIF's famous pumpkin scones at a quiet table in a corner. This was becoming a habit.

Not wanting to make a long day unnecessarily longer through idle chatter, I said, "Over to you, Martin."

"This weekend has exposed me to teaching that is largely new to me. I'm a relatively recent convert to Christianity and, besides, the church I attend rarely preaches on eschatology. Recalling the few exceptions, I would say their view differs markedly from Chuck's. I don't wish to pit one view against another but to bounce off you some reflections I've had during the convention.

"At a home group I attend, we've been studying the book of Galatians. In it there's a passage that I was reminded of during Chuck's sessions today. It probably has nothing to do with Revelation so my thinking may be right off the planet. I'd like your comments anyway. In Galatians 4, Paul uses as an allegory the story of two of Abraham's sons, one born to a slave woman and the other to his wife Sarah. Note verses 24–26:

> These things are being taken figuratively: The women represent two covenants. One covenant is from Mount Sinai and bears children who are to be slaves: This is Hagar. [25]Now Hagar stands for Mount Sinai in Arabia and corresponds to the present city of Jerusalem, because she is in slavery with her children. [26]But the Jerusalem that is above is free, and she is our mother.

"What caught my attention is that we have here two women who represent two cities, the old and the new Jerusalem, and two covenants. In Revelation we have two women, the Babylonian prostitute and the bride of Christ, both of them connected with two cities: Babylon, which Luke has argued is old Jerusalem, and the new Jerusalem, the bride of Christ. I'd like to suggest that a subtitle for the book of Revelation could appropriately be, 'A Tale of Two Cities,' with acknowledgements to Charles Dickens. But am I seeing connections where they don't exist?"

David, whose body language betrayed indifference to the topic, unexpectedly responded to Martin's question: "Your recent studies in Galatians triggered off a connection with Revelation because women and cities feature in both. Paul's allegorizing targets Christians who are being influenced by legalistic Jews. He has no thought of eschatology. I see no justification for your proposed subtitle on the basis of Galatians. I am sure John did not write his Revelation with any sense of indebtedness, at this point, to Paul."

"You might be right, David," said Luke "but Martin's proposed subtitle has merit on the grounds of the content of Revelation irrespective of Paul's purpose in Galatians. The book *is* about two cities, two women, and even two covenants."

"A case could be made for more than one subtitle," I said, "but I rather like 'A Tale of Two Cities,' not just because I'm a fan of Dickens with a dog named after one of his characters, but because it's such a neat way of summarizing what for many is a very complicated book. So much of the bad news in the first part of the book revolves around Babylon, the old Jerusalem; so much of the good news in the second part of the book revolves around the new Jerusalem."

"'A Tale of Two Cities' is a great title for the last book of the Bible," said Luke, "and in some respects it sums up a good deal of the Bible as a whole." Luke then turned and thanked Martin for his observation.

"I've appreciated chatting with you guys," said Martin, "and wrestling with questions some of which are yet to be resolved. I'm sorry that the service here tomorrow clashes with the one in my local church so I'll not only say 'Goodnight' but 'Goodbye,' for now anyway."

Martin went off on his own and the rest of us drove home and tried to creep to our respective rooms without waking Charlotte and to get some sleep in readiness for "The Urgency of the Hour" in the morning.

48

Highlight of the Conference

Attendance at the Sunday morning service exceeded expectations. Chuck's challenge to invite friends accounted for some of the strangers; others seemed to be church people who were skipping their regular service for a chance to hear Chuck before the tent came down. Paul Fitzgerald turned up. I had not seen him at any session of the convention. When he entered the tent, he walked down the main aisle, looking around as if he were lost, or in awe of the many people present, or was he looking for Anna? My question was soon answered. Seeing Josh near the bookshop, he called out, "Hey Josh, have you seen Anna?" Rather than dialogue at a distance, Josh approached Paul and greeted him warmly. Though I was seated not far from where they stood, neither had noticed me.

"Have you seen Anna?" Paul asked again.

A lengthy pause before answering suggested Josh was unsure whether he was being asked if he'd seen Anna in the tent this morning or whether he'd seen her elsewhere. He opted for the former, no doubt to avoid a conversation about Anna's illness, knowing the family was keeping it quiet and not knowing how much Paul knew. He simply said, "I've not seen her this morning."

"Don't tell me she's not coming," Paul muttered in mild annoyance. "I could be out surfing this morning but came especially to see her and she's not here."

Paul's reaction indicated ignorance of Anna's illness or, at least, of its seriousness. "When did you last see her?" Paul asked.

I could feel Josh was cornered. He answered, "Yesterday." I hoped, for his sake, that his answer would end Paul's interrogation but he continued:

"Where did you see her?"

"At her home."

"You mean you skipped a meeting of the convention to visit Anna."

"Yep."

"Why?"

"I'm not at liberty to say."

Paul's mildly annoyed tone ratchetted up a notch or two as he said, "Josh, I don't like what I'm hearing. You haven't been flirting with my filly have you, Josh?"

Josh's visit to Anna could hardly be called "flirting" but he hesitated, perhaps because his strong feelings for her confused him. Paul did not wait for an answer: Josh's failure to respond to a simple yes-no question was interpreted as a "Yes." He pursed his lips, shook his head in disgust, and dashed away muttering, "And to think I regarded him as a friend."

Josh looked devastated. He hesitated, as if considering whether to chase after Paul as he headed for the exit but, before he could make up his mind, Mark Mullins started the service by inviting the crowd to stand for an invocatory prayer. Paul disappeared into the forest of standing worshippers and Josh, disconsolate, slumped into the nearest seat.

After an opening hymn, Mark introduced Andy: "Some of you have not met our pastor, Andy Zimmerman, so I've asked him to say a few words."

Andy's Southern drawl and touches of humor as he welcomed the crowd, resonated with the audience, creating an atmosphere in stark contrast to the dejected Josh. He then said, "Dr. Chuck Harmon has been God's man for our first second-coming convention and, as the pastor of this church, I believe he's been the person we needed to stimulate the growth of our congregation. We've been privileged to share him with the wider Christian community and I'm sure I speak for all of you in expressing our gratitude for his making himself available this weekend." Loud applause followed as Andy sat down.

As was usual on Sunday mornings, Stan Mullins gave the announcements, but today he was not his usual self. The matter-of-fact Stan was unusually buoyant. He began with a story about Sherlock Holmes and Dr. Watson who were taking a camping break from criminal investigation.

> From his sleeping bag, Holmes asked, "Watson, are you asleep?"
>
> "I was till your question woke me. What do you want?"
>
> "What do you deduce from the stars above us?"
>
> "That there are millions upon millions of them and that our planet is but a speck in a vast universe."
>
> "No, you idiot," said Holmes, "you should have deduced that some rogue has stolen our tent."

Stan then said, "We don't want this tent to be stolen so it must be pulled down tomorrow. Before that can happen, the inside of the tent must be cleared of books, chairs, the keyboard and the platform. If you can be here at nine o'clock tomorrow morning to help, we would be very grateful."

Stan's manner showed he was obviously thrilled with the success of the convention and, one sensed, a little proud of the new direction the church was taking. He made a strong point of inviting those looking for a church to consider SCIF, "the church with the pastor all the way from the United States of America, the church where everyone's welcome, and the church where Buderim's best pumpkin scones are served for morning tea." Perhaps SCIF was about to enter a growth phase. Charlotte was beaming at my side and, looking around at other members of the church, they all, apart from Josh, had a similar "he's-talking-about-*my*-church" look on their faces. Stan invited Andy back to lead in a pastoral prayer.

"Before I pray," he said, "I would like to request prayer for our family. We love being in Australia and we love serving in the church here on the Sunshine Coast. If you sense that the next word I'm going to say is 'but', you're not wrong. But our daughter Anna [Josh perked up] is suffering from a recurrence of nephritis, a disease she contracted as a child. Sadly, her health has deteriorated rapidly to the point where she may soon have to undergo regular dialysis and need a kidney transplant. She's in desperate need of believing prayer so, as a family, we would be grateful for such support." Andy's voice began to quaver and he struggled to continue. With appropriate sensitivity, Mark Mullins came to the microphone, put his arm around Andy and, with a doctor's understanding of her condition, prayed for Anna and the family then, to relieve Andy of the responsibility of the pastoral prayer, he prayed for the members of SCIF and for the wider community.

The sad look on Josh's face was still there but he now seemed to be present rather than somewhere else. He even joined in the singing of "He's Coming Soon" prior to Chuck's final message, "The Urgency of the Hour." However, he remained downcast for the rest of the service.

Chuck began by reading three sentences from the last chapter of the book of Revelation: Verse 7: "Behold, I am coming soon!" Verse 12: "Behold, I am coming soon!" Verse 20: "Yes, I am coming soon." Chuck continued: "Rather repetitious, isn't it? It's repetitious for a reason: Jesus repeats 'I am coming soon' because he *is* coming soon." Amens sounded all over the tent. "But," said Chuck, "the repeated words sound an urgent message, a message that needs to be heeded by the world at large and by every person in this tent, no matter who you are."

Having set the direction his sermon would take, Chuck unpacked the urgency of the hour for the world at large by elaborating on the "war to end all wars" that didn't; on a United Nations that had not united the nations; on the slaughter of Tutsis by Hutus in Rwanda; on Sunnis and Shias fighting in the Middle East; on floods of refugees fleeing Islamic militants; and on bomb blasts from Paris to Pakistan, from London to Libya. If that were not enough, Chuck exposed corruption in political corridors, drug cartels in South America, sexual slavery in Asia, and child abuse in religious institutions. "For such a world," said Chuck, "judgment is coming and it's coming soon. The only hope for a world hurtling out of control is the return of Christ. And he's coming soon."

I agreed with Chuck that we lived in a very needy world but questioned his claim that the return of Christ was the world's only hope. Was the gospel not the answer to the world's problems? Were the incarnation, atonement, and resurrection of Christ not the elements of God's strategy for the renewal of humanity?

The image Chuck created in my mind was of a besieged remnant in an increasingly hostile world, much like a band of settlers huddled in a stockade encircled by wild Indians brandishing tomahawks and shooting flaming arrows. With their only hope the arrival of the cavalry, they sing, "Hold the fort for I am coming."

To me, Chuck endorsed a pessimistic mindset that failed to do justice to the work of Christ and the power of the gospel. It was as if the mustard seed in Jesus' parable was not destined to become a big enough bush in which birds would bother building a nest. Chuck's gloom-and-doom view of the world and his interventionist solution triggered a contrasting and emotional experience from my past. I was at a missionary rally. We were singing a hymn to the beautiful tune "Londonderry Air." When we reached verse 3, particularly the second half where the music rose in keeping with "But this I know," my eyes became moist with tears, tears of victory at the prospect of optimism realized.

> I cannot tell how He will win the nations,
> How He will claim His earthly heritage,
> How satisfy the needs and aspirations
> Of east and west, of sinner and of sage.
> But this I know, all flesh shall see His glory,
> And He shall reap the harvest He has sown,
> And some glad day His sun shall shine in splendor
> When He the Savior, Savior of the world, is known.

Such optimism resonated with my spirit as giving greater honor to the gospel and greater satisfaction to Christ as he reflects on the travail of his soul and the uncountable fruit of his sufferings.

I emerged from my reminiscing to find Chuck focusing on the Christians in the tent with a warning not to be caught napping by the soon return of Christ but to be living and serving with an any-moment mentality. "He's coming soon; he's coming soon."

His final challenge was to non-Christians with a clear and powerful presentation of the gospel. He stressed humanity's separation from God through sin, God's means of reconciliation through the death of Christ, and the dire consequences of being alienated from God when Christ returns. "The urgency of the hour," he said, "is to repent and trust Christ today. Tomorrow may be too late because he's coming soon; he's coming soon."

As Mrs. Beecroft quietly played the introduction to the closing hymn, Chuck read the first verse:

> Come, every soul by sin oppressed;
> There's mercy with the Lord,
> And He will surely give you rest
> By trusting in His Word.

He then invited those who were not ready to meet the soon-to-return Christ to come forward as the hymn was sung. He paused after each verse, read the next verse and reissued the invitation. To his credit, Chuck did not indulge in emotionalism and manipulation but many responded. The last verse read:

> Come, then, and join this holy band,
> And on to glory go
> To dwell in that celestial land
> Where joys immortal flow.

Chuck revisited his theme: "He's coming soon; he's coming soon. At that time some will go to glory to dwell in that heavenly land. Will you be among them? If you're not sure and you want to be, come as we sing. Time is short: he's coming soon." I turned to look back up the aisle. People were still coming and, to my surprise, I saw Paul Fitzgerald among them. He looked straight ahead as he came, his face showing signs of a seriousness I had not seen in him before.

The response to Chuck's message was unique for SCIF and the unexpectedness of it meant the members of the church were unprepared to handle the situation. Mark Mullins took the initiative for chairs to be set up in a quiet corner beside the platform and for Chuck to speak to those who had responded. Meanwhile, Charlotte and I, along with other church members moved towards the counseling area to help as needed. Mark recruited others and appropriately matched counselors with inquirers. I noticed he directed John Delaney towards Paul Fitzgerald.

Morning tea was a protracted event extending from the close of the meeting to well after the completion of the counseling session. When Charlotte and I arrived, the hall was abuzz with joyful conversation. Robyn Bradford was her ebullient and ubiquitous self as she moved from table to table with an infectious excitement. Not that her catalytic influence was needed. All around people were rejoicing: some in the new experience of conversion; others in the privilege of having led someone to Christ; still others in the overall success of the weekend.

Charlotte was keen to get home as she had promised lunch to our house guests, David and Luke, before they drove back to Brisbane. I anticipated that the joyful morning-tea conversation would continue around the meal table with, perhaps, the addition of a final robust eschatological discussion. I had a couple of questions arising from the morning's service. I just might use them to demonstrate *my* catalytic influence.

49

Dodgy Means to the End

The spinach quiche and Caesar salad justified the expressions of gastronomical satisfaction directed at Charlotte. She responded with, "If you are enjoying the quiche as much as I have enjoyed the spiritual food this weekend, I'm a better cook than I thought I was. The highlight, of course, was this morning's service with such an encouraging response to the message."

"I agree, Charlotte," said David. "It was worth coming up from Brisbane for that meeting alone. When I saw all those people going forward to get ready for the soon return of Christ, a question arose in my mind that I would like to put to Ed and Luke."

"We're in the hot seat, Ed," said Luke, as he gave me a wink.

I had not expected discussion to begin so early in the meal and the unsettled look on Charlotte's face suggested an inaudible "Edward" coupled with a concern the discussion might be too robust.

Loud barking from Chuffey prevented David's asking his question and announced the arrival of Josh from next door. He walked up the back stairs and apologized for interrupting our lunch.

"You're most welcome, Josh," said a relieved Charlotte. "Ed," she said to me, "if you draw up another chair, I'm sure Josh would be happy to join us for a coffee."

"Sounds good," said Josh, as he took the seat I offered. He looked very different from the depressed Josh I had seen slouched in the tent earlier.

"What news, Josh?" I asked.

"I'm heading back to Bundaberg this afternoon and dropped in to say goodbye."

"You're going back to work yet your cheerful demeanor looks like you're going to a party," I said with a smile.

"Well, I've had some good news since last we spoke but if I tell you the story, I'll feel like I'm intruding on your lunch-time conversation."

"No need to feel that way, Josh," Charlotte was quick to respond. "You're always welcome and, if you're happy to tell your story, we'd love to hear it. I'm sure I speak for everyone here." She received a triple male affirmation.

"Well," said Josh, pausing reflectively, "this morning I had a run-in with Paul Fitzgerald just before the service started. Paul and I have been friends for years but today we fell out. He virtually accused me of trying to steal his girlfriend, Anna Zimmerman. He stomped off just as the service was starting and I assumed he left the meeting."

Trying hard not to let my body language betray that I had witnessed the episode between Josh and Paul, I said, "I noticed Paul went forward when Chuck gave his appeal."

"I didn't," said Josh. "I was too preoccupied with my problems to notice anything, but at morning tea I learnt what happened."

"Speaking of tea," interrupted Charlotte, "who's for a cuppa?"

The three men who had leaned forward in anticipation of the continuation of Josh's story, sat back a little disappointed but gave their orders for tea and coffee. "Put your story on hold, Josh; I'll be right back," said Charlotte as she disappeared into the kitchen.

"Josh," I said, "I was surprised to hear Andy Zimmerman report on Anna's health during the meeting."

"So was I," replied Josh. "I wish her condition had been made public earlier. My confrontation with Paul may have been avoided."

"I understood the family intended to keep Anna's health to themselves," I said. "Any idea why Andy might have changed his mind, Josh?"

"I asked myself the same question during the sermon," said Josh. "That's probably why I missed most of it."

"What conclusion did you come to?" I asked.

"I think Anna's condition has deteriorated so rapidly that Andy feels it is inappropriate to keep the congregation in the dark. More importantly, I think he feels the need for prayer support, not only for Anna but for the family. Perhaps Andy had not intended to say what he did this morning. Perhaps, as he stood to give the pastoral prayer, he was very conscious that he, the pastor, needed prayer more than anyone, and the thought of his absent and very sick daughter so overcame him that he just came out with it."

Josh himself seemed to be getting emotional so I cut him short: "Anna's condition is certainly very serious. With the prospect of a kidney transplant, it's not too early to be requesting prayer from a wide segment of the Christian population for a suitable donor. I think Andy has done the right thing and we all need to stand with the family."

"We should pray now," suggested David. We nodded and he prayed, followed by Luke and me. When I finished, I opened my eyes thinking Josh might not be up to participating. I looked up to see Charlotte standing at the door with a tray of steaming mugs and a restraining look on her shaking head that said, "Wait a minute, Ed." Her empathy was justified. Josh did pray and as I listened I discerned two things: one, that Josh Wilson was more spiritually mature than I realized; and two, that Josh Wilson was more in love with Anna Zimmerman than I realized.

Charlotte served the tea and coffee with vanilla slices and then said, "Josh, I'm sorry I interrupted your story earlier. You were about to tell us what you learnt about Paul Fitzgerald at morning tea."

"I was in no state of mind to go to morning tea. The only reason I went was to find Dad and Mum to tell them I'd probably be on my way to Bundaberg before they got home. When I entered the hall, I couldn't see them but Elizabeth Wills saw me and approached saying, "Do you know what John's doing?"

"The tone of her voice indicated that *she* knew what he was doing and thought I'd be interested. Unenthusiastically, I replied, "No. What?"

"She said, 'He's counseling Paul Fitzgerald inside the tent. He went forward during the appeal.'

"She had my attention. I told her I thought Paul had skipped the meeting, to which she said, 'John and I arrived a bit late. As we walked from the car park to the tent entrance, Paul rushed past us looking quite agitated. John went after him and managed to persuade him to stay, provided we sat at the back of the meeting so he could make an unobtrusive getaway if he couldn't hack it. He stayed, he came under conviction, he responded, and as John counsels him, I believe he's doing serious business with God.'"

"Have you had any feedback on how the counseling went?" asked Charlotte.

"I sure have. Elizabeth kept me talking until John and Paul arrived. I felt uneasy, unsure about what to say to Paul. I needn't have worried: he started the conversation but not before he hugged me—I felt a bit embarrassed. He said, 'I'm sorry, mate.' He released his grip on me and, looking me straight in the eye, said, 'I've been a scumbag. When I heard Andy talk about how sick Anna was, I thought, "Here I am so out of touch with the girl I profess to love I don't even know that she's seriously ill." To be honest, Josh, I've no right to use the word "love" because, I'm ashamed to say I've been two-timing. Anna's not the only girl I've been chasing. As Dr. Harmon spoke this morning, God showed me that I was a phony. The profession of faith I made was only to impress Anna; my church attendance was only to see Anna. And all the time I was seeing other girls on the side. I didn't know

Anna was ill; you did, Josh, and you had every right to visit her as your sister's friend. Maybe she means more to you than that. If so, good for you; you're more worthy of her than I am.'

"I was overwhelmed. I couldn't take it in, but he wasn't finished. 'Josh,' he said, 'I now believe I'm no longer a fake but a genuine Christian. With John's help I've surrendered my life to Christ. He can come back as soon as he likes because I'm ready.'

"And I got the feeling he meant every word of it. I returned the hug he'd given me, with no embarrassment this time."

"No wonder you're so much brighter than you were earlier this morning," I said.

"One last thing," said Josh. "Andy said I could pop in to see Anna on my way back to Bundaberg. I just might do that," he said, with raised eyebrows and a cheeky grin.

Josh finished his coffee hurriedly and said he had to go. We farewelled him, he went down the back steps and, with a parting friendly bark from Chuffey, he was gone.

For a few moments all was quiet around the table. Charlotte broke the silence: "In spite of my joy at Josh's story, I can feel an afternoon nap coming on. Not uncommon on a Sunday. I'll let you guys continue chatting." David and Luke thanked her profusely for her hospitality, she said her goodbyes and left with, "I'll leave the dishes for you, Ed."

Luke brought us back to the conversation we were having before Josh turned up. "David," he said, "before Ed goes off to do the washing up, I'd like to know what you had in mind when you said that in the light of the good response to Chuck's message on the imminent return of Christ, you had a question for Ed and me."

"With the intervention of Josh's absorbing story," said David, "I thought my question was gone forever. You've got a good memory, Luke. Give me a moment while I do a mental backtrack." He paused and then asked, "Given that Chuck's message was very much focused on a future return of Christ that you guys think may have already occurred, does not the wonderful response to the message, with life-changing effect, as in the case of Paul Fitzgerald, argue for the truth of Chuck's position?"

David had pinched one of my questions but had expressed it better than I could have, reinforced as it was by Josh's news about Paul Fitzgerald. During the service I had considered an answer to the question but decided to leave the answer to Luke. I encouraged David by saying, "A very good question, David. Over the years I've heard many testimonies along the following lines: 'I was brought up in a Christian home. One night, at the age of seven, I thought, "What if Jesus comes back while I'm asleep and I wake up to find Dad and Mum have been taken and I'm left." That night I gave my life to Christ.' What happened this morning is not an isolated example of conversions associated with the proclamation of Christ's return."

I could see Luke champing at the bit as I spoke, probably thinking I had joined the opposition. He lost no time in saying, "Truth by association is as invalid as guilt by association, David. If the child in Ed's story was converted at age seven, it was because he committed his life to Christ not because he believed in his parents' eschatology. Conversions result from belief in the gospel, not belief in a particular view of the second coming. If you start adding that to the gospel you'll have a false gospel."

"That's true, Luke, but the second coming of Christ did play a significant role in my story," I said.

"It did," said Luke, "but again that does not prove the truth of the parents' eschatology."

"Why not?" from David.

"What the child believed had the same effect as if he had said, "What if the house burns down while I'm asleep? What if someone breaks into the house and murders me while I'm asleep?"

"Both of those are possibilities," I said.

"Whose side are you on, Ed?" Luke said, not unkindly. "The effect of one's belief can be very real without the object of that belief being true. I may believe that the sound of an explosion means terrorists are blowing up my house, causing me to run for my life. The running is real but the sound may not be as thought. It could be caused by a car's backfiring or a neighbor's suddenly turning up the volume on his television during a war movie. The child in Ed's story might wake up in the night to go to the toilet, find his parents' bedroom empty, believe they've been raptured, repent and be soundly converted. Actually, his parents have not been raptured but are having a cuddle on the back porch in the moonlight."

David asked, "Are you saying 'the end justifies the means?'"

"Not at all! I'm saying that a good outcome does not justify the means used to achieve it, any more than the betrayal by Judas that led to the death of Christ for the salvation of the world, makes Judas a good man."

"Are you saying Chuck did the wrong thing this morning?" David asked.

"Chuck preached the gospel faithfully and sought to motivate a response to it on the basis of his belief that Christ could return at any moment. He acted in accordance with his convictions. It's not the way I would do it because I don't share his convictions."

"How would *you* motivate a response to the gospel?" I asked.

"Rather than say, 'Christ could come today,' I would say, 'You could die today.' The time of one's death is very uncertain. Visit a cemetery and note the ages inscribed on the headstones. In all the years preachers have been using Chuck's motivational approach, many have died, none has been raptured. Are you 100 percent certain that Christ will come in the next hundred years? I suspect that, like me, you are more certain that most people now living will have died in that time. I believe my approach is quite as motivational as Chuck's but that it has more validity."

Logical as Luke's argument was, David was not about to give up. "Luke, the problem with your approach is that it ignores the ethical imperatives in the New Testament based on the fact that Christ is coming soon. To take but one example, James 5:8: 'You too, be patient and stand firm, because the Lord's coming is near.' If James can make motivational use of the second coming, why can't Chuck?"

"You're right, David. The New Testament writers often urged action on the grounds that Christ's coming was near. The reason they did so was that Christ's coming *was* near. As we were reminded this morning, three times Christ says in the last chapter of Revelation, 'I am coming soon.' The reason Chuck shouldn't do what James did is that Jesus did what he said he would do: he came when he said he would come; he came soon, before some of the disciples died, before that first generation passed. Throughout this weekend we've been singing 'He's coming soon.' Almost everyone has done so sincerely believing that the return of Christ is just round the corner, that 'soon' means 'soon.' David, how come 'soon' means 'soon' now but it didn't mean 'soon' then?"

Luke had just asked my second question. To give David a break from Luke's barrage, I stepped in. "David, all three of us want to know what the Scriptures indicate in relation to the words 'near' and 'soon' as they apply to the coming of Christ. Two verses in the chapter from which Chuck read this morning may help us.

"In verse 10 of Revelation 22, John is told, 'Do not seal up the words of the prophecy of this book, because the time is near.' The phrase, 'the time is near,' is given as the reason for not sealing the prophetic message, in stark contrast to Daniel 8:26 where Daniel is told, 'Seal up the vision, for it concerns the distant future.' Clearly the 'prophecy of this book,' the whole of it, was not in the distant future when John wrote: it was soon, it was near.

"At the risk of over-kill, David, consider the very next verse, Revelation 22:11. Having said 'the time is near' in verse 10, John immediately says in verse 11, 'Let him who does wrong continue to do wrong . . .' I'll guarantee you've never heard a sermon on that verse, David. What would it sound like? Would the preacher say, 'If you're a thief, continue robbing banks; if you're committing adultery, continue your affair?' Certainly no preacher would say that in *our* day but John said it in *his* day. Allow me to paraphrase what John seems to be saying: 'The time is so near that it's too late for change.'"

"Thanks for that Ed," said David. "Those two verses certainly deserve further thought."

The dishes were waiting for me and my friends had quite a drive to get home but I wanted to share a little more before they left. "David and Luke, I've been on a journey for quite some time, asking questions about eschatology and not always getting answers. Where I have drawn conclusions, they are not set in concrete: I may be wrong. If so, I'll be the first to admit it. One thing is certain: I am bound to the authority of Scripture as rightly interpreted and I am committed to my friends. Even if we do not agree, I will try not to be disagreeable and will continue to respect and love you both as brothers in Christ."

"Same here," said David.

"Count me in too," said Luke.

"Finally—I mean it—I am concerned that unless we resolve the issues associated with 'soon,' we may be guilty of a breach of ethics or, to be more blunt, of a massive con job."

"Whatever do you mean?" asked David with a pained look.

"Let's use our imaginations. Suppose you've been asked by the company you work for to do some business interstate. You have a young family. As you farewell them, you say to the children, 'Be good while I'm away. Do what Mummy tells you. I'm coming home soon and when I do, I'll have some exciting surprises for you.' Day after day Mummy reminds the children, 'Daddy will be home soon and he's bringing some lovely presents, so be good.'

"But Daddy doesn't come home soon. The children grow up, get married and have children. They say to their children, 'Your grandpa said he was going away and that he would come back soon with some lovely surprises, so be good. He could come today.'

"But he doesn't. The grandchildren grow up, marry, have children and say to them, 'Your great-grandfather said he was going away . . . ' I don't need to go on.

"Not for a moment am I accusing Jesus of deception, but some biblical interpretations, and the use made of them, reflect negatively on his integrity and I, for one, will not have it. If that puts me out on a limb, so be it."

David and Luke were soon gone and I was left alone—to do the dishes.

50

Eschatological Dangers

At 9:00 a.m. on Monday morning, the church property was bustling with dozens of volunteers folding tent flaps, stacking chairs, dismantling the platform, the sound and lighting equipment, and the book table. The tent had to be emptied by 10:00 a.m. in readiness for the arrival of the marquee rental professionals who would lower the huge tent poles and fold the heavy sections of canvas.

Three hours later, the site was restored to its pre-second-coming-conference condition. The vacant land somewhat mirrored my inner emptiness. I had enjoyed the weekend, the enthusiastic singing of the crowds, the stimulating meal-time discussions with friends—even with Alex Symons—and the thought-provoking addresses by Chuck. Now, all had disappeared with the tent and I was left wondering whether the Sunshine Coast Independent Fellowship would reap any lasting benefits in the New Year; whether the whole thing had been largely a flash in the pan.

"Hi, Ed," said a familiar voice. I turned to see Paul Fitzgerald who, I learnt, had been sweeping the hall, storing trestle tables, and disposing of kitchen garbage. The joy on his face told me that Josh's story had been no exaggeration and that the conference would not be a complete flop: one bright spark would be a worthwhile legacy. Paul thrilled me with an account of his conversion—and I told him so—that left me in no doubt of its genuineness, but I did fear his atheistic father, Max, might be less thrilled about it. Given the lack of encouragement Paul would get at home, I was pleased to hear that John was to meet weekly with him and, as he departed, I expressed the hope that he would continue to attend our home group.

"I certainly will," Ed. "I'm going to need all the support I can get. You have a great Christmas and I'll see you at the first home group of the year, if not before."

I went home, pleased to have caught up with Paul but I was still a bit flat. Charlotte, who had justifiably skipped the working bee, noticed. "You look like you've just eaten a particularly sour lemon, Ed."

"It's probably just the eschatological adrenalin wearing off," I said.

"What do you mean?"

"Over the weekend, I've done a lot of thinking about second-coming issues, about what Chuck said, about what my friends and even my critics have said. I've enjoyed it. Some of the questions I've been asked, as well as those I've asked myself, have stimulated my brain cells and pushed dementia a little further into the future."

"Ease up, Ed. Dementia's not even on the radar."

"It might appear over the horizon sooner than you think if I don't do something about it. When I was at AIMS, Charlotte, my mind was active. I was preparing and giving lectures, studying journals and even writing articles for them. We've been here for two years and I've spent more time fishing than I have on such things. I fear I'm fossilizing. I need a project that will stretch me mentally."

"You don't have lectures to prepare anymore but there's no reason for not writing. You've got an office, a computer, and a good personal library. Why shouldn't Dr. Edward J. Sutherland become a household name because of a bestseller he wrote? Give it some thought. I'm going to take a nap. I've left you a salad in the fridge."

Charlotte's suggestion was a good one. I *did* give it some thought. Over several days, the conviction grew that I should write a book about eschatology in an attempt to clarify my muddled thinking on the subject. For too long I'd been questioning, debating, asserting, doubting, criticizing, and being criticized, about end-times issues. The result? Confusion, perhaps heresy! Was it possible to pull together the disparate strands of my thinking to create a neatly-woven tapestry out of a tattered mess? I wanted to be the "exact man" whom Francis Bacon said was the product of writing. Was he correct? I'd have to write to find out. I recalled a verse from a poem by John Greenleaf Whittier:

> Drop Thy still dews of quietness,
> Till all our strivings cease;
> Take from our souls the strain and stress,
> And let our ordered lives confess
> The beauty of Thy peace.

The words "ordered lives" meant that, if I was going to take the business of writing seriously, I needed to organize my day with dedicated slots for the task. Because Charlotte was at her best in the early morning, I made myself available at that time to help with shopping, in the garden, or around the house as needed. We agreed that after morning tea together I would go downstairs to my office and write, leaving her free to design, paint, photograph, or simply relax. We'd meet again for lunch, then she would take her regular nap and I would continue writing—after washing the dishes.

The road to bestseller status got off to a bumpy start. At our first morning tea, Charlotte asked, "Have you decided on a topic for your book?"

"Yes, dear. I'm going to write about the second coming of Christ and related matters."

"Are you sure that's wise, Ed?" she said with a quizzical look. "Your views are considerably left of center. If you publish them, you'll end up with a reputation as a borderline heretic who should be marginalized, if not excommunicated."

"You're probably right, Charlotte, but I feel I need to write the book for my own sake. I'm a mixture of clarity and confusion and I'd like more of the former and less of the latter. I believe writing the book might help me achieve that goal."

"I don't know," said Charlotte, with a thoughtful frown. "I don't want to stifle your creativity or hinder your desire for clarity, Ed, but you could achieve those ends simply by saving your book to a file on your computer and leaving it there, thus avoiding all the risks of going public."

"That's true, Charlotte. What you suggest would meet *my* needs but there are important matters that should be aired widely."

"Are you saying that your eschatological views are so much better than others' that it would be unfair to deprive the world of your unique insights?"

"Charlotte, I am convinced that our views on eschatology, and how we derive them, may have harmful consequences out of proportion to the views themselves. Whether people adopt my views (they're still pretty hazy) is of less importance to me. The repercussions are of the utmost importance and people need to be alerted."

"I can't wait to read the book," said Charlotte, the frown replaced by a smile. "If the subject is so critical, you *ought* to write the book, Ed, but as a compromise, why not write it under a pseudonym? Your message will still get out, but without the risks."

"A good idea, Charlotte. I'll work on it."

The ordered-life routine took a few weeks to become settled. Some adjustments had to be made. Space was needed for such essentials as the occasional concert date with Charlotte, a meal together at the surf club, or at Sizzlers with the Zimmermans, not forgetting fishing excursions with Jack Wilson—when the whiting were biting.

One thing I wanted for the book was a sense of unity. I did not want it to be a rambling discourse reflecting the disjointed bits and pieces I had acquired through my interactions in venues from a fishing boat to a coffee shop, from a barbecue to the back of a tent, not to mention the many debates I had held with myself. My telling Charlotte that people needed to be alerted to the consequences of false views of eschatology suggested a means of unifying the book and a title for it: *Eschatological Dangers*. As for the name of the book's author, I took a leaf out of a pseudonymous book of poems purporting to be written by three sisters, Currer, Ellis, and Acton Bell, who just happened to have the same initials as the Bronte sisters, Charlotte, Emily, and Anne. I opted for Evan James Sinclair. Who could possibly detect that behind the name was Edward J. Sutherland?

My first task was to get an overall outline of the book. I decided to devote a chapter to each of my perceived dangers. I was reminded of how, in preparing sermons over the years, I had always felt I was half-way there when I had the underlying structure in place.

After a week of strict adherence to my ordered-life routine, I came up with the following chapter headings and an outline to be fleshed out later.

CHAPTER 1: THE DANGER OF IMPUGNING THE INTEGRITY OF JESUS

When C.S. Lewis called Mark 13:30 "the most embarrassing verse in the Bible," he clearly understood "this generation" to mean the people living at that time. Instead of determining how the things Jesus had spoken of earlier (including his second coming) could be fulfilled at that time, he assumed Jesus got it wrong. In an attempt to avoid Lewis's conclusion, interpreters give the meaning "race" to "generation" or apply the text to some future generation as if "this" meant "that." They too are wrong. Jesus prefaced his prediction in Mark 13:30 by stressing that he was telling the truth. We should believe him rather than say he erred or try to make what he said mean other than what he intended. Both approaches question his integrity.

The integrity of Jesus is also put at risk in the interpretations given to passages such as Matthew 16:28 where Jesus says he will return within the lifetime of some of the disciples. Those who attempt to make the text refer to events such as the transfiguration neglect the link Jesus made between his coming and three things: the kingdom, the presence of angels, and the distribution of rewards (verse 27), none of which occurred at the transfiguration, the resurrection, or Pentecost.

The integrity of Jesus is impugned by futuristic interpretations of John 14:1–3. Jesus, after telling his disciples that he is going away, comforts them with the assurance that he's going to prepare a place for them and that he'll return to take them to be with him. What cold comfort to disciples who after 2,000 years are still not with him because he's yet to come for them!

The integrity of Jesus is undermined when interpreters huff and puff to make his plain statement, "I am coming soon" (three times in Revelation 22) mean something else.

CHAPTER 2: THE DANGER OF IMPUGNING THE INTEGRITY OF NEW TESTAMENT AUTHORS

When interpreters ignore the plain time references in the following texts, they cast doubt on the integrity of their authors.

> Romans 13:11–12: And do this, understanding the present time. The hour has come for you to wake up from your slumber, because our salvation is nearer now than when we first believed. [12]The night is nearly over; the day is almost here. So let us put aside the deeds of darkness and put on the armor of light.

Paul's integrity is in doubt if he is urging his readers to action using words like "nearly over" and "almost here" when there are still 2,000 years or more to go.

> Hebrews 10:37: For in just a very little while, "He who is coming will come and will not delay."

The integrity of the author of Hebrews is to be questioned when he uses language such as "a very *little* while" if, in fact, "He who is coming" has not come after a very *long* while.

> James 5:8–9: You too, be patient and stand firm, because the Lord's coming is near. [9]Don't grumble against each other, brothers, or you will be judged. The Judge is standing at the door!

The integrity of James is in doubt when he urges ethical behavior on the grounds of "near" and "at the door" if the coming of the Lord is not near but far off, and if the judge is not at the door but miles away.

> 1 Peter 4:7: The end of all things is near. Therefore be clear minded and self-controlled so that you can pray.

Peter's integrity is impugned in his linking of the two sentences with the word "therefore" if the word "near" does not mean "near."

> Revelation 1:1, 3: The revelation of Jesus Christ, which God gave him to show his servants what must soon take place. ³Blessed is the one who reads the words of this prophecy, and blessed are those who hear it, and take to heart what is written in it, because the time is near.

John's use of the clauses, "what must soon take place," and "the time is near," raises doubts about his integrity when interpreters attempt to reconcile these time statements with a delay of thousands of years.

CHAPTER 3: THE DANGER OF PROMOTING INVALID PRINCIPLES OF INTERPRETATION

To ensure an accurate understanding of the Bible, training in sound principles of biblical interpretation (hermeneutics) is important for all Christians. The relationship between eschatology and hermeneutics is circular. Unsound principles of interpretation lead to erroneous eschatology and the teaching of such eschatology encourages the use of unsound principles by those taught.

The eschatology of many Christians was not derived from a study of the Scriptures but was inherited, often over many generations as part of a denomination's articles of faith, or fed to them through radio and television preachers, books, or study Bibles. The unwary can wrongly believe that what they hear or read is truth because the Bible is freely and respectfully quoted. Without criteria for testing the use made of the Bible, erroneous eschatology can be imbibed along with the invalid methods of interpretation associated with it.

The cross-generational propagation of false views of eschatology leads to entrenched views that adherents feel they must uphold at all costs. If the Bible appears to be at variance with the eschatology, the Bible must be interpreted to support the eschatology rather than the eschatology revised or rejected. In the process, errors such as the following occur:

1. Failure to take into account the original audience. In Mark 13:3–4, four disciples ask Jesus some questions following his prediction of the destruction of the temple in Jerusalem. The rest of the chapter is his response to those questions. When Jesus uses the word "you," it refers to those four disciples, not to people living in the twenty-first century.

We cannot assume that signs that he said *they* would experience (such as "wars and rumors of wars") are relevant to *us*.

2. The application of the questionable double-fulfilment principle when interpreting prophecy. For example, a prophecy such as Matthew 24, associated with the destruction of Jerusalem, is also applied to the future without warrant from the text itself.
3. Failure to understand the nature of apocalyptic literature leading to gross literalizing of texts intended as symbolic; for example, a literal understanding of astronomical disturbances that are simply a tool of apocalyptic literature to represent disturbances on earth.
4. Reliance on phrases such as "prophetic perspective" and the redefinition of words like "imminent" to avoid facing up to the plain implications of time texts.
5. The assumption that because a text can be taken literally, it should be, forgetting that the author's intention must determine whether a text is to be understood literally or symbolically.
6. The unquestioned adoption of an inherited paradigm such as dispensationalism that determines the shape of one's eschatology.

CHAPTER 4: THE DANGER OF PROMOTING RELIANCE ON FALLIBLE AUTHORITIES

The more entrenched the eschatology, the greater the danger of being influenced by less reliable authorities than the Scriptures.

Popular preachers and writers on eschatology who make a name for themselves through their conferences, broadcasts, and literature, can be so well-regarded that their interpretations are accepted without question even though their handling of the Scriptures may be questionable. Such "authorities" appeal to their audience through claiming that events in the daily newspapers are the fulfilment of prophecies in the minor prophets or Revelation; through making a case that a prominent world figure is a likely candidate for the antichrist; or through tapping into moral decline and international concerns as clear indicators of an any-moment rapture.

When an entrenched eschatology is supported by a creedal statement that is centuries old, interpreters who have a long association with the denomination or theological persuasion that adheres to the creed, may give it an unwarranted authority. Their commitment to the creed hinders an open-minded consideration of an alternative eschatology. Even denominations that are not confessional can, over time, develop an unwritten eschatological creed quite as damagingly authoritative.

Creedal statements may at times rely on an inadequate foundation. For example, the Westminster Confession, in support of its statement that Christ "shall come again at the last day in great power," uses Matthew 24:30 which was fulfilled within that first-century generation (verse 34).

When arguing for a particular eschatological point of view, it is not uncommon for proponents to quote early church fathers or to make statement such as "this was the view held by the church till the fourth century." Unthinking listeners can be fooled into believing that the fathers and those living nearer the days of the New Testament have greater authority than modern alternative views. They forget that even before the New Testament was completed there were deviations from the truth with false apostles at Ephesus and a false prophetess at Thyatira. As for the church fathers, it is easy to be selective in quoting them, to forget that they can be used to support doctrines not taught in Scripture, and to assume a consistency among them that may not exist.

CHAPTER 5: THE DANGER OF PROMOTING A PESSIMISTIC MINDSET

Our eschatology affects our outlook. Many Christians have an end-times mentality that regards wars, earthquakes, spiritual decline, the rise of false prophets and the antichrist as indicators that Christ is soon to return. Every news bulletin contains enough bad news to justify their pessimistic attitude about the world's future. They look forward to being taken out of the sordid mess at the rapture and before the horrific great tribulation.

The so-called "signs of the times" are questionable, being drawn from passages such as Matthew 24 and 2 Timothy 3:1–5, the former relating to the destruction of Jerusalem and the latter to conditions Timothy's readers would experience.

The pessimistic outlook limits the power and fruit of the gospel and the progress of the kingdom of God. The gospel is *the* answer to the world's problems and Christ's teaching on the kingdom of God is that what began small will become big. Daniel 2 speaks of a kingdom that God sets up and that grows till it fills the whole earth. This good news calls for a willingness to spread the gospel in the sordid mess with an optimistic mindset that the kingdom of God will expand to the glory of God and the honor of Christ's atoning work.

Though I had one more chapter in mind to add to the outline, I thought I would run what I'd written past Charlotte for some feedback. At breakfast one morning I handed her a copy.

With a cup of coffee in one hand and my notes in the other, she read them thoughtfully as I watched her face for signs of encouragement. The occasional nod suggesting approval was outnumbered by frowns that were more difficult to interpret. Did she disagree with what I had written or was she concerned that it was too provocative, even dangerous? I soon found out.

"Ed, you've identified some challenging concepts and I like the way you have tied the chapters together with the dangers thread but much of what you have written confirms the need for you to write under a pen-name."

"I've already decided on one," I said.

"Good for you, Ed. What is it?"

"Evan James Sinclair."

"Edward, the initials of Evan James Sinclair are the same as those of Edward Jeffrey Sutherland. What kind of camouflage is that?"

51

Inauguration or Consummation?

The New Year saw a considerably enlarged post-conference SCIF that included conversion growth resulting from Chuck's message on "The Urgency of the Hour," and transfer growth of conference attendees who preferred our church to their own. Others came at the invitation of members: Paul Fitzgerald brought a fellow surf lifesaver and John and Elizabeth a couple of students from USC. The air of excitement at the prospects for the year ahead was in sharp contrast to the sadness in the Zimmerman family over the state of Anna's health.

At our first Wednesday lunch for the year at Sizzlers, Andy and Linda outwardly rejoiced at the success of the conference and the growth of the church but we could tell they were hurting inside. Andy gave voice to his pain: "Anna has lost 80 percent of her kidney function. If we can't find a kidney donor very soon, she'll have to go on dialysis, something we'd love to spare her from. We are so grieved to see her deteriorating health and so helpless to do anything about it."

"Andy and I would gladly give her one of our kidneys," said Linda, "but we both have blood type AB and that is incompatible with Anna's type A. Sam's blood is type B which is also unsuitable. We really are in a desperate situation. Dr. Mark Mullins is on the lookout for us but so far no donor is in sight."

"How is Anna handling her illness?" asked Charlotte.

"Amazingly well," said Linda. "She's the one who needs encouragement but often she's the one who cheers us. Only yesterday she blessed us by quoting a hymn that regularly sustains her. I found it lifted my spirits so much I made a copy of the words. Let me read them to you. They were written by a Swedish poet, Lina Sandell and translated by A.L. Skoog.

Day by day and with each passing moment,
Strength I find to meet my trials here;
Trusting in my Father's wise bestowment,
I've no cause for worry or for fear.
He whose heart is kind beyond all measure
Gives unto each day what He deems best—
Lovingly, its part of pain and pleasure,
Mingling toil with peace and rest.

Every day the Lord Himself is near me
With a special mercy for each hour;
All my cares He fain would bear, and cheer me,
He whose name is Counselor and Power.
The protection of His child and treasure
Is a charge that on Himself He laid;
"As thy days, thy strength shall be in measure,"
This the pledge to me He made.

Help me then in every tribulation
So to trust Thy promises, O Lord,
That I lose not faith's sweet consolation
Offered me within Thy holy Word.
Help me, Lord, when toil and trouble meeting,
E'er to take, as from a father's hand,
One by one, the days, the moments fleeting,
Till I reach the promised land.

When Linda finished reading, there was a quiet pause, then we spontaneously linked hands round the table at Sizzlers and prayed earnestly for the Zimmerman family, for Anna in particular, and for a suitable kidney donor to be found soon.

The sad news about Anna was very sobering for Charlotte and me. I thought of Josh and wondered how his visit to Anna on his way back to Bundaberg had gone and whether he was fully aware of the seriousness of her condition. I was reluctant to mention either Josh or Paul in our conversation with Andy and Linda. Paul's conversion might make him more acceptable to Anna *and* her parents, not to mention the increased competition for Josh. I would love to have batted for Josh but it was none of my business.

For the rest of the week, I worked on completing the outline of my proposed book, *Eschatological Dangers*. I responded to Charlotte's exposure of the flaw in my pseudonym by changing Evan Jeffrey Sinclair to Charles Fortescue. She liked it and the tender kiss I received assured me my cover would not be blown.

The final chapter in my outline was the most demanding as it sought to pull a number of key issues together and, if I was on the right track, it was the most important for the wider Christian community. The "if" reminded me to hold my views with an open hand but highlighted the risk I was taking. My fool-proof pen name, however, gave me courage to share what I felt might well be the truth, and it offered comfort should it prove to be wrong.

CHAPTER 6: THE DANGER OF MISTAKING THE PURPOSE OF CHRIST'S RETURN

The question for consideration is whether the intended purpose of Christ's return was to launch a new phase in the overall plan of God *within* human history or to wrap up human history at the *end*. In short, was it intended to inaugurate or to consummate?

The vexed question of timing arises. If Christ returned before some of his disciples died, the answer is "inaugurate"; if his return is thousands of years later, the answer is "consummate." How we decide between these options will affect our understanding of the purpose of Christ's return.

Since chapter 6 will argue for inauguration, it is important to make a case for an early return of Christ before considering the purpose of his coming.

Support for an Early Return of Christ

1. The plain statements of Christ that his coming was near when he spoke
   a. Before his disciples traversed the cities of Israel (Matthew 10:23).
   b. Before some of his disciples died (Matthew 16:27–28).
   c. Before their generation ended (Matthew 24:30, 34).
   d. Before long: his three-fold "I am coming soon" (Revelation 22:7, 12, 20).
2. The plain statements of New Testament writers that Christ's coming was near
   a. Romans 13:11–12: "And do this, understanding the present time. The hour has come for you to wake up from your slumber,

INAUGURATION OR CONSUMMATION? 267

because our salvation is nearer now than when we first believed. ¹²The night is nearly over; the day is almost here. So let us put aside the deeds of darkness and put on the armor of light."
- b. Hebrews 10:37: "For in just a very little while, 'He who is coming will come and will not delay.'"
- c. James 5:8–9: "You too, be patient and stand firm, because the Lord's coming is near. ⁹Don't grumble against each other, brothers, or you will be judged. The Judge is standing at the door!"
- d. 1 Peter 4:7: "The end of all things is near. Therefore be clear minded and self-controlled so that you can pray."
- e. Revelation 1:1, 3: "The revelation of Jesus Christ, which God gave him to show his servants what must soon take place. ³Blessed is the one who reads the words of this prophecy, and blessed are those who hear it, and take to heart what is written in it, because the time is near."
- f. Revelation 22:10: "Then he told me, 'Do not seal up the words of the prophecy of this book, because the time is near.'"

3. The last days

Further support for an early return is found in the meaning of the New Testament phrase, "the last days." It is not uncommon for Christians today to make the statement, "We are living in the last days" by which they mean the end is near and the second coming of Christ is just round the corner. It is strange that they do not give the same meaning to the phrase when it occurs in Scripture. Given that the first coming of Jesus occurred in the last days (Hebrews 1:2), those who make the statement might need to consider that the first and second comings were much closer together than they think. The day of Pentecost occurred in the last days (Acts 2:16, 17), language hard to justify for a period that so far has lasted about 2,000 years. Even harder to justify is John's phrase "the last hour" (1 John 2:18).

The Purpose of Christ's Return

1. To execute judgment on decadent Israel

After pronouncing a series of woes on the Jews of his day for their neglect of the law, their hypocrisy, and their persecution of the righteous, Jesus predicted judgment and desolation "upon this generation" (Matthew 23:23–38). He told parables that prefigured such judgment

(Matthew 21:40, 41; Luke 19:27), a judgment that came with the destruction of Jerusalem in AD 70, an event associated with his return.

2. To inaugurate judgment on a broader scale

   Jesus said that at his coming in glory with his angels before some of the disciples died, he would issue rewards according to works (Matthew 16:27–28). Jesus also said his coming in glory would occur within the generation of his hearers (Matthew 24:30, 34) and that it would be associated with the judgment of the righteous and the unrighteous (Matthew 25:31–46). Such judgment is normally thought to occur at the end of time but if Christ's time statements are taken seriously, one of the purposes of his coming within that generation was to execute judgment on a broad scale.

3. To inaugurate a new age

   A misleading translation in the King James Version of Matthew 24:3 contributed to a misunderstanding of the last days. According to the KJV, some disciples asked Jesus about the sign of "the end of the world," a phrase with consummation overtones. However, the phrase should have been translated "the end of the age," not the age we are living in but the age the disciples were living in. Their question was prompted by Jesus' prediction of the destruction of Jerusalem which occurred in AD 70. When the temple fell at that time, an age came to an end, the age of the old covenant with its priests and sacrificial system. Jesus' return is linked with the fall of Jerusalem (Matthew 24:30) and thus terminates one age and inaugurates a new age.

   When the New Testament speaks of "this present age" (Titus 2:12), it refers to the age that ended with the fall of Jerusalem, not the age that is present to us. When it speaks of "the coming age" (Hebrews 6:5), it refers to the age of the new covenant, the age *we* are living in. The Greek word *mellō* used in Hebrews 6:5 could justify the translation "the age that is about to come."

4. To inaugurate the kingdom of God

   Both John the Baptist (Matthew 3:2) and Jesus (Mark 1:15) said that the kingdom of God was near. Jesus was more explicit when he showed how near it was by linking it with his coming before some of his disciples died (Matthew 16:28).

5. To inaugurate the future aspect of salvation

   Jesus told his disciples that when they saw the events associated with the destruction of Jerusalem, they should lift up their heads because their redemption was at hand (Luke 21:28). Paul told the Romans that the day of salvation for them was near (Romans 13:11–12). The Hebrews were told that Christ would appear to bring salvation to those who were waiting for him (Hebrews 9:28).

Christ's coming in glory is accompanied with a trumpet blast and the gathering of his elect, normally associated with a yet-to-come rapture but, according to Jesus, it would occur within that first-century generation (Matthew 24:30–31, 34).

The consumption mindset may be good news for Christians living at the end but what of those who die before the end? Are they, like the Old Testament believers, destined to Sheol/Hades? Are they, like Abraham, waiting for the city with foundations (Hebrews 11:10, 16)? Abraham was still waiting when Hebrews was written but "something better" was promised (Hebrews 11:39). The fulfillment of that promise was at hand: the Hebrews had "come to Mount Zion, to the heavenly Jerusalem, the city of the living God" (Hebrews 12:22), "the city that is to come" (Hebrews 13:14). The presence of the Greek word *mellō* would allow for the translation, "the city that is about to come."

The inauguration mindset has good news for *all* believers. At death they are clothed with an immortal body, no waiting. In 2 Corinthians 5:1–5 Paul recoils from the thought of leaving his body, his earthly dwelling, at death and being unclothed while he waits for his new body, his heavenly dwelling. He regards such a prospect as grounds for groaning. Has Paul had to endure being "naked" for 2,000 years? It all sounds very like the somewhat dismal outlook that Old Testament saints had at the thought of death. The writer to the Hebrews (11:39–40) says of the Old Testament believers that they died without experiencing what was promised, then adds, "God had planned something better for us [first-century Christians] so that only together with us would they be made perfect." Their being made perfect may parallel the phrase, "the spirits of righteous men made perfect," an experience to which the Hebrews had come (Hebrews 12:23).

Eschatological Dangers had a long way to go but before starting on the long task of expanding and refining my brief chapter outlines, I sent a copy to Luke Rodman asking for his comments and for permission to use some of his ideas. I stressed that the book was to be published under the name of Charles Fortescue and threatened dire consequences if he ever linked it with Ed Sutherland. The following day I received his reply:

Dear Charles Fortescue,

I address you in this way for fear that an email about your forthcoming book addressed to your real name might have fearful repercussions.

Now, about your book, Ed, oops, I mean, Charles, the outline augurs well for the literary fame of Charles Fortescue, or should that be "theological notoriety" of Charles Fortescue? In any case, I happily give it my imprimatur.

By all means use material arising from our varied interactions but, if you are determined to adopt a cloak-and-dagger approach to the project, you'd better not acknowledge your indebtedness to me by name, for two reasons: one, even a third-rate Sherlock Holmes would be onto you in no time; and, two, if you do go down over the book, I don't want to go down with you.

I wish you every success.
Luke.

PS: I don't like your chances of finding a publisher given that your (our) brand of eschatology is not currently where the money's found.

After reading Luke's note, I didn't rush into the kitchen to show Charlotte. The thought of "going down" or attaining "theological notoriety" would only unsettle her. At least I was free to use Luke's ideas and I did have his encouragement to continue. Whether his wish for my "every success" would be fulfilled remained to be seen.

52

Fantastic News

I worked hard to prepare the book for publication, all the while suspecting that Luke was right: finding a publisher might be a challenge. I maintained a weekly fishing excursion with Jack for fear that if I didn't, he might initiate a conversation that I imagined would go like this:

> Jack: "How are you spending your time these days? What could be more important than fishing?"
>
> Me: "I'm writing a book."
>
> Jack: "What's it about?"
>
> Me: 'Theology.' I'd use that word expecting it would end the conversation.
>
> Jack: "What branch of theology?" He *would* ask that.
>
> Me: "Eschatology." I'd hope that big word would shut him up.
>
> Jack: "You mean the second coming of Christ and end times?"
>
> Me: A reluctant "Yeah."
>
> Jack: "Give us a break, Ed."

When I finished the first draft of *Eschatological Dangers*, I sent a copy to Luke for his feedback before making final touches and searching for a publisher. He was generally happy with what I'd written but did raise an important issue.

"Ed," he wrote, "you rightly showed that creedal statements may at times rely on a misinterpretation of biblical texts. That in itself does not prove that the creedal statements are wrong. There may be other Scriptures that, rightly interpreted, *do* support the statements."

Luke was right: a creedal statement may be correct but based on a faulty foundation. Rather than discount the Westminster Confession, it was simply necessary to support it with an alternative text that validly affirmed its future second-coming statement. I knew there was a long list of Scriptures pointing to an early return of Christ, within that generation. I also knew that many today acknowledged such a return but also insisted on a still-future return.

Years ago I had written to such a person, the author of a good book on the earlier return. I asked him for Scriptures confirming the still-future return. How disappointed I was to receive a reply that he was too busy to answer my question. I think he *was* too busy. I had taken the time to read his book and was a sincere seeker after the truth, not out to have an argument or prove a point. In the time it took to tell me he was too busy, he could've mentioned a reference or two. Or did he not have a reference or two for his position?

Although I was still not sure what the author *should* or *could* have said in his reply, Luke's comment caused me to include material in *Eschatological Dangers* that involved stepping down from a know-it-all position to one where humble pie was on the menu; from a clear-cut position to one that acknowledged some frayed edges and an element of mystery; to a position that insisted on the need for further serious exegetical work. It called for a willingness to say, "I don't know," or, even, "I could be wrong." The material I added to the relevant place in my draft copy was as follows:

"Without doubt there was *a* (note the emphasis) coming of Christ before some of the disciples died. Much that is associated with a still-future coming was fulfilled at that time. However, of the many texts that refer to Christ's return, some may apply to a yet-to-occur return, that is, a return that consummates.

"The answer may be waiting for further serious and honest exegetical work in the Scriptures or we may even have to rest back on the truth of Deuteronomy 29:29: 'The secret things belong to the LORD our God, but the things revealed belong to us and to our children forever . . . '

"As for the creeds and confessions, they should always be respected, but never thoughtlessly. It is very easy to parrot them. The creeds are summary statements, condensations of truth, and they serve their purpose best when those who recite them have a solid understanding of the extensive theology that lies behind them. Christian theology is much bigger than the words in a creed.

"When a creedal statement accords with Scripture, correctly interpreted, we can confidently confess our allegiance to it; if supporting texts are used that, when correctly interpreted, do *not* support a statement, we should search the Scriptures to see if there is support elsewhere; if the Scriptures contradict a creedal statement, they take precedence; where we are unsure, wisdom dictates that we continue to affirm a creedal statement, pending further light, rather than abandon it and thus beg the question."

Our weekly meetings with the Zimmermans were put on hold because Anna needed constant attention and regular dialysis treatment. I wasn't surprised to receive an email from Josh Wilson. His two visits to Anna had troubled him but the regular updates he received from Andy and Linda (at his request) only added to his concerns. He was particularly upset that Anna had requested there be no visitors. He remained in Bundaberg. Charlotte and I felt for him and included him in our prayers whenever we prayed for the Zimmermans.

One Friday morning while Charlotte and I were relaxing at morning tea on the back veranda, my mobile rang. It was Andy. He began by saying, "If Charlotte's within earshot, switch to speaker phone." I did so and we heard Andy say, "We've just had a call from Mark Mullins. He's tracked down a kidney donor with the right blood group for Anna. Praise the Lord! We're so thrilled. We rejoiced with Andy and when he hung up, I emailed Josh with the good news knowing he'd be overjoyed.

Two days later at church, Andy announced the good news to the members. They responded as excitedly as if they knew nothing about it but the SCIF grapevine ensured most did. Mark Mullins caught up with me after the service and I assumed he would give some follow-up to Andy's announcement. He said nothing. Instead, he said, "Max Fitzgerald accosted me at the Lions Club meeting on Thursday night. His vitriolic words went like this:

"'If I was annoyed when my son Paul began to get involved in your church, I'm furious now. I thought it was just a passing fancy connected with some girl he had his eyes on. He didn't talk about what went on there and I didn't ask him. Now he's forever talking. He tells me he's been born again, whatever that means; that he's been converted. He's started talking about religion in the house. I won't have it and I blame you and your kind for the damage that's been done to him through your indoctrination and psychological manipulation. Mark my words: I'll get this nonsense out of him if I have to belt it out of him.'"

"Sounds nasty," I said.

"It's not all bad. Max went on to say, 'I'll give him this though: I may not like it that he's embraced religion, but I like that he's less in love with Paul Fitzgerald, and that he's showing more respect for me and his mother—he even helps round the house without having to be asked. I'm feeling a bit ambivalent: on the one hand I don't like what he's believing but I do like how he's behaving.'"

"And what did you say, Mark?"

"I think I blew it."

"How so?" I asked.

"Max had given me an obvious opportunity to witness to him but I missed it and merely said, 'Food for thought, Max.' He turned and went off with a 'Humph' leaving me with a sense of failure that I hadn't made the most of the situation."

"Don't beat up on yourself, Mark. Max is an intelligent man and a meal of 'food for thought' may be just what he needs. We should pray that he comes to acknowledge the connection between Paul's 'believing' and his 'behaving.' When he sees it and reflects on it, he will be preaching to himself and that sort of preaching often penetrates better than the preaching of others. To put it another way, truth that gently knocks on the back door may gain access more readily that truth that hammers on the front door."

Mark had not initiated conversation about Anna so I did. "Great news about a kidney donor for Anna," I said.

"Fantastic news," said Mark. "The donor is a fit person with the right blood type so we anticipate that Anna will regain her health and live a satisfying life."

"How long will all this take, Mark?" I asked.

"After the operation, Anna will be in intensive care for a day or two but she could be home in a week and back on deck, if all goes well, within a month."

"We'll look forward to that," I said, thanked Mark for sharing and took Charlotte home. She'd been talking to Andy—Linda was home with Anna—so we compared notes over lunch.

Anna's operation went smoothly. Visitors were not encouraged initially but update emails kept folk informed. Once home visits were permitted (about three weeks after the op), Josh was on the Zimmerman doorstep, and so were we. We were amazed at the change from the recently under-weight, puffy-eyed Anna to the lovely Anna of former days. Andy and Linda's delight in the recovery of their dear daughter was so infectious, it spread throughout the church so that Sunday morning services and the morning teas that followed were joyful occasions indeed. Josh's church in Bundaberg didn't see much of him. What a celebration of praise we had when Anna made her first appearance at church. Everyone wanted to speak with her so I held back since Charlotte and I had visited her several times at home.

On the last such occasion, she was seated on a Cape Cod chair on the front veranda with a piece of paper in her hand. She looked up as we got to the top of the stairs, greeted us and said, "I've had a letter from Paul. May I read it to you?"

With a "By all means," from Charlotte and a "Certainly," from me, she began. Rarely have I been more focused than when she read:

Dear Anna,

I am not the same Paul you used to know and you, I'm pleased to hear, are not the very ill Anna you used to be. Thank God.

You have no doubt heard of my conversion. It has been revolutionary in more ways than one. Life used to revolve around Paul Fitzgerald; now it revolves around Christ and others. "Others" includes you, Anna, but in a new way. Once you were a pretty girl (one of several, I confess with tears) whom I was chasing with ulterior motives and a professed love that should have been in inverted commas. Now I love you as a sister in Christ, without inverted commas, because I am learning about the kind of love described in 1 Corinthians 13.

Anna, my priorities have changed. I am no longer pursuing my former lifestyle, or even girls for that matter. I am even questioning my future in the business world with an MBA. The other day I was reading John 15:16. I sensed that as Jesus appointed his disciples to go into fruitful ministry, he might have a similar vocation for me. It's early days yet but I am available if that's what he wants of me down the track.

I am so sorry for the pain I must have caused you by my dishonorable behavior but be thankful, as I am, that God used you to get me where I would hear the truth about Christ and experience new life in him.

Life at home is difficult but I will stay here for the present in the hope of demonstrating, particularly to my dad, that God is real.

Anna, I hope we can continue to be friends, with a brother/sister relationship as fellow members of SCIF and the wider family of God.

Your brother in Christ,
Paul Fitzgerald.

Anna had difficulty finishing the letter without choking up. When she finished, I could not speak: I was choked up too. Charlotte was dabbing her eyes. Anna was the first to speak.

"I've wanted to read the letter to you both because Paul's letter has raised a number of questions. I'm glad Charlotte is here to give a woman's perspective and, Ed, I've seen you in action at USC answering curly questions so thank you for listening. As I read the letter, did you sense that Paul was politely ending our relationship?"

"That's how it came across to me," said Charlotte. "What did you think, Ed?"

"I think he's ending it in one sense but continuing it in another sense, at a higher level."

"So no more Saturday night dates?" asked Anna.

"That's a reasonable conclusion," said Charlotte, "at least not just the two of you in a copper-red Mazda Miata."

I had a question: "Anna, what's your reaction to what Charlotte has just said?"

"I was attracted to the old Paul because of his bronzed Aussie physique and his daredevil ways. He was fun to be with, but his old ways rubbed off on me. My spiritual life went backwards and my relationship with my parents suffered. Now that there's a new Paul, I find your question hard to answer."

Charlotte spoke: "Anna, before I met Ed, I was going with a guy called Mike. He was a fine Christian fellow but I was not sure if he was the one for me. To use your own words, that question was 'hard to answer.' Because Mike and I were dating and were pretty close, I realized that I was going to find it hard to know the answer because my stirred emotions were clouding my judgment. I shared this with Mike and he suggested we put our relationship on hold for three months. During that time I socialized more widely, my emotions settled down, and I was able to see things more objectively, as though I was looking through new spectacles. Guess what I saw or, rather, guess whom I saw?"

"It wouldn't be Ed by any chance?" said Anna. Not waiting for an answer, she added, "And the rest is history."

"Spot on," I said. "I was much better than Mike."

Charlotte patted my leg.

With a measured tone in her voice, Anna said, "One part of me would like to continue dating the revolutionized Paul. That part of me wants to interpret Paul's letter as sanctioning such a course. Another part of me resonates with your story, Charlotte. Thank you for sharing. To be honest, with a lot of time to think in recent days, I believe Paul's letter at the very least may be putting our relationship on hold. What you have shared confirms that's what I should do."

"It won't be easy, Anna, but be assured we'll stand with you," said Charlotte.

"We certainly will," I said. "Let me add just one further thought, Anna. If you are wanting to put the relationship on hold in order to gain greater clarity about God's choice of a partner in life, you will need to put it on hold mentally as well as physically. Only then will your spectacles be clean."

"I understand. Please pray for me."

We did.

53

One Coming, Two Outcomes

I offered *Eschatological Dangers* by Charles Fortescue to Australian and American publishers and waited for their response. Three weeks later, I received a letter with an American stamp on the envelope. I opened it in excited expectation that was short-lived:

> Dear Charles,
>
> Having read your book, we regret to advise that sales from the retail outlets we supply are unlikely to justify the costs of publication.

A day later, a Sydney publisher wrote:

> Dear Mr. Fortescue,
>
> We regret to advise that we are unable to publish your book as its theology is incompatible with our doctrinal position.

Luke's prophecy was being fulfilled. The third reply was even more discouraging:

> Mr. Fortescue,
>
> The books we publish are intended for a market that adheres to statements of faith that reflect the centuries-old doctrines of Christianity. We consider the views expressed in your book to be at variance with these doctrines and thus to be heretical. We therefore advise that you do not publish the book.

I wrote a dispirited email to Luke:

ONE COMING, TWO OUTCOMES 279

> Hi Luke,
>
> You will see by the three attachments that your doubts about my finding a publisher have been confirmed. The last of the three rejections makes me want to put the manuscript in the attic and hope that a distant descendant discovers it, thinks it a rare find in a climate less entrenched in inherited eschatology, and makes a fortune.
>
> You have my thoughts on the matter. What would you do with it?
>
> Ed (Charles Fortescue is dead).

Luke usually responded promptly to my correspondence but on this occasion he didn't. The remaining publishers did and they were all negative. I went fishing more regularly with Jack and concentrated on our home group in an attempt to alleviate my disappointment.

The attendance at home group was boosted by the increased attendance at SCIF following the conference. We picked up Paul's friend from the surf life-saving club and the two students from the Real Life group at USC brought by John and Elizabeth. Adding to the group was the return of Josh Wilson. Stan Mullins had recruited Bundaberg locals to staff the hardware store allowing Josh to return home. Anna's recovery had gone well so she was glad to be present. In short, the young people outnumbered the likes of Charlotte and me but we were delighted, as were Jack and Carol Wilson. The original intention that the group focus on youth was being realized. We showed remarkable restraint when the enthusiasm of the youth stimulated vibrant discussion with challenges to traditional views. Respect and grace from both sides, however, ensured that a dynamic harmony prevailed. Wednesday night was the highlight of our week.

Andy had decided that in May he would preach a series on Second Thessalonians. He asked that home groups use the passage expounded each Sunday as a basis for discussion mid-week. On the Wednesday night after his first sermon of the series, the discussion threatened our dynamic harmony with more dynamic than harmony. The controversial text was 2 Thessalonians 1:6–8:

> God is just: He will repay back trouble to those who trouble you ⁷and give relief to you who are troubled, and to us as well. This will happen when the Lord Jesus is revealed from heaven in blazing fire with his powerful angels. ⁸He will punish those who do not know God and do not obey the gospel of our Lord Jesus.

To help members of the group get a handle on the text, I asked some questions:

"What do we learn about the Christians in Thessalonica from verse 6?"

"They are being persecuted," said Elizabeth.

"That's bad news; what's the good news?" I asked.

"Relief is in store for them, according to verse 7," said Carol Wilson.

"When is that going to happen?"

"At the second coming," said Cathy Mullins. It was her night to attend.

"And what is in store for the persecutors?" I asked.

"They're going to cop it," said Paul.

"When is that going to happen?"

"At the second coming," said one of the new USC students.

"Well done, everybody," I said. "You've unpacked the text neatly. I've been asking all the questions. Now it's your turn. Who has a question?"

John Delaney spoke up. "Ed, it was made plain at our recent second-coming conference that Christians will be taken out of the afflictions of this world at the rapture but it doesn't seem to be mentioned in the passage."

I could sense controversy brewing so I relayed the question: "What do others think of John's observation?"

Jack Wilson spoke up: "I read somewhere that it's a sound principle of biblical interpretation that what is *not* taught in one text cannot be dismissed if it *is* taught in another."

John seemed to be happy with Jack's answer so the group waited silently for further questions. Cathy Mullins had one: "Jack, I think your principle has merit but does it apply to this text?"

"Why not?" Jack asked.

"It is clear from verse 8 that the second coming in the text is a coming in judgment. If the coming were preceded by a reference to the punishment of the persecutors, there wouldn't be a problem for your position. Instead, the persecuted Thessalonians are to receive their relief when Christ returns in judgment, not at a rapture as expected."

I could see Jack was a little unsettled and was preparing to respond but his son Josh beat him to it. "As I read the text, there is one coming that will have two results: one, the persecuted will get relief; two, the persecutors will 'cop it,' to quote Paul."

Paul smiled and said, "I'm with you, Josh." Anna smiled too but I was unsure at what or whom she was smiling.

Jack now had his thoughts together. "Whatever our understanding of the passage before us, we cannot deny the rapture because it's clearly taught in 1 Thessalonians 4:16–17." He said this with an air of finality that assumed the matter was ended.

Cathy Mullins was not convinced: "Jack, you are right that we cannot adopt the interpretation of one passage at the expense of another. However, Josh's point about one coming's being associated with two events in no way questions the truth of 1 Thessalonians 4:16–17. The words 'one coming' are really the sticking point. It is hard to deny that the passage we are studying tonight speaks of one coming achieving two outcomes. As for the 1 Thessalonians 4 passage, there is nothing in it to exclude the possibility of other things happening at the same time such as the punishment of the wicked."

Carol Wilson spoke up. "Jack, here's where your principle kicks in. You said earlier, that 'what is *not* taught in one text cannot be dismissed if it *is* taught in another.'"

I began to feel for Jack: his family seemed to be ganging up on him. I only hoped Lauren didn't join the gang. Charlotte obviated that by saying, "Maybe we've got to reconsider not the fact of the rapture but the timing of it. Perhaps there are not two stages to the second coming but one coming that does what both passages teach."

The frown on Jack's face was hard to interpret. Was he annoyed that the home group was undermining clause 24 of the SCIF Statement of Faith? Was he beginning to doubt his entrenched two-stage view of the second coming? Was he angry with me for allowing my views to creep into the church through the home group of which I was the leader? On this score I took some comfort from the fact that all I had done was ask questions. All the controversial stuff had come from others. Whether Jack would see it that way was unknown.

I was about to suggest that we spend some time in prayer for the members and ministry of our church when mild-mannered Elizabeth asked a disturbing question: "If the persecuted Christians at Thessalonica were to receive rest from their sufferings when Christ returned, since he hasn't returned so far, have they not yet experienced relief?"

Elizabeth's question was sincere and well-intentioned but I could see a very big worm escaping from the can. No one answered her question and Jack's frown, if anything, was deeper. In a different context, I would have had something to say but grace and a meaningful look from Charlotte in my direction caused me simply to say, "I'm sorry, Elizabeth, but time has gone so we'll have to place your question in the food-for-thought category so we can finish the meeting with a time of prayer.

As we walked home, Charlotte commended me for my restraint in not imposing my own ideas on the home group but she was concerned at Jack's concern. "I hope Jack doesn't provoke the leadership team to act against a perceived breach of the doctrinal statement by shutting down our home group. I love our group and would hate to see it close down. Surely the keen participation of our young people in thinking through the meaning of the Scriptures is a good thing."

"I agree totally, Charlotte. We'll have to work and pray for its continuation."

When Charlotte went to bed, I turned on my computer and saw that Luke Rodman had finally responded to my post-publisher-rejection email.

> Dear Ed,
>
> I hope you haven't done anything stupid, like burnt your manuscript, or erased your hard drive. I know how you must feel. It's hard to get up again after the dejection of rejection.
>
> I believe in your book, Ed. The Christian public may not want it but they need it. When children prefer jelly beans to nutritious food, parents devise ways of making them want what they need.
>
> I've been thinking a lot about your book and I'd like to suggest that we work together on getting it off the ground and out where it's needed. To put my money where my mouth is, I'm prepared to pay for 100 self-published copies to get things rolling. I'll ask around about local publishing options. Charlotte is an arty type who could help with an attractive cover.
>
> When we get our first run back from the printer, we'll put a 30 percent mark-up on them and get some funds for the next run.
>
> Please send me a digital copy of the book so I can get to work.
>
> Luke.

Charlotte gladly produced an impressive cover for *Eschatological Dangers* and the completed manuscript was sent to Luke.

I was a bit reluctant to go fishing with Jack on Friday, just two days after the controversial implications of our study in 2 Thessalonians. Was it just my imagination that he seemed a bit cool or at 5:00 a.m. was he still waking up? I determined that if anyone brought up the topic of Wednesday night's meeting, it wouldn't be me.

After the sun rose and we'd caught a couple of trevally and a flathead, Jack perked up. I wanted to say how great it was to have Josh at the home group but feared the mention of "home group" would trigger confrontation. As if Jack read my mind he said, "It sure is good to have Josh home but he's getting to the stage where he should be settling down and living independently of us."

"Do you see any prospect of that, Jack?"

"I think he's keen on Anna but the feelings don't seem to be reciprocated. Furthermore, there's the competition from Paul, probably stronger now that he's been converted. I worry about my son. He needs to be more assertive in pursuing his interest."

"He's a fine lad, Jack. I wouldn't worry. He deserves a special girl and such a girl will find him and be more than satisfied with her catch."

"Speaking of girls," said Jack, "Elizabeth Wills is a talented and thoughtful girl. She certainly stirred the pot the other night with her question about whether the Thessalonians were still waiting for relief from their sufferings."

"Elizabeth sure is a lovely lass," I replied, hoping he wouldn't follow up on her challenging question.

"Actually, Ed," said Jack, as if he continued to read my mind, "Elizabeth's question was not the only confronting issue. Her boyfriend's comment and the subsequent discussion with Cathy Mullins that cast doubt on a rapture separate from the second coming, was quite disturbing."

My attempt to avoid controversy having failed, I responded cautiously. "I could see you were concerned about the rapture issue, Jack. I tried to keep my distance from the topic but young and old were determined to grapple with it."

"Ed, your leadership of the group was admirable. I am not criticizing you or those who engaged with the text as they did. On the one hand, I felt my entrenched eschatological position was being challenged; on the other hand, I was thrilled to see folk thinking intelligently about the Scriptures, including my wife and my son.

"Carol and Josh did well," I affirmed.

"Ed, the old cliché says, 'You can't teach an old dog new tricks.' It may be true in certain contexts but it shouldn't be true when it comes to wrestling with new ideas such as those that surfaced on Wednesday night. Over the last two days, I have realized that the Scripture we studied at the home group may contain new tricks that even this old dog must be open to learn."

"That's a very mature position to adopt, Jack, and I commend you for it."

I took my trevally home to Charlotte for breakfast. She enjoyed it but was even happier that her fears about the possible closure of the home group were groundless in light of Jack's openness to fresh ideas.

54

A Startling Revelation

The first hundred copies of *Eschatological Dangers* came off the press before the end of the month. Luke sent me fifty copies with the names of bookshops on the Sunshine Coast to contact as possible outlets. The other fifty he would distribute. Charlotte was thrilled with the book, gave me a very endearing hug, collared a dozen for her own distribution network, and solemnly pledged to safeguard its true source.

I was pleased with the professional appearance of the publication. Charlotte had produced an attractive cover that, in addition to the title and author's name, depicted a conventional sign reading "Danger: Men at Work" with "Men" crossed out and replaced by "Entrenched Eschatology" above a caret mark. At the end of the book, Luke had added an appendix entitled, "Study Guide for *Eschatological Dangers*." It contained five or six questions for each of ten study sessions, each question cross-referenced to a relevant part of the book. I wondered if one day SCIF home groups might use it without, of course, knowing the real identity of Charles Fortescue.

Though I appreciated Luke's initiative in adding the study guide, I was less impressed with his second initiative. On the last page of the book he had, without consulting me, invited responses to the book: "Readers who wish to comment on the material in *Eschatological Dangers* are welcome to contact the author." An email address followed: *charlesfortescue@letterbox.com*. While my initial reaction to the email address was slight annoyance, I changed my mind when I foresaw the emails pouring in (pandering to my pride) and the work of replying filling the gap left by the completion of the book. The change of mind softened my reference to the email address in a note to Luke:

Hi Luke,

Congratulations! The book looks great. Many thanks for your hard work in getting it published and for the study guide you added. I'm hoping it will induce churches to use it in Bible study groups. Charlotte's catchy cover should get buyers' attention.

I told you Charles Fortescue was dead and you've not only resurrected him but appointed him to respond to readers' emails. I'll forward all the tough ones for you to answer.

Your partner in the book trade,
Ed.

Charlotte was encouraged when a friend who sells home-made candles at the Eumundi market agreed to display copies of the book. I was encouraged when two of the local bookstores agreed to take ten copies each with the promise of more if sales warranted. In our approaches, we had to be careful not to unmask Charles Fortescue, not difficult for Charlotte as she could say, "The book was written by a dear friend of mine." I had to take a less ingenuous tack: "I know the author very well; he's a noted biblical scholar with a message for Christians everywhere." Pleased with my sales pitch, I included it in an update to Luke on distribution statistics. He replied that his own approach was working well without any need to mention the author. "Humph," I said to myself. Luke had only five copies left and suggested we order a further 200.

Over the next few months, sales confirmed Luke's optimism and emails from readers began to arrive addressed to Charles Fortescue. At first they were discouraging. One reader wrote:

> In your list of dangers you should have included the danger that books like yours, at variance with "the faith which was once delivered unto the saints," would proliferate.

I didn't bother to respond. I assumed he was too entrenched for me to dig him out. Another wrote:

> You need to take note of 2 Timothy 2:15: "Study to shew thyself approved unto God, a workman that needeth not to be ashamed, rightly dividing the word of truth" (King James Version). Dispensationalists rightly divide the word of truth into seven dispensations. They are therefore "approved unto God" and are workmen that need not be ashamed. You don't rightly divide the word so you are not approved and should be ashamed of yourself.

I replied, "Please read the New International Version rendering of 2 Timothy 2:15," but I doubted if he had access to a copy.

When readers asked questions, I was generally happy to respond although I was never quite sure if they were honestly seeking answers or saying, "You can't answer this question because your position is wrong." I gave them the benefit of the doubt and did my best to answer them without being too dogmatic. One reader asked:

> If the judgment of Matthew 25 occurred along with the fall of Jerusalem, what reckoning is there for those who live after that event?

I replied: "Before getting to the point of your question, to confirm that the judgment of Matthew 25 occurred in connection with the fall of Jerusalem, compare the description of Christ's coming in glory with his angels in Matthew 25:31 with Matthew 24:30–31. Clearly both passages refer to the same event, an event to occur before that generation ended (Matthew 24:34). As for judgment post-AD 70, Hebrews 9:27 says we are 'destined to die once, and after that to face judgment.' The text may be saying that instead of waiting for a mass judgment at some future date, after AD 70 each person will be judged individually following death."

Another reader asked:

> If a resurrection took place at a first century coming of Christ, have those who die after that event missed out?"

In my response, I summarized Luke's case that the Babylon of Revelation represented Jerusalem and added: "Revelation 14:13 says that those who die in the Lord subsequent to the fall of Jerusalem (Babylon) are blessed. There is something special from that point on, as if it is a turning point for believers with respect to conditions in the after-life. J. S. Russell puts it well: 'The plain meaning of this is that the *Parousia* [coming] marked the introduction of a new epoch in the condition of departed saints and in the prospects of all who after that epoch commenced should die in the Lord.' It would seem that, instead of being disembodied at death, believers in this 'new epoch' receive their immortal bodies at death. Perhaps this is what Jesus meant in John 11:26 when he said, 'Whoever lives and believes in me will never die.'"

I was surprised to get a comment from Arthur Bradford. I checked whether Charlotte had given Robyn a copy of the book and was pleased to hear she hadn't. Perhaps they'd been to the Eumundi market. Arthur's point (or was it Robyn's), addressed to "Dear Mr. Fortescue," read:

In Acts 1:11, the angels at the ascension of Christ told the disciples that he would come "in like manner as ye have seen him go into heaven" (KJV). The words "in like manner" rule out a first century coming because Christ didn't return then "in like manner" to his ascension. The disciples saw him ascend. No one saw him return.

In my reply to Arthur I said, "The Greek words translated 'in like manner' in Acts 1:11 are identical to the words translated 'as' in Matthew 23:37: 'How often I have longed to gather your children together, as a hen gathers her chicks under her wings.' It is clear that the Greek words do not require the meaning "in like manner in every respect" as your question implies. As chickens shelter their young so Christ wished to shelter the Jews of Jerusalem. The specific details with respect to the manner of sheltering are different. As Christ went at his ascension, he would return but the specific details of each need not be the same according to the Greek words used."

My weekly schedule over the next few months involved fishing (I had my priorities right), home group, cautious book promotion, playing the part of Charles Fortescue, and Sunday services. Occasionally Andy invited me to preach. I made sure not to say anything that could be interpreted as disrespect for the SCIF doctrinal statement.

Home group continued to be a delight. The blending of young and old through mutual respect and harmonious cross-generational communication reflected the oneness of the body of Christ as I'd rarely seen before. On the subject of blending, on two consecutive Wednesday nights, Josh Wilson sat next to Anna Zimmerman. I dismissed it as pure coincidence and Paul's body language showed no signs of disapproval. I thought no more of it till I noticed the same seating arrangement obtained at church on Sundays.

Charlotte broached the subject on the way home from a morning service: "Ed, I think cupid may have hit the target in Josh and Anna."

"Just because they sit together at church and home group?"

"And he drives her home from home group and church," said Charlotte.

"Yeah, but he's a thoughtful fellow and he has an avocado Mustang that he likes to drive and show off. Don't read too much into it, Charlotte."

"To read into something is to read what's not there. I'm reading what *is* there and I tell you, 'Josh and Anna are an item!'"

I wasn't convinced and, since Charlotte and I had not spoken recently with Josh or Anna about relationship matters, I felt we should both plead ignorance of what was happening on the romantic front. However, we were not to be left in the dark for long. The following Wednesday night after most of the home group members had departed, we were helping Jack and Carol clean up when Josh appeared at the kitchen door with Anna and said he'd like to chat with the four of us. He invited Lauren to join us as we settled into lounge chairs and looked to Josh to start the ball rolling. He did and it bowled us all over.

"Anna has agreed to marry me." After a slight pause to let the announcement sink in, our delight was expressed in handshakes and congratulations from the men; and hugs, kisses and tears—of joy—from the ladies.

When the seven of us finally resumed our seats, Charlotte gave me an "I-told-you-so" look. I gave her a "You're-right-again" smirk and said, "You're a dark horse, Josh." The Wilsons seemed stunned as they stared at Josh in anticipation of his story. Clearly the news was as fresh to them as to us. Carol's hands were cupped on either side of her nose as she struggled to take in what she'd heard; Jack clasped his hands behind his head which was shaking from side to side in disbelief; and Lauren's face lit up with delight and a knowing look that told me she was privy to Anna's growing interest in her brother.

"You're right, Ed," said Josh, "I am a dark horse. I've always been a rather private person who keeps his thoughts and feelings to himself. My sharing them tonight is partly an apology for having kept you, Dad, Mum, and Lauren, in the dark. I hope you'll forgive me when you hear my story."

"Of course we will, Josh," said an emotional Carol.

Josh continued: "I'm pleased that Ed and Charlotte are here because they have assisted Anna and me in the journey that has brought us together. I've had my eye on Anna since the day I looked at her in the rear-vision mirror of Ed's car on the trip from the Brisbane international airport to Buderim. I've kept her in view but I've always been careful not to give too much away. I knew Anna and Paul were spending time together and my shy temperament baulked at interfering."

"Where does Paul fit in the story now?" asked Jack.

Anna answered, "After his conversion, Paul wrote to tell me that he wanted our relationship to be on a new brother/sister footing. He is sensing that God may be leading him into Christian service and his focus is on knowing God's will rather than chasing girls like me."

"How did you feel about that?" asked Carol.

"That's where Charlotte helped me. She shared how her emotional attachment to a guy called Mike was clouding her judgment. They put their relationship on hold resulting in greater objectivity that led to her discovering Ed." All eyes turned, with a smile, in my direction and Charlotte gave my leg a squeeze.

Anna continued: "Carol, I accepted Paul's decision and retreated physically and mentally. Josh had been kind to me, visiting me as my health deteriorated, and I saw him as just a nice guy, not as a substitute boyfriend."

"What was happening with you following Paul's conversion, Josh?" I asked.

"At first I thought that Anna and her parents would be more approving of him and that there was no hope for me."

Anna spoke again. "During my recovery, Josh visited me quite regularly but never revealed his feelings for me. However, my feelings were getting stronger by the day. No longer was he just a nice guy but I saw him as that special someone with whom I would be delighted to spend the rest of my life. I'm sure Josh must have seen it in my eyes but my interest in him seemed not to be reciprocated."

"What was going on, Josh?" I asked. "I've known for a long time that you were interested in Anna."

Tears came to Josh's eyes as he struggled to respond. "I had a secret that I could not reveal till I was absolutely sure that Anna loved me. I was afraid that if I revealed my feelings she might express an interest in me that would lead to my telling her the secret. I was afraid that when she heard it she might be forced to make a commitment to me that she didn't want to make."

"I don't understand, Josh," said Anna.

"You've lost me," said Jack. Carol's concerned look seemed to say, "What unknown darkness lies in my son's past?"

Josh looked at Anna with teary eyes and said, "Anna, the day I visited you and you showed me the letter you received from Paul, the tenderness with which you looked at me said, "Josh, it's you I love and I so much want to know if you love me." At that point I stopped my play acting and gave you the kiss I had been saving for the girl of my dreams, the kiss I longed to give you but couldn't because of my secret."

"I'm still lost," said Jack.

"Please explain," urged Lauren.

Still looking lovingly into Anna's eyes, Josh stood and said, "Anna, you and I have something special in common." He paused before he said, "We both have only one kidney. That's my secret."

A shocked silence was interrupted by Anna's rushing into Josh's arms and hugging him with uncontrollable weeping. The rest of us continued to watch in teary silence. I am sure others were thinking as I was: "Josh has given one of his kidneys to the girl he loves but he kept it a secret till he knew, not only that she loved him but that she would marry him." I didn't blubber like Anna but I came close. Now I understood what Josh meant about not wanting to force Anna to make a commitment that she might not wish to make in different circumstances.

When Josh and Anna finally sat down, the silence continued. Jack and Carol were no doubt mystified about their son's sacrifice of a kidney without their knowing. They deserved an explanation and Josh did his best to give it.

"When Anna's father described the seriousness of her condition and requested prayer at the convention for a kidney donor, I did some research online. I learnt about the problems of getting the right match, about what was involved in a kidney operation, about the recovery time, and the post-operation quality of life. I arranged an appointment with Mark Mullins to get further information. My love for Anna was such that I thought the least I could do was see if I was a suitable donor. Mark arranged a blood test for me and the result showed I had blood type O which made me a universal donor. I could donate no matter what Anna's blood type was.

"I had three weeks' holidays owing to me so Mark arranged for my operation to take place in Bundaberg and for the kidney to be flown to Brisbane in time for Anna's operation. My surgeon used the laparoscopic technique which has a shorter recovery rate. I was therefore able to get back to work after my holidays looking as well as before. You can imagine my joy when I heard that Anna's operation went well.

"Mark told me that the Zimmermans had asked who the donor was but he was a model of secrecy and protected my anonymity. I was determined that no one would know until Andy and Linda consented to my asking for Anna's hand and she consented to give it. All that is in the past and I am now happy for Andy, Linda and Sam to know my secret. I'll let Anna tell them when I take her home tonight. I would like all of us to keep the secret a secret."

Sensing that his parents were not entirely relaxed, Josh said, "Dad and Mum, I'm so sorry you are only now finding about my gift to Anna. Be assured that I acted as I did, not through a lack of love for you, but to save you stress over whether I was doing the right thing and whether the operation would be successful. Please forgive me if you think I should have done things differently."

Jack and Carol embraced their son. Words were not needed. He was forgiven and they too were at peace and very proud. As Lauren gave her brother a hug, I overheard her whisper, "You're an awesome brother and you've made an awesome choice."

Josh and Anna excused themselves so they could catch the Zimmermans before they retired. Charlotte and I also left so the Wilsons could have time to themselves to process the surprises of the evening.

55

The Jigsaw Comes Together

A year, almost to the day, after the raising of the marquee for the second-coming conference, another tent was erected in the church grounds. The crowd of helpers and the level of excitement exceeded the previous occasion: SCIF was about to celebrate its first wedding in years, the marriage of Anna Zimmerman, the pastor's daughter, to Josh Wilson, an elder's son. The service would be held in the church and the reception in the tent, beautifully decorated with flowers grown locally at Buderim and provided by church members.

The whole church family was invited and many were involved. Paul Fitzgerald was best man, Lauren Wilson was Anna's bridesmaid, and Sam Zimmerman was the page boy sporting a black bow tie and carrying the rings on a white silk cushion. Andy served two roles, as father of the bride and officiating minister. A revived Second-Coming Conference Band accompanied the bridal procession with Mendelssohn's "Wedding March," Matthew Beecroft beaming throughout. Linda Zimmerman sang "O Perfect Love" and, while the marriage register was being signed, Elizabeth Wills surprised everyone by taking out of a case, not her clarinet but a saxophone. She played a virtuosic rendition of Rolf Løvland's song "You Raise Me Up" which everyone enjoyed though it was new to many.

At the reception, the ladies of the church provided a sumptuous buffet meal that the best of professional catering services could not have equaled. Jack Wilson showed exceptional skills as master of ceremonies, inserting humorous transitions between official speeches. At one point he said, "You may be wondering why Elizabeth played a saxophone solo after, not before, the vows were taken. It was because our church doesn't approve of pre-marital sax."

I can still remember snippets from the speeches, formal and informal. Paul said he couldn't imagine a couple more suited to each other or more worthy of each other. Lauren said she couldn't have asked for a better sister-in-law and Sam Zimmerman said, "I've always wanted a big brother and now I've got one." Linda Zimmerman said, "I read somewhere that 'behind every successful man there's a surprised mother-in-law.' It's not true. I know my son-in-law *will* be successful so I *won't* be surprised." Robyn Bradford said, "Josh and Anna, may you have a long and happy life together, should the Lord tarry."

Everyone was moved by Anna's speech: "Not long ago I faced an early death with no prospect of being together with anyone, but through the sacrificial love of a kind kidney donor, to whom I will be forever grateful, I am not only well but privileged to marry the most wonderful man in the world."

Many in the tent had moist eyes as they listened to Anna but none as much as those who knew the identity of the sacrificial donor. I noticed Mark Mullins was more emotional than his wife Cathy. Had the good doctor maintained his patient confidentiality to that extent?

After the wedding, life settled back to the routine of my post-publication weekly schedule. The monthly increase in the sales of *Eschatological Dangers* allowed me to reimburse Luke for his investment in the project and kept me busy as Charles Fortescue, responding to questions and comments from readers. One day I received an email from an unexpected source:

> Dear Mr. Fortescue,
>
> Your book was donated anonymously to the library of the college where I am a faculty member. The word "eschatological" in the title caught my attention since I have had an interest in end times for many years.
>
> I found your book at variance with my eschatological views at many points so I initially dismissed is as unorthodox and unworthy of consideration. However, two things kept nagging at me: one, that I was guilty of having swallowed, without serious analysis, what my eschatology mentors fed me; and, two, that I had at times defended my eschatology, largely inherited, even in the face of Scriptures that opposed it. The nagging stopped when I decided to re-read your book with an open mind.
>
> I can't say I now agree with everything you wrote but I was challenged to do two things:
>   1. Make sure that my position does not cast doubt on the integrity of Jesus or New Testament authors; and
>   2. Listen to the text without reading it through spectacles manufactured by my inherited eschatology.

Both of these challenges are daunting because if, in embracing them, I see that I have been wrong at significant points, I will need a good deal of courage to admit it.

Yours sincerely,
Robert Donaldson (Dr.)

I suspected Luke was the anonymous donor of my book to the AIMS library. The irony of Alex Symons's son-in-law reading the "heresy" of Edward Sutherland amused me but I was glad for both our sakes that Charles Fortescue was on trial not me. I wrote back to Robert:

Dear Dr. Donaldson,

I appreciate your honesty in admitting the influence of your inherited eschatology and your willingness to rise to the two challenges you identified. They are worthy challenges and, as you imply, risky challenges.

My own journey towards the position expounded in the book has been a struggle, not unlike that of an explorer battling his way through a thicket towards an open plain. The open-plain metaphor may give the impression that the struggle is over and there are no unanswered questions. Not so: the word "towards" indicates that I have not reached clarity on all points.

To change the metaphor, I have been working on a jigsaw puzzle. The border is largely in place and many of the pieces are where they belong. Other pieces wait to be slotted in. The temptation to force them in is always there but I know a piece does not belong when I have to exert undue pressure to make it fit. I also know when a piece *does* fit, not only because pressure is not needed but because, when it is in place, it has a sense of belonging, and of adding to the partially completed picture. What I must not do is rashly scrap that partially completed picture because I face difficulties with unplaced pieces. What encourages me is that the pieces that are in place already display a picture that is more like the one on the lid of the jigsaw box than the picture I inherited.

You wrote that you would need courage to admit you were wrong. Don't rush in that direction. Even now, I try to hold my views with an open hand. The words of Augustine of Hippo help me to that end.

He wrote: "In matters that are so obscure and far beyond our vision, we find in Holy Scripture passages which can be interpreted in very different ways without prejudice to the faith we have received. In such cases, we should not rush in headlong and so firmly take our stand on one side that, if further progress in the search for truth justly undermines this position, we too fall with it."

I wish you well as you work on the puzzle.

Kind regards,

Charles Fortescue.

I heard no more from Robert Donaldson but months later his name came up unexpectedly. It was a Monday morning. Jack and I went fishing together, enjoyed more for the robust but friendly conversation we had over Andy's sermon of the day before than for the fish we caught. We disagreed on several points but were never disagreeable. After gutting and filleting our catch on the river bank, I crossed the road towards our house, climbed the front stairs and found Charlotte reading the morning's mail.

Without asking if I caught any fish, she said, "Listen to this, Ed." She held up the latest copy of the AIMS magazine, *Aiming Higher*. In spite of our unceremonious departure from the college, our names had never been taken off the mailing list. I dropped into a low-slung canvas deck chair and stretched my legs over its extended arms as Charlotte read a paragraph under the heading, "Faculty Notes":

> Dr. Robert Donaldson leaves the college at the end of this semester after three years as lecturer in New Testament. The board has advertised for a suitable replacement in the hope of an appointment before the start of the new academic year.

"He hasn't lasted long," I said. "Perhaps he doesn't get on with the chairman of the board, Alex Symons, his father-in-law." I thought no more about it until David Barnes caught up with us while he was holidaying at Caloundra. We reflected on the years we spent as faculty colleagues at AIMS and even on the SCIF second-coming conference. David was still committed to Chuck Harmon's eschatology but it didn't affect our relationship. He was another Jack Wilson. For me, the two of them reflected the sentiments of Anthony Norris Groves: "Talk about loving me when they agree with me. Give me men who will love me even when they disagree with me and that will be the stuff with which to build a church."

It was Charlotte who brought up Robert Donaldson's name: "David, a couple of months ago, Ed and I were surprised to read in *Aiming Higher* that Robert Donaldson is no longer part of the faculty."

"That's correct."

"What happened?" I asked.

"Robert was asked to resign," David said reluctantly.

"Over what issue?" I asked.

"You're putting me on the spot, Ed. I'm telling tales now so please keep this to yourself. The board felt that Robert was teaching material that did not fit with the college's doctrinal statement."

"While you're on the spot, David, you may as well continue telling tales and inform us of his unorthodox views."

"It all started with a book that was anonymously donated to our library."

I could see where David was headed. I interrupted him with, "You mean to tell me that one book in the library led to his sacking."

"As I said, that's where it started, months ago. The dismissal only came at the end of a process," said David, a little out of sorts, perhaps through a sense of guilt that he'd already said too much.

Charlotte asked, "Do you mind if I ask the name of the book donated to the library?"

"The book was called *Eschatological Dangers*. It was written by a Charles Fortescue, an author I've never heard of. The publisher was also not well-known. I suspect Charles Fortescue self-published the book knowing that a respectable publisher would not be interested in such rubbish."

Charlotte had a wonderful opportunity to look knowingly in the direction of Charles Fortescue but, to her credit, she gave nothing away. I was less disciplined so, had David been looking my way, he may well have guessed from the grin on my face that Charles Fortescue was none other than Edward J. Sutherland. By the time he *did* look in my direction, I had resumed a straight face.

Wanting to know the rest of the story and hoping David had overcome his guilt feelings, I pressed him to continue: "That was how it all started, David. What happened next?"

"Well, Robert read the book and told me he was not happy with what he read. It conflicted with his eschatology at many points. Surprisingly, he re-read the book and when next he saw me he said, "David, I hastily dismissed Fortescue's book as unorthodox but having read it again, I think there might be something in it.""

"What do you think caused him to change his mind?" I asked.

"I asked him that very question," said David. His answer surprised me. He said that his unthinking adherence to the eschatology of his upbringing and education had caused him to fall into most, if not all, of the traps that Fortescue warned against in his book."

"Can you be more specific?" I asked.

"For example, he said he had been brought up on the *Scofield Reference Bible* and that he believed the study notes in it without question. His church taught the same ideas and in theological college they were again reinforced. He therefore felt he had imbibed erroneous hermeneutical principles, unwittingly impugned the integrity of Jesus and New Testament writers, forced awkward texts to fit his inherited paradigm, and accepted the views of people like Darby, Scofield, and popular authors about end-times, without obeying Paul's injunction in 1 Thessalonians 5:21 to 'test everything.'"

"But David," I said, "surely it's a good thing that he has begun to think for himself, to espouse a sound hermeneutic, and to avoid forcing the text to fit his eschatology rather than the other way round."

"Ed, you're acting as an apologist for Charles Fortescue whose ideas, from what Robert shared, are not unlike your own. We've been down that track before and I don't want to go there again. That's not the view we teach at AIMS and that is why Robert Donaldson had to go."

"For simply holding a personal viewpoint that you and others didn't agree with?"

"You don't understand, Ed. His personal view is his business but he brought it into the classroom. In his lectures on Mark's gospel he gave a Fortescue-type interpretation of Mark 13. He recommended his students buy their own copy of *Eschatological Dangers*."

"No wonder our sales have gone up," I said to myself. To David I said, "Would you regard the degrees offered at AIMS as academically credible?"

"Certainly," he said. "We and many other theological colleges are part of a network that has the highest government accreditation."

"The way Robert Donaldson has been treated would cause your accrediting body to be very concerned," I said. "It sounds like AIMS is sticking a funnel into the top of students' heads when they arrive and then pouring in a rigid curriculum without the opportunity to debate its validity in the face of alternatives. David, that borders on brainwashing. It certainly does not make for thinking Christians. You teach theology, David, a great subject, but the aim should not be to pour theological facts into students' funnels but to teach them to think theologically, to engage with the text with an open mind."

"You might have a point there, Ed," David admitted, "but we have a duty to protect our students from the kind of nonsense Charles Fortescue peddles."

"Have you read *Eschatological Dangers*, David?"

"No," he replied, a little sheepishly.

"Perhaps you should read it before you label it 'nonsense.' Besides, David, you can't act as nanny to your students for the rest of their lives. When they leave the nursery they are going to encounter the Charles Fortescues of this world and, not having been taught to think, his book sales will only increase."

"You sound like you've changed your tune and no longer adhere to Fortescue's brand of eschatology."

"Not at all," I said. "I believe Robert Donaldson has taken to Charles Fortescue's ideas because he's begun to think, something he'd admit to having neglected in relation to eschatology in the past. It's been costly but he's been prepared to pay the price because he's convinced that what he's embraced is closer to the truth than what he's abandoned."

I felt I'd been a bit harsh on David. Charlotte's look confirmed my feeling. To lighten the atmosphere a bit, she said, "David, just today I baked a carrot cake which will go well with a cup of tea or coffee. Which would you prefer?" He gave his order, I apologized for my forceful manner (not the substance of what I said) and engaged in small talk about his holiday and his family in an effort to leave AIMS behind.

When Charlotte returned with drinks and cake, she undid my effort to change direction by asking David, "Have there been any other changes at AIMS in recent days?"

David thought for a moment, perhaps wondering if he was being asked to divulge further not-for-public information. He said, somewhat hesitantly, "Alex Symons is no longer chairman of the board."

"Is he ill?" asked Charlotte.

"No," said David. "He's his old self but, as you know, it was he who arranged for his son-in-law, Robert Donaldson, to be appointed in Ed's place. With Robert's departure from perceived orthodoxy, Alex was regarded by some members of the board as having lacked discernment in the appointment of Robert in the first place, as having been guilty of nepotism, and as having been less than upfront in the reason given for Ed's dismissal. The college board passed a motion calling for Alex's dismissal as chairman, should he choose not to resign."

"There *is* a God!" I cried. "Justice is not dead!"

"Edward!"

Epilogue

If you've struggled through the thicket with Ed Sutherland to this point, well done! You have probably disagreed with him on many occasions and may even have emerged from the thicket convinced he was heading in the wrong direction.

Whatever direction you take, it is hoped that the book will contribute to even some of the following outcomes.

- The creation within the Christian community of an atmosphere that allows for the open and honest sharing of doubts and questions without fear of ridicule or rejection.
- The identification of pre-understanding that hinders hearing what a text is actually saying.
- The art of asking the right questions about a text as a step towards eliciting the right answers.
- Tenacity to cling to the truth contained in texts that are clear, rather than to muddy such texts with an assumed understanding of texts about which godly scholars differ.
- Courage to go out on a limb with the truth though it clashes with conventional ideas.
- Commitment to the Scriptures as the ultimate authority and discernment to recognize when such commitment is compromised by adherence to inherited views, doctrinal statements, popular teachers, and denominational affiliation.

- Fear of impugning the integrity of Christ and the biblical authors by distorting the intended meaning of their words through the use of invalid principles of interpretation.
- A healthy skepticism of eschatological scenarios that minimize the effectiveness of Christ's work and the power of the gospel to address the deep-seated problems of humanity.
- A willingness to pray sincerely the ancient Hebrew prayer with which this book began.

> From the cowardice that shrinks from new truth,
> From the laziness that is content with half-truths,
> From the arrogance that thinks it knows all truth,
> O God of truth, deliver us.

Study Guide

The following material, based on chapters in *Through the Thicket*, can be used for personal reflection on issues raised in the book, as a catalyst for home-group Bible studies, or to stimulate discussions in college classes on eschatology, hermeneutics, or apologetics.

STUDY 1: THOUGHTFUL OBSERVATIONS

Reading: *Through the Thicket*, chapter 2; Matthew 10:23

1. When Ed Sutherland asked if there was anything surprising in Matthew 10:23, Alex Symons had nothing to say. Comment on the following reasons that people read such a verse and see nothing surprising in it.
    a. They have previously studied the text and reconciled it, rightly or wrongly, with what they believe.
    b. They have glossed over the words in the verse without giving due consideration to their intended meaning.
    c. They have dismissed the text as belonging to the too-hard basket.
    d. They are afraid to state what it seems to be saying for fear of an Alex-Symons-type reaction.
2. Share occasions when one (or more) of the above reasons has applied to you.
3. What surprised Luke Rodman in the verse?

4. What motivated Alex to respond so strongly to Luke's provocative statement about Christ's return?

5. What deeper, unspoken motivation, might cause one to respond as strongly as Alex did?

6. What evidence is there that Luke was not being dogmatic in making his statement about Christ's return?

7. Evaluate Luke's supporting evidence for his statement about Christ's return. Does the evidence justify Ed's saying, "I was impressed with his thoughtful observations."

8. Comment on Luke's understanding of Jesus' words, "I tell you the truth," in relation to:
    a. Luke's "thoughtful observations."
    b. Alex's interpretation of the verse.

9. What is your reaction to the following quotations from the chapter?
    a. Alex to Ed: "How could you let that bearded idiot get away with such garbage?"
    b. Ed to Alex: "Luke was listening to the text more than you were. You rattled off a pat interpretation designed to make the text fit your predetermined eschatology as if what you believe has greater authority than the word of God."

STUDY 2: THE END OF THE AGE

Reading: *Through the Thicket*, chapters 4–5; Matthew 24:1–3; Mark 13:1–4; Luke 21:5–7

1. In the light of the texts in Matthew, Mark, and Luke, consider the following:
    a. The disciples are behaving like a group of tourists visiting Jerusalem. Note how enthusiastically they want to share their impressions of the temple buildings with Jesus.
    b. What would be their reaction to Jesus' prediction of the destruction of the temple, a prediction that was fulfilled in AD 70? Note John 2:20 and consider that according to the Jewish historian Josephus, some of the white stones in the temple were fifty feet long, twenty-four feet wide, and sixteen feet thick.
    c. Why did Jesus preface his prediction with "I tell you the truth"?

2. In Matthew 24, four of the disciples (named in Mark 13:3) asked Jesus two questions: "When will the temple be destroyed?" and "What will be the sign of your coming and of the end of the age?"
    a. The first question is understandable given the bombshell Jesus had dropped. What problems do you see with the other question?
    b. The King James Version translated "age" as "world." Was this helpful or misleading? Why?
3. The two questions concern three events: the destruction of the temple; the second coming of Christ; and the end of the age. The Greek construction of the second question and the use of the singular "sign" in relation to the two events in the question—the second coming and the end of the age—indicate a close connection between them.
    a. Articulate the close connection?
    b. The phrase, "the end of the age," is unclear. The end of what age? What are the options?
    c. The disciples were Jews. Put yourself in their shoes, remembering the importance of Jerusalem and its temple for Judaism, and reflect on the meaning they may have intended when asking about the end of the age.

STUDY 3: SIGNS OF THE END

Reading: *Through the Thicket*, chapters 6–7; Matthew 24:1–8; Mark 13:1–8; Luke 21:5–10

1. The disciples asked for a sign. In response, Jesus gave them a number of precursors to the events they had asked about.
    a. Note the repetition of the pronoun "you." To whom does it refer?
    b. Among the signs are the incidence of false Christs, wars, rumors of wars, famines, and earthquakes. How does the word "you" cast doubt on the way Christians today quote the signs as evidence of an imminent return of Christ?
2. With respect to the signs Jesus gave for his coming and the end of the age—wars, rumors of wars, earthquakes, famines, and false Christs—consider the following:
    a. All of these phenomena have occurred many times, over many centuries, in many countries since Christ made his prediction?

When Christians have experienced them, they have felt the end may be near but the end has not come. How accurate, or even helpful, were the signs? Did Christ get it wrong or have we misunderstood him?

b. Would the signs be more helpful if they occurred, not in isolated parts of the world over long periods of times, not some of them, but all of them, in one generation, in a small corner of the world where, without the aid of modern media, Christ's disciples would learn of them if not experience them? Note: The historical references for the signs in chapter 7 are intended to support just such an occurrence.

c. With two options before us, all the signs in one generation, or scattered signs over many generations, which option best offers signs that act as signs; offers a satisfactory answer to the disciples' question; and safeguards the integrity of Christ?

STUDY 4: ESCHATOLOGY AND CHANGE

Reading: *Through the Thicket*, chapters 8–9

At the leadership meeting, Stan Mullins and his son Mark expressed two conflicting views of change. Read their statements below and consider the questions that follow.

Mark Mullins: "Our church has lost a generation with little hope of regaining it short of radical change. Change comes at a price: the relinquishing of power; the intrusion of the unfamiliar; the struggle by old dogs to learn new tricks; a bigger budget; the construction of a larger church building; a renewed mindset that stops harking back to the 'good old days' and begins to look optimistically to better days ahead."

Stan Mullins: "All this talk about declining numbers, a lost generation, growth, and a larger church building betrays ignorance of the times. We are in the last days, brothers, when decline is expected. Jesus said, 'When the Son of Man comes, will he find faith on the earth?' This is the Laodicean age, the age of lukewarmness, the age immediately before the return of Christ. We need to be suspicious of large numbers. The mega-churches are apostate with their shallow sermons, their emphasis on entertainment rather than edification, on worldly music rather than godly worship. We are privileged to be part of the remnant. We must maintain what we have and heed Paul's warnings to Timothy about conditions in the last days when people will 'depart from the faith' and will have only an outward 'form of godliness.' Paul goes on to say, 'From such turn away.'"

1. Mark spoke about the cost of change. How relevant are the points he made to church growth today?
2. What words in Stan's statement reflect his eschatology? Critique his argument.

STUDY 5: THE LAST DAYS

Reading: *Through the Thicket*, chapter 10

1. Evaluate Ed's understanding of the texts he considers concerning the last days:
   a. 2 Timothy 3:1–5
   b. Acts 2:15–17
   c. Hebrews 1:1–2
   d. 1 John 2:18
2. How does his conclusion differ from that of Robyn Bradford?
3. Discuss Ed's question, "The last days of what?"
4. If you were one of the disciples who, in the context of Jesus' announcement about the destruction of the temple, had asked for a sign about the end of the age, what age would you have been thinking about? Why?
5. Compare Ed's case with that of commentators who apply "last days" to the entire period between the first coming of Christ and a yet-to-occur second coming of Christ?

STUDY 6: UNIVERSAL PREACHING OF THE GOSPEL

Reading: *Through the Thicket*, chapter 11; Matthew 24:9–14; Mark 13:9–11

1. Read the texts given in chapter 11 in support of Luke's statement that "In the New Testament it is not uncommon for apparently universal language to be used with a limited reference." Do the texts provide justification for his statement?

2. Why do many regard Matthew 24:14 as evidence that the end of the age did not occur in AD 70?

3. Read the following paragraph, noting particularly the words in italics, and reflect on the possibility that the sign in Matthew 24:14 *was* fulfilled by AD 70.

> In Romans 1:8, Paul said the faith of the Romans was known "*all over the world.*" In Colossians 1:6 he said, "*All over the world* this gospel is bearing fruit and growing"; and in verse 23 he wrote: "This is the gospel that you heard and that has been proclaimed to *every creature under heaven.*"

4. In support of the fulfilment of Matthew 24:14 in the days of the apostles, compare Matthew 24:9–14 with Mark 13:9–11. In Mark's account, the pronoun "you" (the disciples) occurs throughout, and the widespread preaching of the gospel is mentioned in the middle (verse 10, the parallel to Matthew 24:14) between the witness of the apostles (verse 9) and their Spirit-inspired testimony when standing trial (verse 11). What does this suggest?

5. Compare Matthew 24:14 with the great commission in Matthew 28:18–20. How do the words "all nations" (verse 19), the pronoun "you" (the disciples), and "the very end of the age" (verse 20), support the fulfilment of Matthew 24:14 in the days of the apostles?

STUDY 7: THE DAY IS ALMOST HERE

Reading: *Through the Thicket*, chapters 12–13, 16

Read Romans 13:11–12 and consider the following:

1. Putting aside pre-conceptions, if you lived in the first century and were part of the church at Rome, how would you understand Paul's phrase, "the day is almost here," when you heard these verses read? Why?

2. After giving your own response to the following comment by Jamieson, Fausset and Brown, evaluate Ed's response in chapter 13.

> The passage was "in the line of all our Lord's teaching, which represents the decisive day of Christ's second appearing as at hand, to keep believers ever in the attitude of wakeful expectancy, but without reference to the chronological nearness or distance of that event."

3. Evaluate Ed's response to the quotation from the *People's New Testament* commentary:

> Some have thought that Paul referred to the speedy second coming of the Lord. He did not know the time of that event, nor did any man, but it might be that he shared the hope of the early, suffering church, that it would be speedy.

4. What point is Ed making in relation to Romans 13:11–12 with his illustration of a family trip to Sydney (chapter 16)?

5. Critique John Macarthur's exegesis of Romans 13:11–12 in his sermon located at http://www.gty.org/Resources/Sermons/80-124.

STUDY 8: THE ANTICHRIST

Reading: *Through the Thicket*, chapters 14, 29; 2 Thessalonians 2:1–12; Revelation 13:11–18

1. Over the years, speculation has produced candidates galore for the role of antichrist. Summarize Ed Sutherland's arguments in chapter 14 against such speculation.

2. In chapter 29, Ed converses with Mark Mullins about Paul's teaching on "the man of lawlessness" (NIV) in 2 Thessalonians 2. Critique Ed's understanding of the passage. Does it favor a first-century or a twenty-first-century fulfilment? Why?

3. It is not uncommon for calculations to be made of English names resulting in 666. Letters in Hebrew, Greek, and Latin had established numerical values but who decides the values for letters in the English alphabet? Revelation 13:18 invites the original first-century readers to "calculate the number of the beast." Why is the text a problem for modern-day calculations, barcode connections, and antichrist speculation?

STUDY 9: CREEDS AND CONFESSIONS

Reading: *Through the Thicket*, chapter 22.

1. Churches generally belong to one of four categories when it comes to statements of faith. Some have no such statement; some, like SCIF, have their own local statement; some, like the Presbyterians, have a

denominational statement; and others adhere to an historical statement such as the Apostles' Creed. Share your church's position. Are there strengths and weaknesses in the various categories?

2. Evaluate Andy's five benefits of a Statement of Faith. Do they justify SCIF's adoption of such a document? Would your church be better or worse off to follow suit?

3. Andy sounded two cautionary notes with respect to doctrinal statements. Read them and then share instances known to you where churches or individuals have given too much authority to their doctrinal statement or have treated non-essential truths as if they were essential.

4. Express Rupertus Meldenius's statement below in your own words.

    In essentials unity,
    In non-essentials liberty,
    In all things charity.

5. Give examples known to you of departures from each of the three lines in the statement. What consequences followed such departure?

6. Remembering that non-essentials may be very important, apply Andy Zimmerman's two questions for distinguishing essential from non-essential truths to the following:
    a. the virgin birth
    b. baptism
    c. a particular mode of baptism
    d. the resurrection of Christ
    e. speaking in tongues
    f. a pre-tribulation rapture

STUDY 10: ANSWERING THE HARD QUESTIONS

Reading: *Through the Thicket,* chapters 23–24, 29

Unbelievers like to ridicule Christianity as an outmoded human construct in the same category as belief in the tooth fairy or Santa Claus. Sadly, many Christians are unprepared to answer the questions thrown at them. A number of the commonly-used questions and possible responses are found in the three chapters prescribed for reading.

One way to prepare to handle the tough questions is to role play encounters with an unbeliever. Read the chapters carefully for ideas and act out the following scenarios with someone else playing the part of an unbeliever. Respond to each from a Christian perspective.

1. You are on a bus and a fellow passenger reading a newspaper with headlines of innocents mown down by a terrorist truck driver says, "How people can believe in a God who allows such things to happen, I'll never know."
2. You invite a neighbor to church to hear a special speaker and are met with, "No way I'm going to church. There are too many hypocrites there."
3. You seek to influence a work colleague to embrace Christ and are told, "I've tried that and it doesn't work."
4. You try to share your faith with a fellow student who responds with, "Why would I be interested in a religion that has a history of violence perpetrated in the name of God."
5. You are a student of science at a university and your tutor says, "Science has eliminated God by filling in the gaps that God was brought in to explain."
6. In chapter 29, Dr. Mark Mullins converses with Max Fitzgerald. Using the chapter as your script, play the role of Mark and have someone else read Max's responses. When you are finished, discuss the effectiveness of Mark's approach and then repeat the exercise using Mark's ideas for your conversation while expressing them in your own words.

STUDY 11: THE INTEGRITY OF JESUS

Reading: *Through the Thicket*, chapters 26–27; Matthew 24:34

Matthew 24:34 is a difficult text for two reasons: one, at face value it seems to raise doubts about the integrity of Jesus since some of the predictions he claimed would occur within that generation seem to have failed; two, the attempts to safeguard the integrity of Jesus have led to replacing what appears to be a straight forward meaning of the text with a range of interpretations that are less convincing than the plain meaning. We cannot dismiss these difficulties lightly if in so doing we cast doubts on the character of Jesus or handle the Scriptures carelessly.

1. In Ed Sutherland's session with the USC students on Matthew 24:34, what problems did they raise in their questions?
2. How did Ed respond to these problems?
3. From your reading of *Through the Thicket*, chapters 26–27, what attempts have other Christians made to get around the problems of Matthew 24:34?
4. How did Ed Sutherland respond to their attempts?
5. Evaluate the handling of Scripture by those who have different views of Matthew 24:34.
6. What approach would seem most effective in addressing the Bertrand Russells of this world, not to mention C.S. Lewis with his comment on Mark 13:10, the parallel verse to Matthew 24:34, that it is "the most embarrassing verse in the Bible"?

STUDY 12: THE KINGDOM OF GOD

Reading: *Through the Thicket*, chapters 28, 30

1. According to Matthew 16:27–28 and Mark 8:38—9:1, has the coming of the kingdom occurred or is it yet to occur?
2. What events are said to occur in conjunction with the coming of the kingdom?
3. How do these events rule out the transfiguration, the resurrection, and Pentecost as the occasion for the coming of the kingdom?
4. What words in the passage from Mark indicate that the coming of the kingdom would be more than a curtain-raiser to a main event?
5. Ed Sutherland said members of the kingdom should "walk tall." Why?
6. Consider the interpretations of the parables of the mustard seed and of the yeast (Matthew 13:31–33) given by Ed and Lauren. Which interpretation did Jesus have in mind? Which of the two promotes an optimistic mindset? What erroneous principles of interpretation led to Lauren's view?
7. Ed also said members of the kingdom should "get involved." Which of the following roles could Christians fulfil in order to do kingdom work? Give reasons for your answers.

- missionary
- carpenter
- supermarket check-out operator
- evangelist
- lawyer
- pastor
- politician

8. Read Daniel 2:31–35, 44–45 and express, in your own words, the truth that helped Martin Forbes to remain optimistic in spite of daily depressing news reports.

STUDY 13: A VERY LITTLE WHILE

Reading: *Through the Thicket,* chapter 33; Hebrews 10:25, 36–38

1. In Hebrews 10:25, the writer urges his reader not to neglect gathering with other Christians, "all the more as you see the Day approaching." Drawing on 2 Peter 3:8, Andy maintained on the basis of this verse that language suggesting an event was near could, from God's perspective, mean it was a long way off. Are the Hebrews seeing the Day approaching "from God's perspective" or from a human perspective?

2. Do the words "all the more" suggest the writer has the divine or human perspective in mind?

3. Read Matthew 24:33. The words "near, right at the door" certainly sound like the Day is approaching. What teaching of Christ in Matthew 24 might have caused the Hebrews to "see the Day approaching?"

4. Hebrews 10:37–38 begins with the word "for," meaning "because." The text gives a reason, for what?

5. Reflect on the experiences of the Hebrews as described in Hebrews 10:32–34. They had persevered under very difficult circumstances and are urged to continue to persevere (verse 36), for the reason given in verse 37. If you were one of the Hebrews, how would you understand the author's intention in using the phrase "a very little while" (verse 37)?

6. Is the writer expecting his readers to understand "For in just a very little while" from a supposed divine perspective that intends "For in two thousand years . . . "?
7. If you have access to commentaries on Hebrews, see how they handle the apparent imminence in the texts from Hebrews 10. Are they convincing? Do they huff and puff to make the text fit a pre-conceived eschatology? Would the Hebrews be convinced?

STUDY 14: ESCAPE OR ENDURE?

Reading: *Through the Thicket,* chapters 35–36; Hebrews 11:32—12:3

1. The biblical examples of men and women of faith who were in groups 1 and 2 are all Old Testament examples. The New Testament has many examples of the two groups. Acts 12, for example, mentions two prominent leaders, one in group 1 and the other in group 2. What were their stories? Contrast Stephen's experience in Acts 7:57–60 with Paul's experience in Acts 14:19–20.
2. Share the stories of people known to you who have had group 1 experiences.
3. Share times in your own life when you were in group 2.
4. Ed asked what determines the group we're in. Discuss Elizabeth's answer: "I got some help with that question from Andy's reference to the prayer Jesus prayed when he was troubled: 'Father, glorify your name.' I think your question should be '*Who,* not *what,* determines the group we're in?' And the answer is 'a sovereign God who will do what brings him the greater glory.'"
5. Reflect on Elizabeth's answer in the light of the following:
    a. Consider the story in John 11: Lazarus gets sick so his sisters, Mary and Martha, send an urgent message to Jesus. Jesus replies that Lazarus's sickness is "for God's glory" (John 11:4). When Jesus turns up, too late by four days to heal Lazarus, both sisters respond, "If you had been here, my brother would not have died" (John 11:21, 32). Given their response, what group did they expect to be in when they sent the message?
    b. During those four days, which group *were* they in? Would the glory of God feature in their thoughts during those days?

c. Read John 11:38-40. At the graveside, do the sisters expect a display of the glory of God when the stone is removed? They see God's glory anyway. Which group are they in now?

d. Elizabeth was correct: God acts for his greater glory. Does he get greater glory by healing sick Lazarus or by raising dead Lazarus? Note also John 11:45.

6. Why is "Father, glorify your name," not always an easy prayer to pray?

7. What answers are found in Hebrews 12:1-3 to the following questions?
   a. What helped Jesus to endure?
   b. What will help us to endure?

8. Ed asked, "Is there a distinction between things that hinder and sin?" Jack and Josh gave personal stories in answer to the question. Share similar experiences of your own.

STUDY 15: A PANORAMIC VIEW OF REVELATION

Reading: *Through the Thicket,* chapters 40-41

1. Dr. Chuck Harmon used Revelation 1:19 as the basis for an overview of the book of Revelation. Luke Rodman agreed with the application of the three tenses in the text to the book but he still disagreed with Chuck. Explain.

2. For Chuck, most of Revelation relates to what is still future after 2,000 years.
   a. Luke thinks Revelation 1:1, 3 casts doubt on Chuck's view. Do you agree?
   b. Evaluate David's views on Revelation 1:1, 3.
   c. In the last chapter of the book (Revelation 22:6, 10), the time phrases in Revelation 1:1, 3 are repeated. How does this help Luke's view and undermine David's view?
   d. The blessing promised in Revelation 1:3 presupposes that the recipients of the book would understand what was written. Discuss this in relation to the two views.

3. Chuck said, "The very first verse of the book says it is a revelation of 'what must soon take place' and verse 3 says, 'Blessed are those who hear it and take to heart what is written in it, because the time is near.' How blessed we are to be part of the rapture generation." What

principle of interpretation is Chuck ignoring in his handling of Revelation 1:1, 3?

4. Give reasons why you agree/disagree with Milton Terry's statement: "But if the things contemplated were in the distant future, these simple words of time must be subjected to the most violent and unnatural treatment in order to make the statements of the writer compatible with the exposition."

5. In his message, Chuck said, "We are in the last days of the last days, brothers and sisters. The Laodicean age has been with us for 200 years and in decline throughout that time. Christianity is at its lowest point ever and only the divine intervention of the rapture can rescue the believing remnant from the encircling morass."
    a. Are there grounds for Chuck to believe that the letter to the Laodiceans (Revelation 3) represents our generation?
    b. In study 12, we looked at optimistic and pessimistic mindsets. What kind of a mindset does the quotation from his message represent?
    c. What is God's answer to the "encircling morass?"

STUDY 16: THE RAPTURE AND THE TRIBULATION

Reading: *Through the Thicket*, chapters 42–43

1. Chuck's sobering description of the tribulation gave way to jubilation at the mention of a rapture that would ensure Christians would escape the predicted terrors.
    a. With so much of Revelation purporting to describe a yet-to-occur tribulation, how do you react to the lack of teaching in Revelation about the rapture prior to the tribulation if the church is supposed to escape the tribulation?
    b. David Barnes's proposal that Revelation 3:10 referred to the rapture seemed reasonable on the surface. Evaluate Ed's response to it.
    c. In the light of Ed's response, discuss the danger of reading Scripture superficially without probing its intended significance by means of thoughtful questions.

2. The rapture is associated with the last trumpet (1 Corinthians 15:51–52; 1 Thessalonians 4:16–17). Ed Sutherland sees a connection with the seventh trumpet of Revelation 19:11–15.

a. What similarities does Ed see between events associated with the last trumpet and the words of Jesus in Matthew 16:27-28?
   b. What are the implications if Ed is correct?
   c. What is the connection between Revelation 11:19 and Hebrews 9:8?
   d. What light does this connection throw on the timing of the seventh trumpet?
3. Read the parable in Luke 19:11-27.
   a. Compare the return of the king and the allocation of rewards to Matthew 16:27-28, noting the time phrase in Jesus' words.
   b. Evaluate Ed's interpretation of Luke 19:14, 27.
4. Read the parable of the tenants in Matthew 21:33-46.
   a. What similarities are there to the parable in Luke 19?
   b. In Matthew 21:40-41, Jesus says that "when the owner of the vineyard comes . . . he will rent the vineyard to other tenants." What does Jesus intend by this according to Matthew 21:43?
   c. What time frame is implied for the fulfilment of these events?

STUDY 17: BABYLON IS NOT ROME

Reading: *Through the Thicket*, chapters 45-46

1. Imagine you are sitting in the gallery with Ed Sutherland as the lawyer Luke Rodman argues the case that Babylon represents Jerusalem. Weigh Luke's evidence with respect to his use of the following texts:
   a. Revelation 11:8
   b. Isaiah 1:21
   c. Revelation 16:19; Ezekiel 5:1-5, 12; Luke 21:11, 24
   d. Revelation 17:6; Luke 13:33; Matthew 23:33-36
2. Ed sees a problem for Luke's view in Revelation 18:24. Discuss Luke's response to the problem?
3. Luke imagines an interview with Jesus on the subject of Jerusalem's role as a persecutor. Does the interview strengthen or weaken Luke's case? How?
4. Revelation 17:3 depicts the prostitute sitting on the beast and Revelation 17:16 depicts the beast destroying the prostitute. Discuss these images with respect to whether Babylon represents Rome or Jerusalem.

5. Consider the implications for understanding the following if Babylon does represent Jerusalem:
   a. The time statements in Revelation 1:1, 3.
   b. The "great tribulation" mentioned in Matthew 24:21 (KJV).
   c. The significance of the phrase "from now on" in Revelation 14:13 in the light of Revelation 14:8.
6. Evaluate the eight points in Luke's summary of his reasons that believers who die *after* the fall of Babylon are better off than those who die *before* it.

STUDY 18: THE MILLENNIUM AND THE NEW JERUSALEM

Reading: *Through the Thicket*, chapter 47

1. How have you pictured life in the millennium? How much of your picture is supported from Revelation 20, the only Bible book that mentions the thousand years?
2. Discuss the list of "four considerations" that Ed felt might make Chuck less dogmatic about his view of the millennium? How do the considerations affect your view?
3. The second consideration says, "If the first verse (of Revelation 20) contains symbolic language, Chuck should consider that such language might be found in other verses also." Suggest examples of figurative language elsewhere in the chapter.
4. How would you respond to someone with a very literal approach to Revelation 21–22 who said, "If 'gold' and 'pearls' don't mean 'gold' and 'pearls' then the accuracy of the Bible is in question"?
5. Critique the following:
   a. The conversation via text messages between Ed, Martin, and Luke in the back of the marquee during the Saturday evening meeting.
   b. Ed's reflections on Revelation 21 and 22 in the paragraph beginning: "Verses from Revelation 21 and 22 that he read served only to confirm my earlier doubts . . ."
   c. Martin's suggested sub-title for the book of Revelation, *A Tale of Two Cities*.

STUDY 19: ESCHATOLOGICAL DANGERS

Reading: *Through the Thicket,* chapter 50

Answer the following questions about the outline to Ed's book, *Eschatological Dangers.*

1. The integrity of Jesus is said to be questioned when interpreters do not take his plain statements seriously but reinterpret them to accord with their preconceptions. Read the following passages and for each ask the questions below: Mark 13:30; Matthew 16:28; Revelation 22:7, 12, 20.
    a. Leaving preconceptions aside, what appears to be the plain meaning of the text?
    b. Why do some people give the text a different meaning?
    c. How do they reinterpret it?
    d. Evaluate the reinterpretation.
2. Doubts about the integrity of New Testament authors arise when people mishandle their texts to suit their eschatological framework. Consider questions a)–d) above in relation to the following texts: Romans 13:11–12; Hebrews 10:37; James 5:8–9; 1 Peter 4:7; Revelation 1:1, 3.
3. Ed lists six errors that sometimes occur when interpreters make texts fit their eschatology. Do you agree that they *are* errors? Share examples of where you have observed one or more of the errors in your own or others' handling of Scripture.
4. Reflect on your own mindset.
    a. Is it mainly pessimistic or optimistic?
    b. How can eschatology contribute to one's mindset?
    c. What biblical truths promote optimism?

STUDY 20: INAUGURATION OR CONSUMMATION

Reading: *Through the Thicket,* chapter 51

1. Do the Scriptures listed below make a strong case for an early return of Christ or can the texts be convincingly interpreted to make a stronger case for a future return of Christ? Give reasons for your answers.
    a. Matthew 10:23
    b. Matthew 16:27–28
    c. Matthew 24:30, 34
    d. Revelation 22:7, 12, 20.

    e. Romans 13:11–12
    f. Hebrews 10:37
    g. James 5:8–9
    h. 1 Peter 4:7
    i. Revelation 1:1, 3
    j. Revelation 22:10
 2. Some Christians hold that Scripture teaches *a* coming in AD 70 to inaugurate some of God's purposes and a yet-future return to consummate the remaining purposes. Critique Ed's case that each of the following purposes belongs to an inauguration paradigm.
    a. To execute judgment on decadent Israel
    b. To inaugurate judgment on a broader scale.
    c. To inaugurate a new age
    d. To inaugurate the kingdom of God
    e. To inaugurate the future aspect of salvation

STUDY 21: ONE COMING, TWO OUTCOMES

Reading: *Through the Thicket*, chapter 53; 2 Thessalonians 1:3–10

1. Why did John Delaney think the rapture was not taught in the passage?
2. Jack Wilson responded to John's suggestion with: "What is *not* taught in one text cannot be dismissed if it *is* taught in another." What point was Jack making to John?
3. Illustrate Jack's principle in relation to biblical topics other than the rapture.
4. John was happy with Jack's response; Cathy Mullins was not. Why?
5. Explain what Carol Wilson meant when she said, "Jack, here's where your principle kicks in."
6. Discuss Josh Wilson's reading of the text that it points to one coming with two results.
7. How do verses 6–10 suggest Josh's view might be correct?
8. Discuss Elizabeth's question: "If the persecuted Christians at Thessalonica were to receive rest from their sufferings when Christ returned, since he hasn't returned so far, have they not yet experienced relief?"

9. The cliché, "You can't teach an old dog new tricks," tends to prove true with respect to theology as we get older. Discuss.

STUDY 22: PUTTING THE JIGSAW TOGETHER

Reading: *Through the Thicket*, chapter 55

Answer the following questions in the context of a jigsaw puzzle's being an analogy reflecting the task of biblical interpretation in relation to eschatology.

The Border of the Puzzle

1. Discuss: The shape of our eschatology is often inherited rather than discovered.
2. Discuss: The more entrenched our eschatological paradigm, the more likely we are to assume that all the jigsaw pieces must be made to fit in.
3. Discuss: There are serious consequences if the parameters of our eschatology are misshapen.

The Lid of the Box

4. Discuss the ways in which the following can deflect our focus from the lid of the jigsaw box (the word of God).
    a. Traditional views
    b. The writings of the church fathers
    c. Doctrinal statements
    d. Notable theologians of the past
    e. Popular preachers and writers of the present

Inserting the Pieces in the Puzzle

5. Pieces that belong do not have to be forced. Give examples of interpretations that you feel uneasy about because they seem to be forced.
6. What influences people to accept forced interpretations even though they don't feel comfortable with them?
7. Revelation 1:3 promises a blessing to first-century readers, which implies that they understand what they're reading. Why do some twenty-first-century interpretations of the book not fit well with this?

8. Discuss: When erroneous presuppositions act like a pair of spectacles worn by readers of the text, they may feel comfortable with misplaced pieces.
9. Illustrate how the attribution of a double-sense to prophetic texts can lead to forced insertion of pieces into the puzzle.
10. Illustrate how the following can contribute to the misplacement of pieces in the puzzle:
    a. ignorance of the intended meaning of apocalyptic descriptions of astronomical disturbances;
    b. failure to distinguish between literal and figurative language;
    c. failure to take into account the original audience of a text.
11. Discuss with examples: Pieces are forced into place when what is clear is muddied to make it fit with an entrenched interpretation of what is unclear.
12. Give examples of the reinterpretation of the words of Jesus to make them conform to an assumed understanding of the picture on the lid of the box.

Bibliography

Andrews, H. T. "Revelation." In *A Commentary on the Bible*, edited by Arthur S. Peake. London: Nelson, 1919.

Baldwin, Joyce G. *Haggai, Zechariah, Malachi: An Introduction and Commentary*. London: Inter-Varsity, 1972.

Barrett, C. K. *A Commentary on the Epistle to the Romans*. London: Adam & Charles Black, 1957.

Butler, M. A. *The Big Picture of Church History*. Marayong, NSW: Herald of Hope, nd.

Clarke, Adam. *Commentary on the Whole Bible*. https://www.studylight.org/commentaries/acc.html.

"Devil's Plans Exposed: Candidates for the Antichrist." http://www.laverdaduniversal.org/candidates.html.

Earle, Ralph. *The Book of the Revelation*. In *Beacon Bible Commentary*. Kansas City: Beacon Hill, 1967.

Enns, Paul. *The Moody Handbook of Theology*. Chicago: Moody, 1989.

Gentry, K. L. *Perilous Times: A Study in Eschatological Evil*. Texarkana, AR: Covenant Media, 1999.

Gregg, Steve. *Revelation, Four Views: A Parallel Commentary*. Nashville, TN: Thomas Nelson, 1997.

Heavenor, E.S.P. "Job." In *The New Bible Commentary*, edited by F. Davidson, 387–411. 2nd ed. London, UK: The Inter-Varsity Fellowship, 1954.

Hughes, Philip Edgcumbe. *A Commentary on the Epistle to the Hebrews*. Grand Rapids: Eerdmans, 1977.

James, Timothy A. *The Messiah's Return: Delayed? Fulfilled? Or Double Fulfilment?* Bradford, PA: Kingdom, 1991.

Jamieson, Robert, et al. *A Commentary, Critical and Explanatory, on the Old and New Testaments*. http://www.biblestudytools.com/commentaries/jamieson-fausset-brown/romans/romans-13.html.

Johnson, Alan. *Revelation*. In *The Expositor's Bible Commentary*, vol. 12, edited by Frank E. Gaebelein. Grand Rapids: Zondervan, 1981.

Johnson, B. W. *The People's New Testament*. http://www.biblestudytools.com/commentaries/peoples-new-testament/romans/13.html.

Lewis, C. S. *The World's Last Night and Other Essays*. New York: Harcourt/Brace, 1952.

Micklethwait, J. and A. Wooldridge. *God Is Back: How the Global Rise of Faith Is Changing the World.* London: Penguin, 2009.

Milligan, Wm. *The Revelation of St. John.* http://www.clydeserver.com/bairdtrust/node/17.

Mounce Robert H. *The Book of Revelation.* The New International Commentary on the New Testament. Grand Rapids: Eerdmans, 1977.

———. *Matthew.* New International Biblical Commentary. Peabody: Hendrickson, 1991.

Newman, Randy. "Ask Before You Answer." *Christian Reader* January/February (2004) 60–63.

Pentecost, J. Dwight. *Things to Come: A Study in Biblical Eschatology.* Grand Rapids: Dunham, 1958.

Russell, J. Stuart. *The Parousia: The New Testament Doctrine of Christ's Second Coming.* Bradford, PA: International Preterist Association, 2003.

Stott, John R. W. *Balanced Christianity: A Call to Avoid Unnecessary Polarisation,* London: Hodder and Stoughton, 1975.

Terry, Milton. *Biblical Hermeneutics: A Treatise on the Interpretation of the Old and New Testaments.* Grand Rapids: Zondervan, 1976.

Watkins, Terry. "Warning: 666 Is Coming." http://www/av1611.org/666.html.

Wilcox, Michael. *The Message of Revelation.* Leicester, UK: Inter-Varsity, 1991.

www.ingramcontent.com/pod-product-compliance
Lightning Source LLC
Chambersburg PA
CBHW050617300426
44112CB00012B/1545